Gender and Fascism in Modern France

Contemporary French Culture and Society

edited by Richard J. Golsan, Mary Jean Green, and Lynn A. Higgins

Gender and Fascism in Modern France

Edited by Melanie Hawthorne and
Richard J. Golsan

Dartmouth College
Published by University Press of New England
Hanover and London

Dartmouth College
Published by University Press of New England, Hanover, NH 03755
© 1997 by Trustees of Dartmouth College
Printed in the United States of America
5 4 3 2 1
CIP data appear at the end of the book

"Female Anti-Semitism during the Dreyfus Affair: The Case of Gyp" is a revision of an article
entitled "Profession, Antisemite: Ideology and Gender in the Life and Works of Gyp," which
appeared in *Nineteenth-Century French Studies* (fall–winter 1994–95).

For Patty and Nancy

Contents

Melanie Hawthorne and Richard J. Golsan

Acknowledgments

There are many people I must thank for their contributions to this project, most notably my colleague Joe Golsan, whose idea this collaborative endeavor was. I am also grateful to the Modern and Classical Languages Department of Texas A&M University and its head, Steven Oberhelman, as well as to the administration of the university and its former students, for making possible a sabbatical year through the Faculty Development Program. This period of leave away from the classroom and from service and administration gave me the time needed to complete this project. Other support came from the Honors Program and the Women's Studies Program of Texas A&M University; their willingness to invest in scholarship is exemplary. I owe a great debt to those who read and commented on various drafts of my chapter, including Lynn Higgins, Pamela Matthews, Mary Ann O'Farrell, and Margaret Waller. Their suggestions for improvement were invaluable, though any errors or infelicities that remain are, of course, my own. Finally, thanks to all the contributors, without whom there would be no book.

M.H.

A number of friends and colleagues have been most helpful in offering advice and support throughout the life of this project, and I would like to thank them here. Rosemarie Scullion, Mary Jean Green, Robert Soucy, Larry Reynolds, and Jim Rosenheim all shared their expertise and critical acumen in reading drafts of the introduction and, on many occasions, offering encouragement as well. Special thanks are due Melanie Hawthorne, whose patience, care, and intellectual passion sustained the project from start to finish, and to Lynn Higgins, whose support, advice, and interest as always exemplify the finest virtues of this or any other profession.

R.J.G.

We would like to thank collectively the following individuals and and organizations for their help and support. Charles Snodgrass, Laureen Tedesco, and Krista May were most helpful in preparing the manuscript for publication. At Texas A&M University, support for the publication of this book was generously provided by the Center for Leadership Studies and its director, Arnold Vedlitz; the Department of Modern and Classical Languages; and the Interdisciplinary Group for Historical Literary Study.

Richard J. Golsan and
Melanie Hawthorne

Introduction: Mapping the Terrain

The essays included in this collection take as their common focus the problematic relationship in France between fascism and reaction on the one hand
and sexual identity and gender politics on the other. They explore this relationship in a wide variety of historical and cultural contexts from fin-de-siècle
France through the Vichy period and up to the present. In so doing, they pose
a number of questions, of which perhaps the most basic is: "Can fascism,
broadly defined, be assigned a sexual identity or gender?"[1] Given that fascism
can be considered the "ideology of masculine superiority radicalized or even
absolutized" and "a symptom of a deep fear . . . and violent rejection of non-
subservient or nonidealized women,"[2] a positive response at the outset would
seem appropriate. Fascism, it would appear, is in its most basic configuration
a masculine—indeed, a pathologically masculine—ideology.

But as the essays here suggest, the issues raised in posing the question are
too numerous and complex to allow for simple answers. Fascism, sexual identity, and gender are all complex and difficult topics in and of themselves, and
even more so when placed in proximity to each other. A brief rehearsal of
these complexities and difficulties is therefore in order by way of both framing
and introducing the essays that follow.

In the case of fascism, more than a half century of intensive research, resulting in enormous quantities of scholarly as well as popular books and articles, has failed to produce either a consensus as to the precise historical
origins of the ideology or a working definition of the term itself. Historians
and political theorists are still debating, for example, whether Nazism
should be considered a redaction of fascism or an entirely independent phenomenon. In *The Birth of Fascist Ideology*, Zeev Sternhell insists that "fascism can in no way be identified with Nazism" since Nazism was based on
"biological determinism and fascism was not."[3] In *The Nature of Fascism*,
Roger Griffin disagrees, arguing that the biological racism of the Nazis was

I

merely the particular form taken by the German version of the nationalist myth underlying all fascisms.[4] The same kind of disagreement prevails also on the issue of whether fascism was essentially leftist or rightist in inspiration. Some scholars have argued that it originated in the revolutionary activism of 1789, while others maintain that it was in fact a reaction against that activism.[5] Many specialists reject these eighteenth-century origins and insist that fascism proper originated as a reaction against the threat of Marxism in the aftermath of World War I. Disagreement on these and other crucial points has been so extensive that, in their preface to the *Dictionnaire historique des fascismes et du nazisme*, Pierre Milza and Serge Berstein lament: "One must accept the evidence. No universally accepted definition of the fascist phenomenon exists, no consensus, no matter how slight, as to its range, its ideological origins, or the modalities of action which characterize it."[6] Robert Soucy expresses a similar view in discussing the more restricted context of fascism between the wars in *French Fascism: The Second Wave, 1933–1939*: "In sum, no static conception of fascism, no ahistorical definition, can do justice to the various doctrinal fluctuations that fascism underwent in France, Italy, and Germany during the interwar period."[7] Despite their pessimism, both Milza and Berstein on the one hand and Soucy on the other go on to offer provocative working definitions of fascism. Given the diversity of opinion on the subject, it is not surprising that these definitions do not coincide.

If efforts to define fascism in generic terms and, as we shall see, within specific historical contexts have been inconclusive, they have frequently proven highly contentious as well. Given the horrors produced by the German and Italian dictatorships during World War II alone, fascism, as one might expect, has been justifiably demonized and "othered," and often for specific political and ideological purposes. Marxist critiques of fascism have invariably focused on its links to bourgeois culture and defined it essentially as an extreme manifestation of capitalism's efforts to defend its interests against the working classes. Proponents of what might be described as the Western cultural tradition have often insisted that fascism was and is a complete aberration, with no real roots in Western culture. As early as 1933, for example, Robert Musil asserted that although the French Revolution and other subsequent European revolutions had been preceded by a plethora of new and fecund ideas found in the works of "famous writers," "it would be to misunderstand the sources of this Third German [Nazi] Revolution by looking for its sources in German intellectual life."[8] As Emilio Gentile has argued, only in the last twenty years have scholars accepted the notion that there is no "fundamental incompatibility" between the terms "fascism" and "culture," and that the notion that there exists a "fascist modernism" is not simply "blasphemy." In the wake of events such as the de Man and Heidegger affairs, and in light of recent scholarship demonstrating fascism's mobilization of culture as a means of, among other things, covering over its ideological inconsistencies,[9] such linkages no longer seem so controversial. Indeed, in *The Birth of Fascist Ideology*, Zeev Sternhell argues that "fascism was an *integral* part of European culture" (emphasis added) and that before it became a political force it was a "cultural phenomenon."[10]

In France, the debates surrounding the definition and origins of fascism have their own complex history, especially as concerns French fascism itself. These exchanges, moreover, have often proven to be particularly acrimonious for several reasons. First, many French historians and political theorists are reluctant to acknowledge that an ideology as brutal, ethnocentric, and "irrational" as fascism could have originated or developed in the cosmopolitan republicanism or Cartesian rationalism traditionally associated with the French heritage. These scholars therefore have a tendency to dismiss apparently indigenous fascist movements and groups either as highly marginal and ultimately insignificant or as having imported their ideology from abroad. Works by foreign scholars especially have challenged both of these assumptions and have linked the origins of fascism *tout court* to various ideologies and political movements in fin-de-siècle France.[11] It is this latter context that is explored by Melanie Hawthorne and Willa Silverman in their essays herein.

No issue, however, clouds the discussion of an indigenous French fascism as much as the history and memory of Vichy. Was the Vichy regime fascist?[12] If not at the outset, did it become so in 1943 and 1944 when, for example, Laval's overtly fascist Milice terrorized the French populace and brutally hunted down Jews, Resistance members, and "Bolsheviks," all enemies of the "true France"?[13] Was Vichy an aberration in French history, imposed by extraordinary circumstances, or was it in fact the authentic expression of a profoundly French ideology, as Bernard-Henri Lévy's highly controversial *L'Idéologie française* argues?[14] Did Vichy's anti-Semitic policies and subsequent participation in the Nazi Final Solution derive from the same racist ideology, or was the latter the result of changing political and historical circumstances and pressures? These issues, and others, have been debated intensely in academic fora, in the media, and at the highest levels of government for a number of years. It is only recently that the controversy surrounding them seems to have subsided somewhat, although scholarly books and articles on the period continue to appear at an astonishing rate.[15]

But even if the subject of Vichy proves less contentious in the future, the debate concerning French fascism, as a historical phenomenon and especially as a political force and ideological presence to be reckoned with in the present and in the years ahead, is not likely to subside along with it. The continuing success of Jean-Marie Le Pen and the Front National, as demonstrated by local electoral victories in the summer of 1995 and Le Pen's strong showing in the presidential elections the previous May, stoke fears of an ongoing resurgence of the extreme Right, a resurgence that has many commentators speaking of a "return of fascism" or a "fascism that is coming."[16] Indeed, already in July 1993, forty left-wing intellectuals had signed a letter published in *Le Monde* calling for extreme measures including an end to dialogue as well as an effort to "isolate the enemy" in order to counter the perceived rise in the level of acceptance not only of extreme right-wing politics but of the ideas of New Right thinkers, especially Alain de Benoist.[17] Bombings in Paris in late summer and fall 1995, apparently perpetrated by Algerian Islamic fundamentalists, may well intensify French xenophobia, which, in all likelihood, can only improve the fortunes of the extreme Right.

Given such a complex political, cultural, and historical landscape, it is hard to imagine—at least initially—how the introduction of sexuality and gender into the discussion of fascism could clarify the issues and provide greater insight into fascist movements and regimes in Europe, and in France in particular. Indeed, several "classic" analyses of fascism that take sexuality and gender into account often have produced "gyno\homophobic" readings that serve as much to condemn femininity and homosexuality as to clarify their role in fascist politics, ideology, and psychology.[18] In the French context, Jean-Paul Sartre's classic—and classically sexist and homophobic—reading of the collaborator—"Qu'est-ce qu'un collaborateur?"—is an excellent case in point.[19] Nevertheless, the fact remains—as many of the essays here demonstrate—that "gendering" fascism through an analysis of literary works and films, as well as of popular books and magazines, can offer illuminating and occasionally surprising results. As these essays also suggest, an appropriate starting point for gendering fascism can be found in examining the role of women and "the feminine" in fascist ideology and psychology as well as in the history of fascist movements, parties, and regimes.

In recent years, a number of historical and theoretical works have addressed these issues in great detail, especially in the context of Nazi Germany and Fascist Italy. Claudia Koonz's *Mothers in the Fatherland* and Victoria de Grazia's *How Fascism Ruled Women: Italy 1922–1945* have provided invaluable and exhaustive historical accounts of the role of women under the fascist regimes, as well as the sexual politics of the ideologies that drove them.[20] To date, no study of comparable quality has been published on the French context.[21]

Among the more theoretical discussions of fascism's relation to women and female sexuality, no work has had a greater impact than Klaus Theweleit's massive two-volume study, *Male Fantasies*. A tour de force that has revolutionized not only the study of fascism's relation to women and female sexuality but, in many ways, the study of fascism itself, *Male Fantasies* appeared originally in Germany in the late 1970s and in translation in this country ten years later. Theweleit's source material for his study includes diaries, memoirs, and novels written by members of the German Freikorps after World War

I as well as other materials from the Nazi era and beyond. From analyses of these materials, Theweleit argues that fascist male sexuality and misogyny were not simply peripheral features of fascist ideology abstractly conceived but in reality the most crucial building blocks of the fascist male psyche.

Theweleit defines fascism in terms of a "fear and hatred of the feminine." The fascist male ego, he continues, is constituted in essence as a flight from the "feminine" within and without the self. It expresses itself in an urge toward violence—often directed toward women—and a longing for warfare conceived "as both a longing for fusion (with the military machine) and legitimate explosion in the moment of battle." The female ego, and feminine desire in particular, are couched in very different terms. They are "free and creative, unbounded."[22]

Theweleit's analyses are certainly provocative and generally persuasive, but they run into difficulties because of his essentialist approach to gender. For Theweleit, gender categories are immutable and tied directly to biological sex differences. As a result, Theweleit deals largely unproblematically with notions such as "masculine" and "feminine" identities and desires. But as much feminist criticism has insisted for quite some time, gender identities may *not* be inextricably linked to biological differences but in fact can be better understood as cultural or social constructs. If this is the case, then there is no necessary continuity between sex and gender. According to Judith Butler, "If gender is the cultural meanings that the sexed body assumes, then a gender cannot be said to follow from a sex in any one way. Taken to its logical limit, the sex/gender distinction suggests a radical discontinuity between sexed bodies and socially constructed gender."[23]

The consequences of this observation are far-reaching. As Butler asserts, the very subject of women can no longer be understood "in stable or abiding terms,"[24] and the same would obviously hold true for the subject of men as well. If gender is in effect "a kind of persistent impersonation that passes for the real,"[25] then notions crucial to Theweleit's definition of fascism, notions such as an essentially primordial and monolithic fascist male desire, become highly problematic.

Given these difficulties, it is not surprising that Theweleit's conceptual model runs into "gender trouble" in other instances as well. For example, Theweleit's system cannot account for an authentic fascism among women.[26] Female or "feminine" desire, as Theweleit describes it, is simply alien to such a project. And yet, as Willa Silverman and Mary Jean Green demonstrate in their essays, in the French historical context, extremely reactionary and fascist politics have by no means been the exclusive domain of men. Moreover, in some cases the espousal of an extreme right-wing or fascist politics by women has even been perceived as an emancipatory gesture allowing for greater equality among men and women.

Turning to the issue of homosexuality and sexual orientation broadly speaking, Theweleit's scheme runs into additional difficulties. For example, male homosexual desire is described almost exclusively as a variation on fascist heterosexual desire. Its appeal is

in its capacity to be associated with power and transgression. Homosexual practice is one of the few remaining gaps through which [the fascist male] can escape the compulsory encoding of feared heterosexuality; it is an escape from normality, from a whole domain of more or less permissible pleasures—all encoded with femininity.[27]

In dealing with specific homosexual acts such as anal intercourse, Theweleit notes that it is not only a form of transgression against the norm but a way to circumvent the danger associated with socially sanctioned forms of pleasure:

[One] reason for the anus to become a privileged site for the persecution of desires may be the opportunity it offers to circumvent devouring femininity while continuing to persecute the threatening animation of contaminated social pleasures. It may, for example, perform this function for men whose fear of re-engulfment by erotic femininity becomes so great that they can no longer countenance the slightest contact with the dangers represented by woman—not even the forms of contact necessary to destroy them. These men seem to fear that proximity to devouring femininity will bring immediate dissolution, annihilation in symbiosis; they will lose self-control and become either violent or feeble. The escape route they seek may well be offered by anal intercourse.[28]

Whether intentionally or not, Theweleit's analysis tends to reduce male homosexuality to an exaggerated or hypertrophied form of fascist heterosexual misogyny. As a result, as David Carroll points out, Theweleit's scheme moves dangerously close, albeit from a somewhat different angle, to the homophobic approach to fascism taken by Sartre and others.[29] It is the reductive nature of all these analyses of the links between fascism and male homosexuality that Andrew Hewitt's essay seeks to challenge.

Lesbianism and especially bisexuality have no place in *Male Fantasies*. This is perhaps to be expected, given Theweleit's exclusive linkage of fascism to male sexuality. In the case of bisexuality, Theweleit's approach forecloses discussion of sexual and gender ambivalences and the relation of such ambivalences to political choices and sympathies. Where these choices and sympathies include fascism or Nazism, they entail serious implications for Theweleit's model. Elizabeth Houlding explores an excellent case in point in her essay on Violette Leduc.

Despite these limitations,[30] the fact remains that in theoretical and historical terms *Male Fantasies* has placed a number of key issues pertaining to both gender and sexuality at the center of present and future discussions of fascism.[31] Indeed, many of the most recent general or "generic" definitions of fascism emphasize an "extreme stress on the masculine principle and male dominance,"[32] accompanied by a solid core of antifeminism and misogyny, whether conceived in physical, moral, or cultural terms, that is, as a primary source of "decadence." In the French context, as Alice Kaplan, Robert Soucy, and others have argued—and as the essay in this volume by Andrea Loselle demonstrates—a visceral, almost rabid antifeminism is all too common among fascist or *fascisant* writers of the interwar and Occupation periods, from Drieu la Rochelle and Paul Morand to Robert Brasillach and Henry de Montherlant. Moreover, the same holds true for political movements, parties, and, during the Occupation, official government policy.[33] In fact, as the essays in this collection strongly suggest, one area of clear continuity between the interwar fascist movements and the politics of Pétain's National Revolution is the role assigned to women in society and the threat they pose when they exceed the bounds imposed on them by a male-dominated hierarchy. Within the thirties movements as well as Vichy, women are lauded to the extent that they remain within the narrow confines of their traditional roles as mothers, spouses, and homemakers. They are also allowed on occasion to become superficial creatures of fashion, as Martine Guyot-Bender shows in her essay. To the extent that they function as mythical national heroes, they are granted greater leeway, as Leah Hewitt notes in her discussion of Joan of Arc. But once these clichéd roles are transgressed, once women are perceived as *rivals* to men, they are subject to vicious attacks and are made responsible, along with Jews, homosexuals, and other "decadent" elements, for the ills besetting French society. Ultimately, for Vichy, only two extremes are possible where women are concerned. National Revolution propaganda endlessly vilifies "bad women" through the use of "obsessive metaphors" and "vengeful metonymies," whereas comparable hyperbole of a very different sort is used to sing the praises of the "mothers of heroes." All these "manichean texts" and "simple oppositional schemas" are, moreover, intended to support a regime that defines itself from the outset as a "virile" reaction to a Third Republic it considers excessively "feminized"—an "effeminate republic of women or inverts."[34]

It is of interest to note that Vichy's condemnation of the feminine, conceived as a threat to heroic, virile, and masculine virtues, does in fact often assume the pathological dimensions described by Theweleit in his discussion of Freikorps memoirs. In her analysis of National Revolution propaganda, Michèle Bordeaux notes that virtuous women—spouses, mothers, etc.—are presented in the singular, whereas bad or dangerous women are almost invariably described in the plural.[35] As such, the latter are reminiscent of the dangerous "hordes" and "floods," the "engulfing images" that terrify the German Freikorps members and threaten to dissolve or annihilate them. In their foreword to the second volume of *Male Fantasies*, Anson Rabinbach and Jessica

Benjamin emphasize the corporeal underpinnings that for Theweleit lie at the heart of this important distinction between "woman" and "women":

Fear of the inner body, with its inchoate "mass" of viscera and entrails, its "soft" genitalia, its "lower half" is translated into the threat of the "masses" in the social sense of classes or especially in those chaotically mixed groups with women . . . in the forefront—mass demonstrations. The mass is diametrically opposed to the need for a rigidly, hierarchically structured whole. The "front" is not simply the place of battle, the locale of violence, but also the body's boundary against self-destruction.[36]

This almost pathological fear of "the feminine" and of women is not, moreover, restricted to the crude stereotypes that characterize Vichy propaganda. Innumerable examples of a comparable fearful animosity toward women and *le féminin* can be found in the works of the fascist or *fascisant* writers discussed in the essays in this collection, but they can also be found in other, more surprising places as well. In the right-wing Pétainist discourse of the Occupation, even among the most subtle and intelligent of the National Revolution's adherents, a virile and aristocratic heroism is always menaced by a feminizing process that threatens to reduce the male to the "merely human." Writing to one of his relations in June 1942 from his job at Vichy, the young Maréchaliste functionary François Mitterrand laments the banality of his situation and his own inertia and concludes, "I am becoming more human, and thus more feminine."[37] Neo-Nietzschean sentiments such as these were not the exception among the Pétainistes, but the rule.

If Vichy and fascist culture in France reveal themselves to be profoundly masculinized in relation to domestic issues and affairs, they often assume a very different stance in relation to the nation's fascist neighbors. In the discourses of both the prewar fascist movements and Vichy's apologists, a subservient, "feminized" role assumes a more positive charge. During the Occupation, collaborationist newspapers and reviews, as well as prominent intellectuals and government ministers, called for France to carve out a future for itself in the "New Europe" by playing an acquiescent and indeed subordinate role to Nazi might.

Toward the end of the Occupation, as the Liberation neared, Robert Brasillach explicitly sexualized Franco-German relations in waxing nostalgic over the fact that the French had "slept" with their more virile conquerors and had found the experience pleasurable. During his trial after the Liberation, it was this assertion more than any other statement made during the war that angered the court and resulted in Brasillach receiving the death penalty.[38]

As Philippe Burrin demonstrates in an essay entitled "La France et le fascisme," a similar submissiveness coupled with a fascination with Nazi might— its "brutal and irrepressible impulses"—characterized the thinking of fascist intellectuals and defined the politics of fascist movements in important respects before the war as well. According to Burrin, the politics of these individuals and movements were geared not toward competing with Nazi Germany and fascist Italy but toward satisfying the latter's imperial ambitions in such a way as to insure that these ambitions posed no threat to France itself. Thus, for example, the Parti Populaire Français (PPF) of Jacques Doriot supported Germany's imperial ambitions in China. Moreover, as Burrin points out, despite its virile rhetoric and posturing, the PPF "lacked the exaltation of warrior-like values, and above all the ambition for domination and supremacy which is the most obvious characteristic of Fascism and Nazism."[39]

As these considerations suggest, the work of "gendering fascism" can produce provocative if occasionally contradictory results. But lest we conclude too quickly that gender analysis can provide the key to understanding fascism and contrasting it with other ideologies and their historical manifestations, two final caveats should be noted. The first concerns the gap between theory and practice. While fascist ideology is unequivocally sexist and misogynistic in its aims and ambitions, putting its ideas into practice has, in certain historical situations, served in fact precisely those goals that the ideology itself was intended to oppose. In *How Fascism Ruled Women*, Victoria de Grazia provides striking examples of this paradox in Mussolini's Italy:

On the one hand, fascists condemned all the social practices customarily connected with the emancipation of women—from the vote and female participation in the labor force to family planning. They also sought to extirpate the very attitudes and behaviors of individual self-interest that underlay women's demands for equality and autonomy. On the other hand, fascism in an effort to build up national economic strength and to mobilize all of Italian society's resources—including the capacity of women to reproduce and nurture—inevitably promoted some of the very changes it sought to curb. Mobilizing politics, modernizing social services, finally, the belligerent militarism of the 1930s, all had the unintended effect of undercutting conservative notions of female roles and family styles.[40]

Although perhaps more cognizant of the gap between theory and practice in its own politics, Vichy, like fascist Italy, found itself obliged to compromise its own stated attitudes in its policies affecting women as a result of financial and other pressures. According to Miranda Pollard, "Vichy's effort to put into practice its goal of returning women to the hearth was undermined by the necessities of the war effort, and fluctuations in labor policy made it inoperable." Pollard goes on to note that in July 1942 the regime removed all labor restrictions on married women, even on those whose husbands were capable of supporting the household.[41] Thus while Vichy's motto "Travail, Famille, Patrie" appeared ideologically continuous in theory, serious fault lines appeared as soon as efforts were made to implement its principles in the troubled social and economic conditions of the Occupation.

Regardless of their respective ideological goals, both Fascist Italy and Vichy France ended up implementing policies that ultimately contributed to the emancipation of women in the workplace, if not in society as a whole. While the existence of these policies does not belie the fundamental antifeminism of the two regimes, it does add one more complicating factor to any equation geared to offering straightforward conclusions concerning the relations between gender, sexuality, and fascism in ideological as well as historical terms.

The second caveat concerns the *exclusive* linkage of misogyny to fascism or the extreme Right. To anyone interested in European culture between the wars, it is no secret that hostility toward women, often accompanied by a cult of virility, was not the exclusive property of the extreme Right, or even just the Right. Misogyny also belonged to the Left, as any number of novels, paintings, films, and other cultural artifacts tend to suggest. Leftist *cinéastes* including Jean Renoir, known for his Popular Front sympathies, were not averse to representing such extreme forms of misogyny as sexual murder in works such as the 1931 film *La Chienne*. The film's central character, a prostitute, exploits and betrays her well-intentioned and gentle lover to the point of driving him to murder. In 1938 Renoir chose to make a film of Emile Zola's *La Bête humaine*, one of whose protagonists, Séverine, drives her lover to murder her husband and then abandons him. Distraught, the lover, Jacques Lantier, strangles Séverine and commits suicide by throwing himself from a train.

This is not to suggest that Renoir's cinema was uniformly sexist and misogynistic. Other works, including *La Grande Illusion* (1937) and *Le Crime de Monsieur Lange* (1936), present heroic and loving women who are very different from the cold and destructive manipulators of *La Bête humaine* and *La Chienne*. The fact remains, however, that in many classics of poetic realist cinema, from Marcel Carné's 1939 *Le Jour se lève* to Jean Grémillon's *Gueule d'amour*, the heroes are driven to suicide and murder by their passion for women, women who are at best ambiguous and at worst incarnations of evil.

Misogynistic attitudes among left-wing artists and intellectuals in the interwar years in France were not restricted, of course, to filmmakers. Novelists such as André Malraux generally assigned women subservient or unsympathetic roles or excluded them entirely from fictional representations of heroic struggles of the Left against fascism, whether in the Far East or in Europe. A charitable reading of Malraux's attitudes is that women have no significant role to play in the politics of the day, since the revolutionary ideal, after all, is intimately bound to the notion of "virile fraternity." A more troubling reading, however, would underscore the degree to which a deep-seated misogyny, whose most extreme expressions typified the works of fascist and *fascisant* writers, also circulated in the cultural productions of the Left. The crisis of male identity brought on throughout Europe by the ravages of World War I clearly transcended the political and ideological categories of Left and Right in interwar France, making any definitive conclusions concerning fascism's exclusive and defining link to sexism untenable.[42]

Where do these remarks leave us? First, to state the obvious, it is clear that fascism was and is permeated by sexism and misogyny, in France and elsewhere, despite occasional pragmatic political decisions that at first glance make this conclusion appear less certain. Second, in historical terms, leftist or antifascist politics in France have in no way automatically coincided with a belief in gender equality. Unfortunately, quite the opposite has all too often proven to be the case, both before World War II and into the postwar years, as Miranda Pollard's essay on *Le Chagrin et la pitié* demonstrates.

But these broad assertions should not lead us to conclude that the study of the relations between fascism and reaction on the one hand, and gender and sexuality in France on the other, can teach us nothing new. In fact, the linkage itself significantly alters traditional perspectives on French culture in this century, thereby not only bringing to light new objects of study but also challenging a priori assumptions that have long overdetermined our basic understanding of phenomena as diverse as the cultural politics of fin-de-siècle France and the memory of Vichy. Ultimately the answer to the question "Can fascism, and more broadly, political reaction, in France be assigned a gender?" is less important than the places the question forces us to look. A number of these places are explored in the following essays.

Willa Z. Silverman

Female Anti-Semitism during the Dreyfus Affair: The Case of Gyp

> What [the anti-Semite] flees even more than Reason is the intimate consciousness he has of himself.
>
> —Sartre, *Réflexions sur la question juive*

> Are you satisfied to be a woman?
>
> Oh! No! —Gyp, interview

Can right-wing nationalism be assigned a sexual identity? Is such an ideology, with its emphasis on force and its championing of anti-Semitism, "masculine" in its essence, as opposed to an inherently "feminine" Left that is tolerant, liberal, and progressive? Does the "masculinist" discourse of right-wing nationalism entail both a profound fear and a rejection of women?[1]

While such a rigid typing of right- and left-wing ideologies in terms of gender seems facile, it does draw attention to the broader question of gender as a category for analyzing ideological affiliation. This essay aims to investigate the interplay of gender and right-wing ideology in the case of the fin-de-siècle novelist, journalist, caricature artist—and woman—known pseudonymously as Gyp.[2] Specifically, I wish to explore the historian Stephen Wilson's contention that "anti-Semitism [during the Dreyfus Affair] [seems] to have had a special attraction for women."[3] This observation initially seems surprising, given the militant role played in the Affair by such *dreyfusardes* as Séverine, Hubertine Auclert, and Marguerite Durand. These women insisted on the necessary convergence of Dreyfusism and feminism and on the solidarity between Woman and Jew as pariahs and victims of injustice.[4]

But alongside these female partisans of Dreyfus figured many prominent *antidreyfusardes*, including Gyp.[5] It was Gyp who, in December 1899, while testifying at the trial of purported nationalist conspirators, chose to state her profession not as writer but as "anti-Semite."[6] This outrageous exchange was recorded by all the major Parisian dailies. It bluntly announced Gyp's vocation during the climactic years of the Dreyfus Affair. For to her literary activities as author of over one hundred *romans mondains*, novels for adolescent girls, and dialogues featuring Petit Bob, her bratty protagonist, Gyp added those of an anti-Semitic activist and propagandist. In so doing, she helped give an ideology shape in the popular mind. As Léon Blum noted in his *Souvenirs sur l'affaire*, to understand fin-de-siècle anti-Semitism, "one ought to refer to the literary and artistic documents of the period, to the novels by Gyp . . ."[7] Charles Maurras even more categorically asserted Gyp's importance, deeming her, after Edouard Drumont, "the writer who has fixed in the minds of French people the most powerful anti-Semitic images."[8] And for Philippe Barrès, Gyp was not merely the master of anti-Semitic popular literature. She was a leading figure of the nationalist Right, indeed "the feminine center of nationalism."[9]

Gyp was nationalism's lone "feminine" center, and the connection between gender and ideology in her case is striking. Her self-loathing as a woman in part explains her loathing of Jews, whom she damned for both their perceived unlimited power and their weakness. Gender also dictated the forms and tenor of her anti-Jewish diatribes. Barred from the ballot box and the Chamber of Deputies, Gyp compensated by using other means—fiction-writing, journalism, caricature, appalling behavior—to influence public opinion. Her marginality obliged her to diversify the forms of her anti-Semitism and to cultivate verbal, visual, even physical extremism. Paradoxically, her gender was essential to her notoriety and effectiveness as an anti-Semitic demagogue.

• • •

Gyp embodied the New Right of the fin de siècle, which the historian Zeev Sternhell characterizes as "revolutionary."[10] Authoritarian and populist, reactionary and revolutionary, archaic and modern, this Right drew initial support from both Right and extreme Left. It aimed to topple, violently if necessary, the scandal-ridden parliamentary Republic, damned for its inability to resolve two questions crucial to France's future, one national (revenge against Germany), the other social (integration of the working class into French society and politics). Nationalism and anti-Semitism, by designating common enemies and providing "a global system of explanation,"[11] united the revolutionary Right, whose members converged from political horizons as diverse as anarchism, monarchism, and radical republicanism.

Gyp was a right-wing anarchist. Her "anarchism," though, was something of a pose, cultivated while slumming at the Chat Noir cabaret. It rarely exceeded a rhetoric of exceptional violence. Authoritarian, this aristocrat with an illustrious Mirabeau pedigree upheld Church and Army. She championed a pantheon of "strongmen"—Napoleon III, Marshal Bazaine, General Boulanger, the marquis de Morès, Paul Déroulède—whom she considered incarnations of her idol, Napoleon. Anarchistic, she shared her friend Henri Rochefort's apocalyptic view of politics, wondering in an 1894 letter to him, written after a wave of anarchist bombings had rocked Paris: "So when is the government going to blow up, with or without a bomb?"[12] In 1914, she hailed the assassin of Jaurès for a job well done.

Gyp's ambivalence toward certain types of authority had led her in the late 1880s to Boulangism, the movement that witnessed the emergence of organized nationalism. General Georges Boulanger, who drew support from both the Right and extreme Left, and who directed his pitch against enemies abroad and at home, proposed a new republic both authoritarian and democratic, militaristic yet also demagogic and vaguely populist, reminiscent of Louis-Napoléon Bonaparte's republican interlude of 1848–51. The grassroots crusade that "le brav'général" inspired marked Gyp's political coming of age. She electioneered zealously for a Boulangist candidate in the Normandy resort town where she summered; distributed seditious posters; orchestrated the rowdy victory celebration; and recorded her participation in the campaign in a pair of satirical works. The Boulanger Affair also introduced Gyp to militants from highly diverse political and social backgrounds—a chauvinistic republican (Déroulède), an ex-Communard (Rochefort), and a young aesthete (Barrès)—who would become her fellow travelers during the Dreyfus Affair.

Contradictory attitudes toward authority, then, led Gyp to the revolutionary Right and the authoritarian-populist model it proposed. And her split between desire and anger when confronted with strong authority issued in part from a coincidence of ideological and psychological factors. Gyp was an infant when her father left his wife and child, and twelve when a careless comrade shot him dead while he fought as a member of the Papal Zouaves to "preserve Christian civilization." The void created by the vanishing of the comte de Mirabeau, who would become the adored, idealized hero of dozens of his daughter's novels, led her to seek paternal authority capable of ensuring order on both the familial and national levels. This mission, which was consistent with her Legitimist and Bonapartist heritage, became urgent for her after Napoleon III's fall and the empire's ensuing collapse when Gyp was twenty.

But this call for a savior also belongs to Gyp's personal fiction of her "maleness," a myth she used to explain her life. Indeed, she constantly stressed her seeming "masculinity." In her *Souvenirs*, she recalled her remarkable athleticism as a child, as well as remarks whispered to her father by a family friend ("Your daughter . . . seems so little like a girl to me . . .") and by her grandfather ("That little girl has all the tastes of a boy! . . . She plays only with soldiers, only likes violent things . . .").[13] For Gyp had cause to regret her gender, as her family constantly reminded her.[14] She was "the last of the Mirabeaus," and a woman: with her marriage, this august ancestral name would become extinct. Her 1927 novel *Napoléonette*, about the Emperor's fictitious female godchild who masked her gender in order to accompany troops during the Napoleonic campaigns, is punctuated with the refrain: "What a shame that you are not a boy!" Gyp was a woman who suffered on account of her sex. As a result, she projected personal fantasies of authority and masculinity onto the national plane, just as she internalized periods of national history that were dominated by strongmen. Striving to combat a perceived "feminization" of France, she campaigned actively to restore to her country the type of male authority she felt lacking in her own life.

While craving this absolute, male authority, though, Gyp rebelled against her subordinate condition. She was an only child, and a female one, raised by a despotic mother and a stern grandfather, a former colonel in the Napoleonic armies. Gyp's adulthood only confirmed her sense of powerlessness. She was a member of a class whose political and social power were waning; a woman married under the dotal system; a female writer supporting her family and competing with literary rivals, among them her own mother. Confronted by a menacing authority she despised, she tried neither to modify nor to reform it, as had her renegade ancestor Mirabeau, but to destroy it. She became a blaster of oppressive authority, whether maternal, conjugal, literary, or political. The meeting in Gyp of a profound need for strong authority and a revulsion toward it produced the makings of a hybrid: an authoritarian anarchist.

· · ·

The essence of Gyp's identification with a nationalist, revolutionary Right was her anti-Semitism. A self-proclaimed "ferocious"[15] anti-Semite, she demanded the expulsion from France of all Jews, but had the charity to add: "I'm not personally asking that they be killed . . ."[16] Her wrath toward the Jewish "race" emanated from some of the myriad sources of anxiety tapped (and also created) by Edouard Drumont, the so-called "Pope of anti-Semitism," whom Gyp considered "a visionary."[17] To the aristocrat Gyp, the Jew represented the bourgeois, who threatened to replace a social hierarchy based on land ownership and privilege with one based on financial capital, but who still insisted on aping the distinctive signs of aristocratic life. The Catholic traditionalist had little trouble identifying the Jew with Satan. Such distortions, of course, always have some grounding, however tenuous; Gyp's resentment of such "parvenus" resulted in part from the spectacular, highly visible success of a small number of middle-class French Jews.[18] To the sentimental Bonapartist of Legitimist descent, the Jew became synonymous with the hated democratic Republic, which brought to power a new, largely bourgeois political class, dethroning the aristocracy in the civil service, magistrature, and elsewhere. Finally, the apologist of "la vieille France"—"the France of old, the pretty

France, bubbly like champagne, always light and always victorious,"[19] to which Rachilde compared Gyp—spurned the Jew as representative of a Maurrassian *anti*-France. The advent of Jewish "domination" at a time when French national identity was in flux marked for Gyp, as one of Drumont's titles mournfully predicted, "the end of a world."

So Gyp's spewing of a torrent of anger and anxiety onto the Jews betrayed to a large extent her socioeconomic and political background. Yet her prejudice differs markedly from that of many contemporaries in its degree of extremism. Like her affinity with the revolutionary Right, Gyp's anti-Semitism also stemmed from her simultaneous embrace and condemnation of power, which was rooted in her ambivalence about gender. The Jewish scapegoat of her invention, whether his name be Dreyfus or, like one of her fictional potentates, le baron Sinaï, was a dual symbol of Gyp's impotence as a woman. He was the archetypal oppressor, crushing the world with his sacks of gold coins; Gyp's novels and caricatures abound with these clichés. In lambasting these "Hébreux," as she sometimes referred to them, she was battling the sense of forcelessness she had felt since childhood, and the shame inherent in being a female, "last of the Mirabeaus." And frustrations with the many prominent Jewish middlemen on whom her professional life depended, most notably her publisher Calmann-Lévy, only aggravated both her hostility and her feeling of victimization.

Gyp's anti-Semitism, then, was the most radical expression of her will to destroy all "oppressors." By her own admission, she was "violent and jocular. And I beat on, preferably, what is serious, or pretentious, or powerful, or cumbersome."[20] Yet while she aimed to eliminate these cumbersome enemies, she also felt attracted to, even identified with them, and indeed wished to supplant them. For like her repulsive, money-grubbing Jews, Gyp was, as she herself acknowledged, "dazzled by the money question."[21] She clearly saw in the Jew the ambition, the will to power she could not always admit in herself, but felt safe to fictionalize. "I want to become strong . . . very strong . . ."[22] is the phrase that runs through her *Souvenirs* like a mantra.

An almighty tyrant, both detested and admired, the Jew was at the same time Gyp's symbol of impotence and decay. In condemning the Jew, she denounced not only strength but its opposite: the weakness, the "feminine" she tried to obliterate in herself. Her anti-Semitism was in part the expression of a deep-rooted misogyny that, to a certain extent, characterized the fin de siècle.[23] She insisted that her artistic persona, Bob, was male, and so too her literary persona, Gyp. Her comment to Ludovic Halévy is typical of her disparaging view of her gender: "Women who write are unpleasant to almost everyone, and I would like to make people forget as much as possible that Gyp is a woman."[24] Aside from designating her artistic and literary personae as males, Gyp often referred to herself as a soldier, reminding Paul Déroulède in

1900 that "I am a very disciplined soldier . . . who follows my leader,"[25] and writing two novels, *Le Cricri* and *Napoléonette*, featuring girl heroines who become soldiers.

Gyp's attitudes toward women exemplify Stephen Wilson's observation that "the Jews were sometimes identified with femininity, and hostility to Jews may have been an expression of women's rejection of their gender and its disabilities."[26] Indeed, the messages of several female contributors to the Monument Henry, the hateful anti-Semitic lists *La Libre Parole* published in late 1898, make this rejection of female sexuality explicit: "A young Frenchwoman who would like to wear trousers and march under the orders of Déroulède"; "A young lady who deplores the fact that she is not a man. Long live the army!"[27] Gyp thus damned in the Jew what revolted and frightened her in others and in herself. Her antithesis and her double, the Jew reflected back to her, in Sartre's words, "an unsettling image, which is [her] own."[28]

Another source of Gyp's consuming anti-Semitism, again related to her unease with gender, was her sexuality. Her Jewish characters, female and male, are either sexually irresistible or repulsive, or both, as shown in "Bob's" drawing of the baronne Raab in *Ohé! Les dirigeants!* (Illus. 1). Another such salacious Jew is Nepthali Schlemmer, "a greasy and sweaty pasha."[29] When this villain tries to seduce his adopted daughter, an adorable blond child nicknamed le Friquet, she retaliates by stabbing him to death. In one of Gyp's drawings, an allegorical female figure of the Republic "opens her arms" to recently naturalized Algerian Jews, depicted as a swarm of hideous insects with spindly tentacles, which lunge toward a plump, alluring Marianne.[30] The tableau, which evokes traditional stereotypes of Jewish men as sexual predators,[31] suggests an extremely unhealthy eroticism (Illus. 2).

A fairly literal interpretation of these ambiguous images of Jewish sexuality might point to Gyp's mixed feelings of erotic attachment and repugnance for certain Jewish men she knew, among them her publisher's son, Paul Calmann-Lévy, a suave man-about-town four years her junior. Sartre equates the "profound and sexual attraction"[32] that some anti-Semites feel for Jews with a fascination with evil, in essence a form of sadism. But Gyp's insistence in many of her novels and drawings on rabid Jewish sexuality is also an angry and fearful distortion of her own repressed sexuality.[33] Her public persona was sensual, even lascivious. But her desire doubtfully expressed itself in more than a superficial way; she was a tease and a voyeur. Arms bare and sheathed in a tight white satin dress, she appeared, to Edmond de Goncourt, "voluptuous, exciting," "unhealthily seductive."[34] The press linked Gyp amorously to Barrès, Anatole France, and Félix Faure. Yet the voluminous correspondence between these men and Gyp does not even hint at this claim. She did surround herself with a coterie of men with whom she flirted energetically and publicly, but they were nearly all elderly or quite young.

Fig. 1. Gyp/Bob. *Ohé! Les Dirigeants!* Sibylle Gaudry collection, Paris.

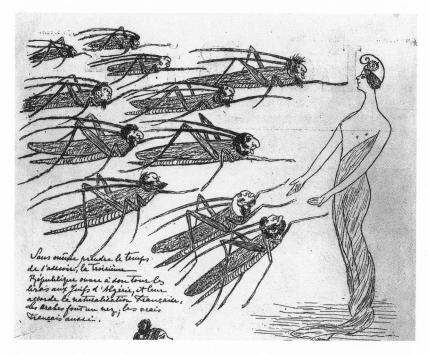

Fig. 2. Gyp/Bob. "Histoire de la Troisième République." *Le Rire* (1896). Sibylle Gaudry collection, Paris.

It is likely Gyp felt anxious about her sexuality. She had little contact with her rentier-husband, Roger de Martel de Janville, who from the beginning of the couple's marriage cheated on his wife "as much as he could and rather showily."[35] What prevented Gyp from doing the same? Her convent-school up-bringing? The harsh legal sanctions against female adultery? Perhaps it was her childhood witnessing of a confrontation between adulterous lovers, a type of traumatic primal scene she later recast in many of her novels. Or perhaps again it was her own confusion about her gender. For Gyp was, in her own words, "un homme de lettres"; an occasional cross-dresser; an outstanding ath-lete with muscular arms. But she was also the *grande dame* with her ballgowns and her salon, a feminist to some, and the mother of three children. Did she see herself as a type of androgyne, a man trapped in a woman's body?

Gyp's sexual anxiety, finally, conflicted with the ideal of respectability on which fin-de-siècle nationalism rested. The "aesthetics of nationalism and re-spectability"[36] dictated new definitions of normal and abnormal sexuality based on the notion of control. Any lack of sexual "control"—whether mani-fested in masturbation, homosexuality, androgyny, or deviance from clearly delineated gender roles—was denounced in scientific and political discourse of the period as ultimately harmful to the nation.[37] Given this emphasis on sexual control and sexual dimorphism as analogies for national vigor, Gyp may have wanted to distance herself from her socially problematic sexuality. So this outsider ritually cast her contradictions and her violence onto other outsiders—women, blacks, city-dwellers, foreigners—but mainly Jews. Effeminate or lustful (for love and gold), rootless and dispersed, these enemies both threatened and confirmed for Gyp her own identity and that of her nation.

• • •

During the Dreyfus Affair, everything in Gyp's life—her relationships, writing, behavior, her entire worldview—was shaped by nationalism and anti-Semitism. Her political militancy confirmed her status as a member of nationalism's inner circle, at once both the consummate insider and, as a woman, an outsider. "Madame Gyp was powerful then," wrote Daniel Halévy of the months preceding Dreyfus's August 1899 retrial at Rennes. "She inspired Lemaître and Guérin . . . Taking this rebellion seriously, we were fearing the worst."[38]

An expert literary and artistic propagandist, Gyp also excelled at that favorite anarchist tactic, "propaganda by the deed," one of the few viable political instruments available to women. She wielded her rebellious personality as a weapon, exhibiting in public the same "unheard-of indecency"[39] that had made her great-grandfather Mirabeau-Tonneau one of the most shocking and despised figures of the Revolution. She was, to one observer, "insatiable,"[40] an embodiment of *furia francese*, who sported a miniature bludgeon destined, she claimed, for the person of Joseph Reinach. She was a permanent and highly audible troublemaker at the rash of trials generated by the Affair, where she could be heard, according to the anti-Dreyfusard press, "yelping"[41] in the back of the courtroom. Her own trial, for libel, pitted her against Ludovic Trarieux, a founder of the Ligue des Droits de l'Homme. She joined the Ligue de la Patrie Française and the Ligue Antisémitique; scoured the streets of Paris for professional rabble-rousers; attended rallies at an anti-Jewish "lodge," the Grand Occident de France; stumped for nationalist candidates; and turned her salon into a nationalist bastion. Friend and confidante of Déroulède and Barrès, of François Coppée and Jules Lemaître (leaders of the Ligue de la Patrie Française), she was considered a go-between among nationalist factions.

Gyp's confrontational style left no one unmoved. It even inspired a self-proclaimed "group of free men" to kidnap her in a *rocambolesque* adventure that became part of Parisian folklore. While to Edouard Drumont, who signed Gyp on in 1892 as one of the earliest contributors to his anti-Semitic daily newspaper, *La Libre Parole*, she was "la bonne Gauloise," anarchist writer Laurent Tailhade envisioned her as a "Walkyrie sucking human blood."[42] Gyp "claws . . . she bites," Abel Hermant concluded. "She wages war."[43]

• • •

It was politics, not writing, that "the feminine center of nationalism" claimed to enjoy; yet in her case they represented two offensives in the same crusade. She was a highly effective polemicist, and to one critic the "undisputed master"[44] of popular anti-Semitic prose, whose success lay partly in the reception of her writings. In some respects, she was simply an extremely astute publicist attuned to the literary tastes of an expanding, and also increasingly politicized, readership. She belonged to a constellation of writers revolving around Drumont,[45] who understood anti-Semitism's mass appeal—and lucrativeness—at a time when, with the progress of Jewish assimilation, it had actually begun to wane. As she stated rather cynically, and with characteristic unconcern for the literary craft: "I have neither self-respect nor esteem for the readers, since I see what they like."[46] And what pleased her readers was not only the anti-Semitic content of her novels but also their unusual amalgam of genres and styles— dialogue-novel, *roman mondain, théâtre du boulevard*, news chronicle. Easily produced, quickly consumed ephemera, Gyp's novels adapted well to the eclectic literary tastes of an equally diverse readership. And they also benefited from the new respectability conferred on anti-Semitism, which by the fin de siècle had become a diffuse, even banal discourse, palpable in medical and scientific literature, ethnographic texts, children's books, even the republican press.

But what of the texts themselves, specifically the cluster of polemical, highly topical works Gyp published at the height of the Affair?[47] It was not her themes that were new; she combined and simplified all the arguments found in *La France juive*, the master intertext for much anti-Jewish literature of that period. Furthermore, several of her plot patterns resemble those of contemporary anti-Semitic novelists. Her characters were familiar, too; her countless venal bankers and exotic *belles juives* belong to the long-established, prolific source of stock characters, descendants of Fagin, Gobsec, Rebecca, Salomé, and others, familiar to Gyp as a prodigious reader and theater-goer.[48]

What Gyp did offer were commanding *romans à thèse,* ideological novels drawing force from their obsessive redundancy, both internal and external. But unlike the better-known, sometimes ponderous anti-Semitic *romans à thèse*— Paul Bourget's *Cosmopolis,* for instance—Gyp's are comic, even farcical in tone, an effect conveyed largely through her use of rapid-fire, emphatically punctuated dialogue, and of verbal and visual caricature. Contemporary critics invariably characterized her anti-Semitic novels as "amusing" or "entertaining." "Face to face with the sinister scapegoat of a new society," Rachilde wrote of Gyp's gleefully vicious attitude, "she simply stuck out her tongue."[49]

Gyp's talent as an anti-Semitic polemicist is exemplified in her novel *Israël,* published by Flammarion in February 1898. The same month Drumont's paper favorably reviewed and prominently advertised its collaborator's latest work. The timing was flawless; the novel appeared during the lull separating the bombshell of "J'accuse" and Zola's first trial from his second one, both of which Gyp covered for *La Libre Parole*. *Israël* arrived just in time to fuel (and for many to justify) the outburst of anti-Semitism generated by the first Zola trial. The anti-Dreyfusard press hailed Gyp and reminded readers of her didactic intent. "*Israël*," one critic wrote, "is a biting satire of the dirty, pretentious and parvenu 'Kikery,' [which] plays such a wretched role in our old modern society and [which] it is good to denounce."[50] And this from *La Nouvelle Revue*: "Gyp delights in running the red-hot iron of her scathing irony over the open wounds that are the humiliation of our society."[51] The reviewer called on Gyp, in the name of the army, to prove "the triumph of Good" and to stigmatize evil. Predictably, *Israël* sold well to a public receptive to such images, and was translated into German the next year.

Resembling the types of "authoritarian fictions" analyzed by Susan Suleiman,[52] *Israël* hammers relentlessly on nationalist and anti-Semitic themes. The novel consists of thirteen loosely connected vignettes in dialogue form, most of them previously published in *La Libre Parole*. Its story unfolds in a present roughly contemporaneous with that of the 1898 reader, and there are many references to specific newspaper articles, politicians, and participants in the Affair. The skeletal plot revolves around a hunting weekend hosted by the comte MacChabé de Clairvaux. He incarnates all the sins of "Israël," as the novel makes clear in chapters ironically titled "Leur Sens Moral," "Leur Tact," and so on. MacChabé has chartered a train so his guests, all chic but destitute aristocrats, can visit his recently purchased château. Countless Manichaean oppositions highlight the Jews' culturally negative qualities: they are clumsy, falling off horses, bumping into furniture, flailing helplessly while swimming; they are urban, ridiculously out of place in the country; they are venal, having "ostensibly stolen in every country and every business venture" (22–23), and fond of hunting only because it entails getting something for nothing. Non-Jews here represent stability, Jews dislocation; citizenship v. naturalization; morality v. immorality; landed wealth v. capital; agriculture v. industry; the man of honor v. the nouveau riche; tradition v. modernity; property v. expropriation; patriotism v. cosmopolitanism. Ad nauseam. While these dyads underscore the Jews' evil nature, it is up to the vicomte de Sangeyne, one of Gyp's "correct interpreters" in the absence of a narrator, to offer the "moral" to this tale of ceaseless conflict. "When the parliamentary Republic cedes to a dictatorship, or to an empire, or to any other type of authoritarian regime," Sangeyne prophesies, "the liquidation . . . is going to be rather painful . . ." (282).

The moral offensiveness of Gyp's Jews has a physical equivalent. In what Fredric Jameson, writing of Wyndham Lewis, describes as a "delirium of metonymy,"[53] Gyp stigmatizes Jews through looks, names, and language. The Jews in *Israël* are nearly all racially tagged by their flab, greasy black hair, fetid odor, and obligatory protruding nasal appendage. In a descriptive gloss that also functions as a type of interpretive commentary by a phantom narrator, a man identified simply as "Le Gros Monsieur" is introduced as "very fat, with yellow and flaccid flab. Puffy eyes, flattened nose, flabby lips. Black hair"(33). This type of cryptic, damning notation, typical of Gyp's style in the *roman dialogué*, reduces characters to marionette-like caricatures. The "fat man's" greasy physique is consonant with his greasy occupation: marketing tablets of concentrated hippopotamus fat for soup-making. This adulterated food contrasts with the natural aliments of the non-Jewish characters, and links the Jews, through equally lubricious metaphors, to excess, decadence, instability, lewdness, bribery.

The Jews' deformed bodies are attached to equally caricatured names; they are grotesque physical and verbal icons. Fin-de-siècle novelists and dramatists often distinguished their Jewish characters by German, Alsatian, or "exotic" proper names. But only Gyp, whose personal and literary trademark was exaggeration, created, in *Israël*, a tribe of burlesque Jews, whose identity is forecast onomastically. They are named Sem and Salomon MacChabé de Mazas, les Cayenne de Rio, Tripoly, Madame de Kuraçao, le marquis de Rancio y Santander, le baron de Wildes Swein, Ubel de Saint Sabbas, Pickledpork, M. Schlemmerai, Nathan Silberschmidt, and Daniel, Ismaël, and Raphaël de Judasküss. It is worth highlighting in this context the crucial importance of names and identity in Gyp's life, and her obsession with them. Her mother had forcibly substituted her thirteen-year-old daughter's second name, Gabrielle, for her first name, Sibylle, deeming her "too ugly"[54] to continue bearing the name of Octave Feuillet's languid heroine. And the extinction, with Gyp's marriage, of the Mirabeau name was viewed as a family tragedy, for which Gyp was held responsible. So she projected onto the Jews the same cruelty her mother had shown her when she chose a name commensurate with her daughter's ugliness. Wildes Swein and Schlemmerai, like Jean-Marie Le Pen's infamous mockery of a French cabinet minister as "Durafour-Crématoire," are Gyp's destructive weapons, part of what Albert Sonnenfeld has called a "polemic strategy in the poetics of anti-Semitism."[55]

Gyp's Jews, like those of some other fin-de-siècle polemicists, babble a guttural, near-incomprehensible *baragouin*. This linguistic debasement signals, like their bodies and their names, a cultural and genetic one. Their consonantal *charabia*, marking them not as exotic but as unassimilable, is a foil for both the measured language of classicism and the slangy folk speech of Gyp's working-class characters (and, very likely, readers). One Jew can hardly speak at all: "[She] speaks in the strangest manner, making a violent effort to articulate"(162). In *Israël*, Gyp's play with language reduces Jews to hostile, garbled sound nearly devoid of meaning, to abstractions, like the masses of bones and hair the gas chambers left behind and that were once people.[56] This nonspeech perhaps most clearly designates the Jew as Other, not the man without a country but, again in Sonnenfeld's words, the "man without a language."[57]

Another of Gyp's strategies in her anti-Jewish crusade was to have her characters propose various "solutions" to the Jewish "question." In her 1895 dialogue novel *Les Gens chics*, Gyp's spokesman, the *grinchu* ("grump"), hints at the possibility of internment. He reminisces about the good old days when Jews were confined to "neighborhoods where a cautious police incited them not to go out . . . [T]here were chains for shutting [them in] . . . that's more like it! . . . Give me that police anytime!"[58] The same character also suggests deportation: "So that's what they're like, the chic people! . . . [H]ow I'd send them back where they came from . . . or elsewhere . . . God, what a cleaning up! . . ."[59] Gyp's suggestions for ridding France of Jews were, of course, reinforced by the larger ideological system of anti-Semitism, to which both she and her readers ascribed. Conversely, *Israël* and other novels by Gyp gave unforgettable shape to these formerly nebulous ideas. In fact, both the novel's ideological line and the imagery that conveys it—"I'd put them . . . in a mortar and grind [them] up at random,"[60] Gyp wrote in 1895—seem to foreshadow the baroque imaginings in the Monument Henry.

Visual caricature, finally, is another penetrating weapon in Gyp's "polemic strategy." A self-taught caricaturist and painter, Gyp belonged to a generation of talented satirical illustrators, among them Adolphe Willette and Jean-Louis Forain, whose success was facilitated by advances in the photorelief printing process. She frequently contributed to the anti-Semitic illustrated press, and supplied several of her novels with "colored images, signed 'Bob.'" In the 1897 dialogue novel *En Balade*, for example, visual caricature complements and again reinforces its verbal counterpart; the crude, childlike style of the drawings seems almost a visual pendant to the *roman dialogué*, with its trenchant notations and barest narrative exposition. A troop of famous historical figures from all eras descends on Paris, hoping to see the Tzar. But their stroll becomes a nightmarish journey through Jewish Paris. In a stylized landscape that hints at the belle époque fad for *japonisme*, the tourists encounter a group of Jewish children; "they are the hope of France," the caption informs (Illus. 3). Like her novels, and arguably more effectively because of their concision and immediacy, drawings like this one distill and synthesize a range of anti-Jewish arguments, and also emphasize the visually centered nature of anti-Semitism. Here, "racial" inferiority is signaled by the children's claw-like hands and kinky hair, which contrast sharply with the "Aryan" looks of the two *nourrices* who frame this horrifying menagerie. The large, flat planes of color, heavily outlined, have something in common with the decorative panels of Vuillard. They distort the Jewish figures, who appear almost abstract but at the same time, because of Gyp's reliance on the traditional iconographic elements of anti-Semitism, shockingly recognizable.[61]

Fig. 3. Gyp/Bob. *En Balade.* Sibylle Gaudry collection, Paris.

Gyp's anti-Semitic texts are indeed stifling spaces. Yet they also contain some curious contradictions that prevent their becoming "dysfunctional."[62] The vapid, aristocratic snobs and dandies in *Israël* are just slightly less reprehensible than the Jews whom they happily exploit; if the Jews have become the new aristocracy, Gyp suggests, the old one is partly to blame through its decadence.[63] And the slangy folk speech of her *petits gens*, her workers and *domestiques*, is in fact nearly as grotesque and incoherent as that of her Jews. For Gyp's "populism"was always of the Chat Noir variety, and barely concealed her nausea over real encounters with *le peuple*. Equally as surprising as Gyp's bleak portraits of aristocrats and *classes populaires* is her rendering of an "atypical," female Jew—who resembles the author! Odette de Cayenne de Rio, perhaps the only "sympathetic" Jewish character in the novel, from Gyp's perspective, despises Jews ("I'm horrified by those of my race! . . . ," 203). Stranger still, she proclaims she will only marry if her assets are legally separated from those of her husband (205). Gyp's difficult legal struggle to separate her assets from her husband's was one of the great personal dramas of her life, and she fictionalized it repeatedly. The traces of nihilism in this novel, and the clue about Gyp's bizarre identification with the Jews, paradoxically ensure the novel's coherence, as they prevent it from becoming a hellish echo chamber.

. . .

Gyp was a highly effective writer and caricaturist who espoused a bad ideology. Her novels of the fin de siècle constitute a right-wing nationalist's account—lying somewhere between chronicle and fable—of the major political upheavals of the Third Republic: Boulangism and the Dreyfus Affair, "l'Affaire des Fiches" and the 1905 separation of church and state. In this era of polemic and vituperation, she perfected a genre, the popular anti-Semitic novel. And in so doing she helped widen the great political debate of the fin de siècle. She continued the campaign of extermination she waged in print on other fronts as well: in the salon and the courtroom, and as a professional, outrageous troublemaker, successfully bringing together anti-Semitic life and works, text and context, word and image as perhaps only a "professional" anti-Semite can. The variety and extremism of her activities are the measure of her triple marginality as a member of the political opposition, an aristocrat, and a woman. But the compensatory strategies necessitated by her position also assured her place as nationalism's "feminine center."

Gyp's nationalism and anti-Semitism must be understood above all in terms of her class, religious, and political background. Yet her gender, and the psychological instability it created in her, also influenced her ideological affiliation. For the wrath she directed against Jews was in part a projection of her self-hatred as a woman, imbued in her since childhood ("What a shame that you are not a boy!"). The mythical Jews she vilified through her political activities and in her novels and caricatures represented for her both the impotence and marginality she deplored in her own condition, and the dazzling economic, social, and political power she aspired to but could not attain ("I want to become strong . . . very strong . . ."). That gender and ideology meshed in Gyp's case does not imply, however, that nationalism and anti-Semitism at the fin de siècle, or during the period that gave rise to fascism, divided along gender lines, nor that anti-Semitism and misogyny were inextricably linked. Misogyny did not, and does not necessarily lead to an embrace of right-wing ideology, as illustrated by the case of André Malraux.[64] Conversely, feminism and anti-Semitism could comfortably cohabit, as the example of Natalie Barney makes clear. Closer to Gyp's case, during the interwar period, is that of Gertrude Stein, who, despite being Jewish and a lesbian, was both contemptuous of women (to the point of adopting a masculine identity) and anti-Semitic.[65] While each of these cases is complex, all serve to highlight the role of gender as an important, and overlooked, component in characterizing the politics and practice of right-wing nationalism and anti-Semitism.

Melanie Hawthorne

(En)Gendering Fascism: Rachilde's "Les Vendanges de Sodome" and *Les Hors-Nature*

Is it a boy or a girl? That's the question everyone seems to be asking about the twentieth-century neonate, fascism. So far, the consensus seems to be that this foundling no one wants to claim must be a boy, as David Carroll has concluded in one of the most recent contributions to the debate: "fascism in general can still rightly be considered an extreme masculinist or virile ideology."[1] Carroll fuels a widespread perception that fascism appeals more to men than to women and that it celebrates masculinity and denigrates femininity. Such observations do indeed seem compelling, yet at the same time they are profoundly troubling.

Troubling because when one looks closer at some of the interventions in this debate, one cannot help asking: where are the women? It is a curious question to have to ask, especially when so much attention is explicitly being paid to issues of gender. On the one hand, there have been some very clear cases of women fascists. The fascinating example of Leni Riefenstahl comes most obviously to mind,[2] but one might also think of Gertrud Scholtz-Klink, who makes such a chilling appearance in the Preface to Claudia Koonz's *Mothers in the Fatherland*;[3] of Mussolini's mistress Margherita Sarfatti;[4] or even of names that are all but forgotten today such as the authors Thérèse Delhaye de Marnyhac, whose "Bouboule" novels are discussed by Mary Jean Green in this volume, not to mention prototypes such as Gyp, analyzed here by Willa Silverman. Nevertheless, while the role of femininity (or its repudiation) in fascism is hotly debated, women themselves often have no presence in the discussion. Thus, while Klaus Theweleit's far-ranging multivolume analysis of the Freikorps and Alice Kaplan's more focused and groundbreaking study of French fascists both focus on fear of femininity, they consistently

27

locate this fear only in men. In his essay on collaboration "Qu'est-ce qu'un collaborateur?" Jean-Paul Sartre—who basically wants to be able to call collaborators sissies, to hit them where it hurts (i.e., in their masculinity)—homophobically argues that collaborators (all men in Sartre's universe, of course, like the resisters) feared they were effeminate and therefore homosexual (rather than men who resisted gender ideology). In what Freud would call reaction formation, they therefore identified with hypermasculine men, the fascists. It has also been suggested that fascism is a form of fetishism. In his *History of Fascism, 1914–1945*, Stanley Payne writes that "only fascists . . . made a perpetual fetish of the virility of their movement and its program and style."[5] In all these cases, the struggle between masculine and feminine impulses and identifications takes place in the male body. How would or could these models apply to women?

This article confronts the absence of women. First, I examine in greater detail their absence from some of the accounts of the origins of fascism touched on above. Then, I try to account for this absence by focusing on the history of nationalism. I argue that since nationalism is a gendered concept, and since a compelling case has been made for the role of nationalism as an essential ingredient of fascism, it should come as no surprise that fascism too is gendered. To illustrate this, I offer a close textual reading of two fictional works by the turn-of-the-century French novelist Rachilde. Finally, I speculate on the implications for women today of the way fascism has been gendered in the past.

The Story So Far: Real Men Aren't Afraid of Women

The models mentioned above purport to explain something of the gender of fascism, but when their underlying assumptions are examined, it appears that each model has excluded a consideration of women at a theoretical level, therefore begging the question of the gender of fascism itself and precluding the possibility that a female fascist could be constituted in the same way as the male analogue. These theories rely heavily on various schools of psychoanalysis (object relations theory, reaction formation, fetishism)—a discipline that had its founding moment at the same time as fascism. But while psychoanalysis may be valuable as a way of reading (and I shall draw on its insights myself later in this article), it may be both vulnerable to charges of ahistoricity and vague about whether it describes ideology or makes some claim about reality.

Consider Klaus Theweleit's analysis in his two-volume study of the Freikorps's attitudes toward women, *Male Fantasies*.[6] Although Theweleit rejects strict Freudian (oedipal) theory, he nevertheless relies heavily on psychoanalytic structures to account for the fear of women and of being (re)absorbed into an indeterminate state he identifies as a precipitating cause of violence in his subjects. He draws principally on object relations theory, albeit a form of object relations that deals in parts, not whole people (1:212). Theweleit argues that the Freikorpsmen lack stable egos (1:208), a problem deriving from the pre-oedipal stages of life when the infant begins to see itself as separate from the mother. The fear of reabsorption, which Theweleit identifies as being at the root of fascism, represents a fear of falling back into a state of nondifferentiation. Because the primary parent from whom the infant must first separate is nearly always a mother (rather than a father), there is a metonymic tranference of fear from reabsorption to femininity.[7]

Presumably women, too, could experience this fear of regression and use the same metonymic transference to connect reabsorption with femininity—though, given cultural gender prescriptions, it might well express itself quite differently—but Theweleit seems to assume that only men would have this fear. His assumption stems both from the pre-oedipal theory he takes as his point of departure and from his essentialist view of gender, evident in his sociobiological borrowings from the work of Elaine Morgan, to explain the association between femininity and water (flooding or flowing).[8] In Theweleit's work there is a slippage, then, from a discussion of historically grounded gender ideology to some essentialist claims about men and women.

Alice Kaplan confronts similar issues in *Reproductions of Banality: Fascism, Literature, and French Intellectual Life*,[9] though her reading of gender is more nuanced and careful. Yet while conceding that "there is no choosing between mother- and father-bound fascist desires" (10), Kaplan emphasizes the former (11) and distributes the roles in her study along gender lines: "Fascist subjects are virile, phallic, their devotion to the language they learn is total, boundary-less, and the language itself is a maternal one. In order for the state to generate a whole new type of man . . . it has to be female. Its subjects are men; fascism itself is a woman, a new mother" (10). The ideology is feminized, but in Kaplan's study it always manifests itself in male bodies: Brasillach, Marinetti, Céline, Rebatet, Bardèche. Kaplan wisely cautions that she "do[es] not mean to condemn biological mothers instead of fathers as the disseminators of authoritarianism" (11), but she nevertheless focuses on the mother-bound desires of men, while leaving aside the question of whether women could have the same desires (could the state become a mother to women, or is it destined to remain a father, patriarchal?). Like Theweleit, Kaplan uses feminist psychoanalytic revisions of Freudian theory—"a whole range of work from Klein and Balint to Theweleit, Chodorow, Flax" (12)—as a basis for her investigation of the cultural metaphors of motherhood and their echoes in fascist voices.

Both Theweleit and Kaplan choose to focus on men, but could their methodology be applied to women? Their theories ground the adult expressions of fascist tendencies in the pre-oedipal stages of life, in the early childhood issues of separation from the mother and identity formation. According to object relations theory, children must learn to differentiate themselves from the mother, a process that entails and leads to the establishment of a separate identity, but how are these infants gendered in object relations theory? If both boys and girls undergo an identical experience at the separation stage, it would appear that both boys and girls may face the same possible detours into fascist desire. But the role of gender in this process of separation and identity formation has not been clearly spelled out. Does separation take place prior to and separately from identity formation (there is "you" and there is "me," but I only gain a sense of "me" after I have made this initial distinction), and what is the role of gender in identity formation, hence in the separation process? Is there a core identity prior to gendering, an ungendered or pregendered concept of self? Or is identity always already gendered, as Judith Butler has suggested?[10]

Conversely, if gender affects the separation process, if the acquisition of a culturally defined gender identity forms part of the process of ego formation (the formation of the subject), then the separation from the mother in the pre-oedipal period is already a gendered process. Boys and girls will undergo different versions of the process, different versions that may affect the formation of fascist leanings. This seems to be the implication of the work of feminist object relations theorist Nancy Chodorow in her much-cited work *The Reproduction of Mothering*,[11] in which she explains the asymmetrical set of developmental issues for boys and girls.[12] According to Chodorow, the most significant problems for girls arise in adolescence around sexual object choice, but for boys the crisis in development occurs in the pre-oedipal stage and concerns the formation of a stable gendered identity with proper ego boundaries. Boys have no stable and coherent image of masculinity to guide their gender identity formation, argues Chodorow, since in industrialized Western society most mothering is done by women. Boys derive the meaning of masculinity, therefore, by negating the image of femininity they perceive in the (female) primary caretakers around them, which leads to a very tenuous sense of masculinity and an exaggerated fear of femininity.

The themes are echoed in Theweleit's account of gender identity problems in the Freikorps, which seems to assume that gender identity is established before separation takes place, so that the process of separation is already a gendered one. According to Theweleit, the male soldier constantly fears reabsorption and femininity (dual, related threats to his identity) and reacts by repudiating the feminine, violently repressing and dominating whatever is perceived as a threat to male ego coherence. Theweleit acknowledges that his study is limited to men's experience of identity formation: the literature he deals with is a "a literature of sons" (1:107). But by locating the origin of fascist violence in the formation of (male) gender identity, Theweleit rules out the possibility that women can undergo the same process. Female gender identity is, by implication, a simple matter of identification, copying the model provided by the mother (though this seems far from uncomplicated to me).

Another psychoanalytic perspective on fascism focuses on homosexuality, either continuing the pathologizing trend of Freudian psychoanalysis (Sartre) or making "queer" use of poststructuralist psychoanalysis (Andrew Hewitt, this volume). Again, such theories draw heavily on ideological ideas about masculinity and femininity, as well as on broad cultural movements, but such explanations seem to apply only to homosexuality in men; their application to lesbians seems either absurd or irrelevant. These accounts take as a starting point the perception that fascism represents a revolt against decadence, a decadence coded representationally in the twentieth century as effeminacy. Culturally, this presents a very powerful argument, but although it includes femininity, it excludes actual women: effeminacy can only be viewed as decadent (i.e., perverse or inappropriate) when it occurs in a male body. The concept of a cultural crisis around an effeminate woman (hetero- or homosexual) seems nonsensical. In the psychoanalytic interpretation, the fascist (male) overcompensates for his underlying effeminacy by becoming hypermasculine and repressing the feminine (homosexual) side of his nature, as described by Sartre, for example, in the essay on collaboration. This model rests on the twentieth-century conflation of homosexuality and effeminacy,[13] as well as on the Freudian mechanism of reaction formation. Whether the reaction against effeminacy is a cultural directive or a psychoanalytic reaction formation, it can apply only to men. The same path to fascism is not open to women. For one thing, while masculinity is perceived to be an achieved status (one has actively to become a man), femininity is an ascribed status (one just is a woman).[14] Furthermore, if one fails to become a man, one remains a woman, but there is no equivalent cultural concept of failing to become a woman or of what a failed woman is. In cultures where gender is perceived to be a hierarchy, "woman" is the bottom of the ladder while "man" represents a step up. A man who fails to move up the ladder remains a woman, but a woman who fails does not move up (or down) the ladder to become a man; a woman cannot move further down the ladder than she already is. In such a sexual economy (arguably the kind prevailing in the historical periods and ideologies associated with fascism), can a woman become a fascist without being a token man and therefore ceasing to be a woman? I believe that some of the examples of women fascists who invoked gender stereotypes to justify their reactionary politics (discussed in more detail below) suggest that she can, but one might not draw the same conclusion from the theoretical literature.

Finally, the case of fetishism excludes women even more dramatically. Fetishism, according to Freud, develops in response to the fear of castration: the boy's sight of the penis-less female genitals alerts him, albeit mistakenly, to the possibility of castration and simultaneously arouses the fear that it could happen to him. In an attempt to repress this knowledge, the boy fixes on penis substitutes or fetishes.[15] Women cannot experience the fear of castration: since they are already castrated, they cannot become fetishists. Although this assertion has not gone unchallenged, the strictly Freudian model excludes women.[16] Unless women somehow assume a male subject position (a position in which they can experience castration anxiety), they cannot follow the same route to fascism as their brothers. Yet if they do assume a male subject position, then to what extent can they be considered fascist *women*?

Each of these theories produces a male fascist body by expulsing, denying, repressing, or subsuming the female. Because the fascist body thus produced always seems to be male, may we conclude that there is something male about fascism? On the one hand, the evacuation of the feminine seems to confirm the intuitive argument that fascism is always a pathological version of hypermasculinity. But I have tried to show that rather than explaining how an ungendered subject inevitably turns into a male and fascist one, when put to the question these accounts reveal that their subjects were always already men. The models that describe the formation of the fascist subject rest upon assumptions that excluded the category of women in the first place.

While it might be reassuring for women to label fascism a male problem, and it certainly seems perverse to claim for women equal access to fascism, nevertheless it seems important to challenge the essentialism of the theories that cast fascism as a problem of masculinity. It seems more than perverse curiosity to ask if fascism could appeal more to women in the present than in the past. It is more than vague speculation to wonder if a female body can be fascist and remain female, and if so, how. It seems urgently important to ask if the abjection of the female in fascism is necessary, or merely historically contingent. These are the questions I shall take up through an examination of the historical roots of fascism.

Is It a Boy or Is It a Girl? The Birth of Fascism

Since sex and gender are assigned at birth, how was sex assigned to fascism at what Sternhell describes as its "birth"? Sex supposedly reflects observable sex characteristics, so what was it about the observable charactersitics of fascist ideology that made it appear male?[17] Although theories about the origins of fascism continue to be debated, it has been suggested that late-nineteenth-century France provided the cradle for this right-wing revolution.[18] I propose, therefore, to examine some cultural expressions of the French 1890s in order to see what these case studies can teach us about the historical connection between fascism and masculinity.

Historians and theorists of fascism have pointed out that one of its essential ingredients is nationalism. According to Stanley Payne, for example, "fascism generally represented the most extreme form of modern European nationalism" (*A History of Fascism*, 11). Zeev Sternhell goes even further, defining "tribal nationalism" as one of the "two essential components of fascism" appearing at the turn of the century (*The Birth of Fascist Ideology*, 9).[19] But as Benedict Anderson has pointed out, "the nation" is an "imagined community."[20] That is to say, nationalism is as much a social construction as gender is. Moreover, part of the social construction of nationalism has historically involved gender, for nationalism in the nineteenth century was a gendered concept: men were part of the imagined community whereas women were not.[21] Both the assignment of nationality and one's representation in the imaginary community of the nation through voting rights illustrate the gendering of nationality. In the case of nationality, men and women were treated differently. For women, unlike men, marriage affected their status in a number of ways, including nationality and citizenship. When a woman married in the late nineteenth century, she all too often assumed the nationality of her husband. Thus if a French man married a "foreign" woman, she became French, but if a French woman married a "foreign" man, he did not automatically become French. This was in accordance with the provisions of the *Code civil*. In nineteenth-century France, according to article 12 of the *Code*, "l'étrangère qui aura épousé un Français suivra la condition de son mari," but (according to article 19) "une femme française qui épousera un étranger suivra la condition de son mari." In the event that the husband was stateless, the French woman became stateless also upon her marriage, and therefore the law was amended in 1889 by the addition of a proviso: "à moins que son mariage ne lui confère pas la nationalité de son mari, auquel cas elle reste française." This asymmetrical treatment of citizenship remained—though it was modified in 1927—until 1973, when the law was changed to reflect social attitutdes about the equality of the sexes.[22]

The inclusion of a person in the imagined community of the nation often led to a belief that the person was entitled to representation in political matters, a form of representation often expressed through the granting of voting rights. Such was the degree of women's exclusion from the imagined community in late-nineteenth-century France that "voting rights for women" were considered an eccentric topic outside the mainstream of serious political debate. Indeed, the assumption that the exclusion of women is normal is so well ingrained that Zeev Sternhell can invoke the political problems caused by "universal suffrage" in France and Germany at the turn of the century without having to clarify that this "universal suffrage" applied only to *men* (see, for example, *The Birth of Fascist Ideology*, 13).

If nationalism is an imagined construct, how have women imagined their relationship to nationalism? If Sternhell is correct that fascism was a cultural

phenomenon before it became a political one,[23] the literature of the fin de siècle may be more revealing than any overtly political writing. To answer this
question, therefore, I propose to look at some cultural expressions by women
in late-nineteenth-century France that offer models of female citizenship.
Since an exhaustive study is impossible, I propose to select a representative
who might be expected to have some (perhaps unconscious) insight into the
matter.

Rachilde

In the 1890s, Rachilde (Marguerite Eymery Vallette, 1860–1953) was a leading
novelist associated with the French decadent and symbolist movements. She
was closely associated with the leading French journal *Le Mercure de France*;
her husband, Alfred Vallette, was the editor and one of the founders, and
Rachilde was a regular book reviewer and contributor. In addition, she hosted a
salon that drew many prominent as well as aspiring writers. Rachilde was part
of that late-nineteenth-century phenomenon of the far Left that was so radical it
could appear right wing.[24] In the case of Rachilde, the difficulty in deciding
where her political sympathies lay is symptomatic of this Left-Right confusion.
On the one hand, for example, Rachilde opposed granting women the vote and
later wrote an antifeminist pamphlet,[25] but it is not clear to what extent these
statements were intended to be provocative rather than serious arguments.

I shall not take on the question of Rachilde's personal politics (a complicated issue in and of itself) in this article. Instead, I wish to focus on the cultural use that was made of her work, which was popular and representative of
certain trends. In addition, through her associations with other writers,
Rachilde was linked to numerous developments in intellectual thought that are
reflected in her novels. To begin with, she had been a close friend of Maurice
Barrès, a writer associated with the development of nationalist thought at the
turn of the century in France through his novels of national rootedness and the
"culte du moi."[26] Barrès and Rachilde had met in or around 1884, shortly after
the former's arrival in Paris, probably through René Brissy, who published
both one of Rachilde's early works (*Histoires bêtes pour amuser les petits enfants d'esprit*) and Barrès's review "Tâches d'Encre."[27] Barrès provided an introduction for the 1889 edition of Rachilde's most famous work, *Monsieur
Vénus*.[28] Rachilde had been physically and emotionally attracted to him for a
time, though by the 1890s she was married to Alfred Vallette and the infatua-
tion with Barrès was long over. On the intellectual rather than the affective
plane, Rachilde did not sympathize with the radically conservative turn in Barrès's thought and later, in 1921, participated in the dadaist attack on him,[29]
though there were undoubtedly conservative currents in her own thinking.

Despite the differences, their friendship and association illustrate something of the way ideas circulated in France at the turn of the century as well as the extent to which Rachilde was part of a network of writers in whose work the embryonic ideas of fascism were expressed and worked out. Both Rachilde and Barrès had been dipped in the same cultural bath and their respective work bears traces of some common elements.

Finally, and no less importantly, Rachilde was also an influence on the Italian futurist and proto-fascist F. T. Marinetti. If Italian futurism is one of the antecedents of (Italian) fascism, and Marinetti is one of the founders of futurism, the infancy of fascism may be said to include the formative years of Marinetti's career. In 1899, Marinetti, then on the editorial board of the *Anthologie-revue* of Milan, wrote to the French novelist Rachilde to praise her work.[30] Marinetti, having spent much time in Paris, was well acquainted with its literary scene, and Rachilde had also published in the *Anthologie-revue* (including the prose poem "Les Fumées"). Believing that Rachilde's work deserved to be more widely known in Italy, Marinetti announced his intention of translating some of it into Italian. Among the works he cites are *Les Hors-Nature* and "Les Vendanges de Sodome," both works from the 1890s.[31] The novel concerns two incestuous brothers, while the short story presents a myth about the origins of (male) homosexuality. The foregrounding of themes of sexuality suggests why these texts appealed to Marinetti, and I believe that the themes influenced his conception of gender roles in the fascist context (for example in such later work as *Mafarka*),[32] but I also want to examine the role of nationalism in these works and suggest that this tells us something about women's imagined relations to nationalism and is part of what Marinetti admired.

The publication dates of the works examined here (1893–1897) coincide with a period of intense development in right-wing thought in France. In particular, 1894 (the year of publication of the collection *Le Démon de l'absurde*) marks an important "first" in the history of fascism, or at least in its etymology. In this year the French word *faisceau* (bundle), the French cognate of the Italian *fasces*, is bundled together for the first time with a reference to racism in a political pamphlet published in Paris. The "doctrine du faisceau" was formulated by (in Alice Kaplan's words) "an obscure French gangster-aristocrat named the marquis de Morès" (xxviii).[33] Rachilde's work thus incubated in the same environment that gave rise to such political activity, and what is etched explicitly in the former work is also echoed in the latter.

Textual Analysis

While the marquis de Morès was preoccupied with race, in "Les Vendanges de Sodome" Rachilde offers a parable about the origins of homosexuality.[34] As a parable, the story presents itself not as a realist representation but as a symbolic account of origins, inviting allegorical interpretation. The narrative recounts how the men of Sodom, out gathering grapes, stone to death a woman who tempts one of them sexually, and that night commit sodomy for the first time. Most of the description concerns the vines and the plain on which they grow, so the few details about the city of Sodom and its inhabitants are telling. The sketchy picture of the city itself—"un mur protégeant une ville" behind which rises "une tour de pierres ivoirines, d'une blancheur d'ossements" (72)—suggests in its spare language both the enclosed, self-contained aspect of the city and the phallic core of civic life, a core that evokes a charnel house. The walled city of Sodom represents security and freedom from temptation for its male inhabitants, but this security appears to rest upon morbid foundations.

The security of the city requires the repression of sexual desire. All the women who might lead men into (sexual) temptation, among them the central character in this story (a young woman named Saraï), were expelled from the city so that the men could save their energy:

Se condamnant virilement à une chasteté de plusieurs années pour ne pas donner le meilleur de leurs forces, durant le temps des récoltes, à ces gouffres de voluptés qu'étaient les filles de Sodome, ne gardant que les mères en gésine et les vieilles, ils avaient répudié jusqu'à leurs épouses, jusqu'à leurs soeurs. (77)

Their sacrifice is premised on the biologically unfounded but culturally powerful zero-sum assumption that the amount of energy is limited and that energy used in sexual activities represents energy subtracted from labor. Their individual desires are thus subordinated to the collective good of the state.

The men of Sodom cannot always remain safely inside the city, however. It is necessary to leave the city to perform essential tasks such as harvesting the grapes. And when they leave the city, they become vulnerable to what they have attempted to expulse, temptation. Saraï (the woman) cleverly chooses the men's weakest moment to tempt them: she waits until they are tired from their exertions and lie down at noon for a siesta, in other words when they are least able to resist temptation. Ever since St. Augustine's pronouncements about the inability to control nocturnal emissions, (male) Western culture has wrestled with the guilty knowledge that the body will betray the mind during sleep. Such guilt was renewed in a secular form at the end of the nineteenth century by theories about the relation of unconscious desire to the conscious mind, especially during sleep and other unconscious states. Charcot's work on hysterics had suggested that the body could display knowledge that bypassed the conscious mind, while Freud's theories went one step further in *The Interpretation of Dreams*, suggesting that, during sleep, the conscious mind was temporarily disabled while the uncontrollable desires of the unconscious would manifest themselves in dreams.

In both theology and psychiatry, then, sleep is a dangerous state because it allows what is normally hidden to manifest itself. The woman who tempts sleepy or sleeping men is thus the return of the repressed in two senses. First, in a figurative, psychoanalytic sense, she represents the sexual knowledge the men have tried to push aside. In the more social sense, Saraï is a sort of scapegoat, but her refusal to carry away the evil she has been designated to represent means that the attempt by the men of Sodom to repress desire by casting out from their midst the person who embodies it has failed. She carries desire back to them and evokes in their sleepy, vulnerable minds the evidence of their unacceptable desires.

Saraï does not tempt all men equally, however. She targets the most vulnerable of the group, a young man named Sinéus, who has been introduced to the reader in somewhat ambiguous and troubling terms as the most handsome of the adolescents. He represents both innocent youth (a virgin, naive and pure) and sexual knowledge: the bees mistake him for a ray of honey, "un rayon de miel" (74). He treads grapes as diligently as the others, but he also capriciously adds fistfuls of wild roses to the harvest (75). It is because Saraï lies down with Sinéus that she arouses the anger of the men of Sodom, though it turns out she has tempted a number of other men, who also have a score to settle with her. The men of Sodom spontaneously reach for stones, and, both as revenge for past temptations and to ward off future ones, they attack Saraï. She takes refuge in a vat under the grapes, which they then proceed to press. Here the parable draws on both theological and popular associations of blood and wine, violently commingled by the men of Sodom. Later that night, when they drink the wine they have pressed, they commit sodomy for the first time, "en les bras de leur jeune frère Sinéus, dont l'épaule douce avait la saveur du miel" (81), an act that closes the story.

This parable of the origin of sodomy thus suggests that it is a repression of the feminine through its incorporation, a parable that fits all too well with certain accounts of the origin of the fascist male body. As in the object relations model, in this version the feminine is not simply repressed but incorporated. When they drink their wine—the "horrible liqueur empoisonné d'amour" (80)—the men are literally ingesting the woman, since her blood has been pressed into the grape juice. It is not the violent act of Saraï's murder that causes the perversity—an act triply perverse because not only homosexual but also pedophilic ("leur *jeune* frère Sinéus") and incestuous ("leur jeune *frère* Sinéus"). In condemning this woman (and presumably others) to live in the desert, they have committed murder before, albeit indirectly. What sets this occasion apart from other instances of transgression is that the wine has a new ingredient. Under the effects of intoxication—not unlike those of sleep in their ability to reduce the "inhibitions" of the conscious mind—the men give in to a desire for each other produced by a mixing of bloods. It is feminization,

implies Rachilde, that gives rise to sodomy, but it is more than just feminization. It is the result of an attempt to live without "wives and sisters."

But there is another male body in this parable, the body politic. Sodom is
not just a walled city but a city-state, one in which women are invisible or else
expulsed. We learn nothing about the women of Sodom who remain in the city
(mothers and the old). All the other women have vacated the public places:
"elles étaient sorties des carrefours, avaient fui des rues" (77); indeed, they
have vacated the city. The women who are left are those who no longer count
as women, those who have been desexualized because they are mothers or because they are no longer sexually attractive. Only the men remain, organized
patriarchally, led by "un vieillard deux fois centenaire" who is "père, chef et
patriarche." The city-state of Sodom is a male-dominated, "patriarchal" society, the kind that might later be called "fascist." It evokes the short-lived Italian fascist state known as the Republic of Salò, which Pasolini made the setting for his last film *Salo: 120 Days of Sodom* (1975), a film based on the work
of Sade but which in Pasolini's version, as in Rachilde's story, combines a vision of an authoritatiran state with sexual politics.

The men of Sodom reject "jusqu'à leurs épouses, jusqu'à leurs soeurs." The
rhetorical force of this sentence draws attention to itself. The biblical incanta-
tory repetition of "jusqu'à," as well as the semantic connotations of the prepo-
sition, underscores the extremism of the action of the men of Sodom. The
words thrown into relief and apposition by the repetition—"épouses" and
"soeurs"—stress not just the femininity of what is repressed (a slippage often
made easier in French—although significantly avoided here—by the dual
meaning of "femmes") but the fact that they represent kinship relations. The
exiled women are wives and those female relatives who become the wives of
other men, sisters.

The emphasis on the repression of particular women (wives and sisters)
rather than on all women suggests that the fascistic tendencies of Sodom are
not simply the product of male effeminacy, though this is part of it. Instead, the
emphasis is on women's roles in kinship networks. The work of Claude Lévi-
Strauss may help explain the relevance of the connection between gender and
kinship. According to Lévi-Strauss in *The Elementary Structures of Kinship*,
social bonds are created when men exchange their sisters for wives.[35] By extension, then, the rejection of wives and sisters presents a threat to those social
bonds, but in order to understand the connection to fascism, we must explore
further.

The connection between sexual and national politics is also evident in one
of the novels admired by Marinetti, *Les Hors-Nature*, which retains the fantasmatic and allegorical qualities of "Les Vendanges de Sodome." Jean de Palacio, for example, describes it as "un agglomérat de mythes."[36] The sketch of
patriarchal society without wives and sisters presented in "Les Vendanges de

Sodome" is played out at length (great length) in this novel, which presents an extended dystopic version of what happens when kinship systems break down. It concerns two brothers, Jacques-Reutler and Paul-Eric de Fertzen, who, like the men of Sodom, are homosexual and incestuous. As in "Les Vendanges de Sodome," the action of the novel takes place when "normal" defense mechanisms have been rendered useless. "Action for action's sake" was recently identified by Umberto Eco as one of the enduring characteristics of Ur-Fascism,[37] and the two sections of this novel explore two modalities of action: "le rêve de l'action" and "l'action de rêve." The dream of action, although deferring real action, is a constitutional element of fascism, while the action of the dream—or "dream work"—realizes action while also inviting psychoanalytic interpretation.

As in "Les Vendanges de Sodome," women are expelled from this closed universe in the first section. Paul fantasizes about creating "un éxil d'héroïque travail où la femme ne sera plus qu'une question d'hygiène" (50). But also as in "Les Vendanges de Sodome," gender and sexuality are a source of conflict and trouble for the social order. As Jean de Palacio notes, the title phrase "Hors-Nature" was a well-accepted and recognized decadent code for "perverse," and by changing the title of the novel (it had originally been called *Les Factices*, a title with its own set of implications),[38] Rachilde was clearly announcing that her novel would defy the norms. But in an important twist on the expectations of who is "perverse" and who "normal," it is not the effeminate Paul-Eric who dreams about going against nature but rather the (excessively?) virile and Germanic Jacques-Reutler, as Palacio notes in his introduction (7). The latter tells his brother: "Tu n'es pas un vrai . . . hors nature, toi!" (324), so that even in the artificial ("factice") realm of the "hors-nature," there are both real and not-so-real outlaws.

Lévi-Strauss's model of the kinship system requires several taboos in order to function: The first is the imposition of exogamy, which, through its role in marriage, becomes the "archetype of all other manifestations based upon reciprocity" (481). The second taboo concerns incest: if every man could marry his own sister, he wouldn't need another man's sister, and, without this need to look beyond one's own immediate family for a spouse, the kinship system would quickly break down. (To paraphrase the Arapesh who was interviewed by Margaret Mead and quoted by Lévi-Strauss, "we don't sleep with our sisters. We give our sisters to other men, and other men give us their sisters," 485). A third taboo is implied by Lévi-Strauss's model but unstated in his work. Exogamy presupposes a taboo against lifelong and exclusive homosexuality or celibacy, at least insofar as these would be understood culturally to preclude marriage. (They may be institutionalized in some cultures in such a way as to be perfectly compatible with conjugal obligations.) We might paraphrase the Arapesh and say that if every man could marry his brother, he wouldn't even need his sister, let alone another man's. The threat posed by homosexuality to the social order, then, is not just the perceived effeminacy, but the removal of some players from the reciprocity game. In other words, homosexuality is not simply a violation of gender roles, but it is perceived as a threat to the social fabric.

The de Fertzen brothers break all three taboos, causing a total breakdown of the kinship system. First and most importantly, they refuse exogamy. Reutler and Paul are compared to Romulus and Remus, the founders of Rome, but, unlike the founders of Rome, they reject the kinship system that would be created through exogamy. Reutler encourages Paul to make a socially advantageous and acceptable marriage early in the novel, but the latter refuses. While he does not refuse to sleep with women, he refuses to marry one. He dallies, for example, with the aspiring actress Jane Monvel rather as Dorian Gray toys with Sybil Vane, and even stages a play he has written (a version of the Pygmalion myth) so that she can become an actress. The opening night of the play is compared to a wedding (157), but the only embrace Jane finds waiting for her is that of death when she accidentally (or was it?) falls during her entrance. As for Reutler, he has lost his ring finger in a duel defending Paul's honor (288). He has never had so much as a "maîtresse . . . digne de ce nom" (290).

Having thus opted out of the kinship system, Reutler and Paul become each other's only kin. Their father, a Prussian officer who had met their mother when attached to the embassy in Paris, dies in battle during the Franco-Prussian war on the very day his wife dies giving birth to Paul-Eric. Both deaths are attributed to Paul-Eric: "Carnassier sans le savoir, puisqu'il a dévoré en naissant et son père, cérébralement, et sa mère, physiquement" (114). Since their parents are dead, the brothers gradually become everything to each other: mother, father, sister, brother, spouse. Reutler serves as midwife at his brother's birth before becoming surrogate mother and suffering a sort of postpartum puerperal fever (118). Paul refers to him as "mon père, mon frère et mon ami chéri" (121). Eventually Reutler declares that he loves Paul-Eric and considers himself his fiancé (269). The problem with this couple, then, is not just that they are composed of the wrong elements (male and male instead of male and female),[39] but that they are too self-sufficient. By being all things to each other, they have no need of others. Nothing circulates; if marriage is the archetype of exchange, there is no exchange, reciprocity, or mutual obligation between the closed unit of the de Fertzen brothers and the rest of the world.

It is in the sense that they refuse kinship that they place themselves "hors nature." Lévi-Strauss explains how the structures of exchange created through marriage transform nature into culture: "the value of exchange is not simply that of the goods exchanged. Exchange—and consequently the rule of exogamy which expresses it—has in itself a social value. It provides the means of binding men together, and of superimposing upon the natural links of kinship the henceforth artificial links . . . of alliance governed by rule" (480). Like the decadents, Lévi-Strauss values the artificial over the natural, but to the extent that marriage comes to be mistaken for the natural order, the return to a presocial self-sufficiency is viewed as an aberration, a deviation from the natural, and "hors-nature." The artificial ("factice") de Fertzen brothers choose not to do what everyone else does "naturally."

But the anthropologist is also a political scientist, for in Lévi-Strauss's work, the relations between families stand metonymically for relations between nations. "If our proposed interpretation is correct," he theorizes, "the rules of kinship and marriage are not made necessary by the social state. They are the social state itself" (490). *Les Hors-Nature* illustrates this conflation of kinship with nationality. The de Fertzen brothers are not just anomalous individuals, they are personifications of nations. Their father was Prussian, their mother French. Thus they are the offspring of a form of national exogamy, but rather than blending both national characters, each brother retains a distinct national affiliation (etymologically, the relationship of being a son). The difference is underscored onomastically. Both brothers have hyphenated first names (Jacques-Reutler and Paul-Eric) in which the first element (Jacques, Paul) is French (their maternal clan line) while the second (Reutler, Eric) is German (the patronymic). Yet both are usually referred to (by the author and by each other) by an abbreviated form of the name that captures their respective national identification (Reutler/Paul, Prussian/French).

In addition to their name, each brother embodies his respective national identity. Reutler, the elder brother, is the Prussian while Paul is the French, despite the fact that they had the same parents. The difference is attributed to place of birth and upbringing, as well as temperament. Reutler "n'est pas poète, lui, il est la lourde science" (72). Born in Germany, he lived alternately in the French château of Rocheuse and in a small town in Swabia. At the outbreak of the Franco-Prussian war, his mother returned to France, where Paul was born in the conditions already described. Reutler has kept the knowledge of these conditions from Paul, and they are only gradually revealed in the novel. While Reutler represents the hard, disciplined, military brother, capable of self-denial of monastic proportions, Paul is the soft, capricious, and capriciously cruel foil to Reutler's hardness.

The national characteristics of Reutler and Paul thus follow isomorphically the gender stereotypes of the late nineteenth century. Reutler is the hypermasculine (soon to be fascist) Germany, while Paul is the effete France in decline, already an old set of stereotypes by the end of the nineteenth century.[40] It was a commonplace of the decadent movement to compare France after the Franco-Prussian war to the late Byzantine Empire, and *Les Hors-Nature* adds to this repertoire the image of Paul, the personification of France, dressed as a Byzantine Princess. The long description of Paul's costume contains all the topoi of decadent figure: "une simarre . . . constellée de pierreries de toutes les nuances"; "une dalmatique en soie, mi-partie pourpre et violette, bordée d'hermine"; "une ceinture écharpe . . . retombait par devant en ruissellement de chaînes d'or, de cordelettes de satin où se mêlaient d'énormes cabochons d'améthyste, de rubis, et les triples croix grecques"; "les bras, nus, surchargés de cercles de métal et de bijoux"; "un diadème . . . dardait les feux aigus des brillants et dégouttait du sang des rubis"; "icone à la fois royale et divine, profane et sacrée"; "ses yeux bleus d'acier flambant dans l'ombre du koheul" (195–97). The Byzantine princess violated by the iron Prussian. With this image at the center of *Les Hors-Nature*, Rachilde captures France's view of itself after the 1870 Prussian war, evokes the aesthetics of the decadent movement, and anticipates the allegory of France violated by Germany noted in post-World War II antifascist discourse such as Sartre's essay on collaboration.[41]

The first part of *Les Hors-Nature*, then, reproduces the same narrative trajectory of "Les Vendanges de Sodome." Men—and by extension nations—refuse "wives and sisters," but their refusal entails a price. As Lévi-Strauss states "every disharmonic regime leads to restricted exchange" (493), but at least in some cases, restricted exchange leads to disharmonic regimes. The restricted exchange of the Franco-Prussian regime of the de Fertzen brothers creates such a disharmonic regime, just as the self-imposed restrictions on wives and sisters led to the disharmony of Sodom. In the second part of the novel, Reutler and Paul have the opportunity to change their minds about admitting women into their regime/family. A solution to the de Fertzens' isolation presents itself in the form of a woman, Marie. Marie is a servant and (like the brothers) an orphan. In Lévi-Strauss's terms this orphan status makes her a free-floating signifier: she does not represent any kinship group that can gain through her exchange. Marie is really the "hors-nature," the outlaw, here, not the de Fertzen brothers as is often supposed, though by "nature" here we should understand rather the socially constructed order instituted through marriage. She was an outlaw when found because she had refused to let herself be raped by her previous employer, a grocer in Besançon who dismissed her because she refused to submit. She ended up in the village near Rocheuse, where she was accused of being a "coureuse de nuit." Because the villagers then expulse her (as the men of Sodom expulsed sexually tempting women), she burns down the church. Because the village rejects her from its society, in other words, she symbolically rejects society and its institutions.

Reutler and Paul encounter Marie in the process of helping to put out the fire, but the circumstances of their meeting signal the sacrificial role Marie is to play. She is found, trapped like an animal in the bushes with her hair tangled in brambles: "les cheveux, des nattes lourdes, accrochés aux branches du roncier. Elle avait dû se faire prisonnière des épines comme une biche se fait saisir au collet" (332). She had been trying to escape the villagers who were pursuing her when she got entangled. This providential discovery evokes the biblical sacrificial ram caught in the bushes sent by God to Abraham to replace Isaac. The substitution of the ram allows Abraham to preserve his kinship group, and Marie will offer such a possibility for the patriarch Reutler and his "child" Paul, but they will refuse.

Reutler and Paul take her in. Although her lot is not an easy one (she is scorned by the other servants, and Paul cuts her hair in a symbolic act of castration), Marie falls in love with Reutler, while Paul falls in lust with Marie. Mistaking Paul's lust for love, and wishing to make him happy, Reutler promises to marry Marie and make her mistress of the estate if she will have sex with Paul. If this pact were to come about, it would restore some of the reciprocity of Lévi-Strauss's exchange. Paul would give "his" woman to Reutler in marriage, signifying an alliance between "Prussia" and "France."

Marie rejects the offer to become Reutler's wife, however, because it is based on economic self-interest, not love. She refuses to accept her role as currency, and instead insists on deciding on her own disposition. Just as she had burned down the church, she burns down the de Fertzen house, in which the brothers are immolated. As the ending of the novel makes clear, the brothers are indeed united by Marie at the end as the kinship system collapses along with the house. They die together, though not simultaneously: Reutler strangles Paul to prevent his suffering. Prussia and France are thus locked in a deadly union that is doomed because not mediated by the exchange of a woman.

The gender confusion in *Les Hors-Nature* is thus only a symptom of a much larger refusal, the refusal to accept the kinship system and the social organization of reciprocity it entails. It is, moreover, a refusal overlaid with nationalist significance, since Reutler and Paul represent not just individuals who reject this system, but political bodies. As, Lévi-Strauss has helped to show, the kinship system (which, it turns out, is indistinguishable from the formation of the state) requires a sex/gender system in order to function smoothly. Refusing to uphold clear gender roles, then, may represent a threat to the maintenance of political roles. The corollary of this argument helps to explain why fascism may look hypermasculine. In effect, maintaining strict gender roles—masculine or feminine—may be of significance to the nationalist state, which has an interest in maintaining its authority. In this sense, fascism is not only hypermasculine, it is also hyperfeminine. Or rather, fascism is hypergendered, it requires gender difference.

Marie's reluctance to be the object of exchange highlights Lévi-Strauss's assumption that women are only passive participants in the state, just as they are passive in the kinship system. In Lévi-Strauss's model, the circulation of women provides the social glue. Woman exists only as a form of currency, a medium of exchange. Comparing the kinship system to linguistics, Lévi-Strauss concludes: "the emergence of symbolic thought must have required that women, like words, should be things that were exchanged" (496). The necessity of this role for women has been challenged, but Lévi-Strauss describes accurately the situation of women in the West in the late nineteenth century (and into the twentieth).[42] Woman is a form of currency (479); she has no personhood. She is part of the body politic but has no body of her own to dispose of through marriage. The nineteenth century was the age of nationalism, as Benedict Anderson has shown, but an age in which men and women were positioned differently in relation to the "imaginary community" of the nation. A man's nationality was that of his birthplace or of his parents (German, French, Italian), but a woman's was that of her father or husband: a woman who married not only took her husband's name by custom but, until relatively recently (1973 in France), also took his nationality by law. Or, put another way, a woman's nationality was womanhood. The exclusion of women from the (male) national body was enacted across Europe through various forms of legislation as well as custom: women could not vote, were defined legally as minors (as in France) or simply as property, could not enter into contracts, serve as legal witnesses, own property . . . The list goes on and is all too familiar.

Marie attempts to resist being cast in this passive role, but her limited success reveals the constraints of the system at the turn of the century. She refuses to become a token of exchange in someone else's system, but she cannot change the terms of the system itself. Since she cannot be a citizen, she cannot act in her own interest. She can only destroy the system, not change it. Marie's situation illustrates what might be called "gendered nationalism." The kinship system described by Lévi-Strauss and famously renamed by Gayle Rubin as the "traffic in women"[43] provides the switchpoint between gender and social structure, sex and politics, and links gender to fascism and nationalism.

Despite the difficulty in offering an absolute definition of fascism, nationalism is a recurrent core element. Whether it is in the work of Barrès or the Nazi transformation of left-wing international socialism into right-wing national socialism, nationalism permeates right-wing ideology. In "The Conquest of Modernity: From Modernist Nationalism to Fascism,"[44] the Italian political scientist Emilio Gentile has argued that nationalism was also an important factor in Italian fascism, since "the cultural roots of futurism and fascism intersect in the common terrain of 'modernist nationalism'" (59). The futurists were attracted to fascist politics, argues Gentile, because they believed it offered "a total mobilization of culture" (79) that would unify the Italian nation and enable it to make a unique and lasting impression on global culture.

Nationalism thus recurs in different national contexts as part of right-wing thought, but nationalism, like fascism, has a gender. Like the fascist body, the national body was male. As illustrated in the work of Rachilde, sex roles are also civic roles. At the turn of the century, to be a man is to be a citizen, while to be a woman is to be a token of exchange. Nationalism presupposes a sense of citizenship from which women were until recently excluded. In the famous recruiting posters proclaiming "Your Country Needs You" and featuring Lord Kitchener or Uncle Sam or some other personification of the nation, only the male citizen is interpellated; "male citizen" is a tautology.

In protofascist ideology of the turn of the century, as Lévi-Strauss helps to explain, Woman is a medium of exchange who circulates in marriage but cannot act on her own behalf. Excluded from citizenship, she cannot participate in the system. If she resists her role as medium, her only choice is to (try to) destroy the system itself, as Marie succeeds in doing. She cannot participate in the system without becoming a man. In the sense that women have historically been excluded from nationalism, the fascist body has been a male one, but this is not to say that fascism is essentially male, only that historically it has been so.

Women and Nationalism in the Twentieth Century

Women's relation to nationalism has historically been different to that of men, and this has affected their participation in political movements. Women's alienation (their status as "other" within the nation) at the turn of the century excluded them from the birth of fascism, but their gradual incorporation into the body politic brought new temptations as well as celebrations. Gaining the vote, an event that followed a "world war" for most women of Europe and North America, changed women's imagined relation to the nation in the twentieth century. It is usually heralded as a moment of celebration by feminists, but ironically suffrage may also encourage an identification with the imagined community of the nation associated with fascism. Thus, as women felt more and more a part of the nation, so the possibilty for sympathy with fascism increased. Claudia Koonz, for example, shows how German women's experience of World War I, combined with their unexpected enfranchisement in 1918, gave women "a stake in the nation that most had not previously felt."[45]

This may help to explain the reactionary attitudes of some of the first elected female politicians. Nancy Astor, the first female representative to the British parliament following women's enfranchisement, later became "one of [Britain's] staunchest and most persistent defenders of Hitler and Mussolini," choosing "to associate herself with the most reactionary, cynical, dishonest, disloyal, and treacherous politicians of the day."[46] It has been suggested, most recently by John Halperin, that she "acted out of ignorance and intolerance and prejudice" (212), but an alternative explanation which preserves some rationality in her judgment is that she acted exactly the way her male counterparts typically had at their first taste of belonging to a nation. In the United States,

the pacifism of Jeannette Rankin played right into the hands of isolationist, ul-
traconservative, and anti-Semitic mothers' groups such as the National Legion
of Mothers of America, which opposed American involvement in World War
II using the (essentialist) rhetoric of maternal concern for their draft-age sons,
though they also sympathized with Hitler's expulsion of the Jews and hated
communism.[47] One such leader, Elizabeth Dilling, even described herself as a
"professional patriot" (Jeansonne, 10). In France, where women were not
granted the vote until after World War II, Margaret Collins Weitz hypothesizes
in her book on women in the Resistance that "not having the vote proved a
negative advantage for women" because they "seldom had a political agenda"
(288). It also seems more than a coincidence that Italian fascism succeeded in
gaining Italian women's allegiance by, in de Grazia's words, "nationalising"
them—her choice of words is perhaps even more accurate than she realized.
By encouraging them to see themselves as a part of the imagined community,
Mussolini gave women the same incentives to adopt right-wing ideology as
men had previously had.[48] Women's increasing sense of political power, then,
can lead to an extreme nationalism couched in the language of traditional gender roles, "family values," pacifism, and other ideologies that help maintain
fascism's "hyper-gender."[49]

Yet women's (contingent) alienation from nationalism at the turn of the
century has also meant that in some ways women were uniquely positioned to
resist fascism and the extremes of right-wing ideology, as a couple of brief examples will illustrate. Confronting the imminent fascist threat in Europe in the
1930s, Virginia Woolf wrote *Three Guineas* as a response, albeit a fictionalized one, to a letter, "a letter perhaps unique in the history of human correspondence, since when before has an educated man asked a woman how in her
opinion war can be prevented?"[50] The remainder of the book sets out Woolf's
pacifist agenda, but it is a gendered agenda, for, as Woolf notes, "to fight has
always been the man's habit, not the woman's . . . Scarcely a human being in
the course of history has fallen to a woman's rifle" (13). Woolf advocates the
education of women, their advancement in the professions, and the protection
of culture and intellectual liberty, so that free and educated women can offer
their independent opinion without economic or personal consideration. Woolf
is convinced that the disinterested advice of such free women will be different
from that of men, though not necessarily for essentialist reasons. Rather, it is
because women have been excluded from full citizenship and as a result have
less cause for patriotism and national identity: "as a woman, I have no country.
As a woman I want no country. As a woman my country is the whole world"
(197). Woolf specifically identifies nationalism as one of the "unreal loyalties,"
from which women had thus far been spared.[51]

Another, more modern, example is Adrienne Rich. I mention her because of
the very noticeable rhetoric of patriotism that permeates her work in collections

from *Your Native Land, Your Life* (1986) to her most recent work to date, *The Dark Fields of This Republic* (1995). She does not resist nationalism, as Woolf does, but instead imagines a different relationship to the nation. In "Sources,"[52] Rich continued the feminist project of "claiming an identity they taught [us] to despise,"[53] by embracing her Jewish heritage. In this process, "becoming a citizen of the world" as she was advised (not by Woolf but by the unnamed "you" of the poem, *Native Land*, 18) would prevent her identification with European Jews, would prevent her from seeing her place in the world, a sense of situation necessary "not in order to stare with bitterness of detachment" but as the grounding for "a powerful and womanly series of choices" (*Native Land*, 27). In the poem series "Eastern War Time" (in *An Atlas of the Difficult World*),[54] Rich invokes the Holocaust to caution that remembering the past is not sufficient, however: "Memory says: 'Want to do right? Don't count on me'" (*Atlas*, 44). Rich, who has assumed the voice of political conscience for late twentieth-century women, has "tried to listen to / the public voice of our time." The antidemocratic threat of fascism calls again at our own end of century, both through the reelection of former fascists internationally and through the domestic terrorism of white supremacist militias, and this time it calls to women as well as men. Rich has "tried to remember and stay faithful to details," not just to remember but to take note of and record "who was in charge of definitions and who stood by receiving them" in (borrowing from F. Scott Fitzgerald) the "dark fields of [this] republic."[55] "This is not somewhere else but here," cautions Rich as she describes "the great dark birds of history"—birds that evoke not only the American eagle but the black spread eagles of the Third Reich—which "screamed and plunged into our own personal weather." An understanding of the gendered role of nationalism in right-wing thought may be useful in understanding the (personal) weather forecast. Among other things, it makes it possible for feminism to analyze the destructive rhetoric of patriotism and nationalism and to articulate the need to resist such rhetorical appeals. It makes it imperative for progressive movements worldwide to recognize the need to engage women politically lest their political enemies capitalize on their neglect and "nationalize" women following Mussolini's model.

We must wait for the full impact of women's assimilation into the nation to take effect before we conclude that fascism manifests itself only as hypermasculinity. (I think of the studies showing how long it took for different, gendered voting patterns to show up after women received the vote in the United States.) Despite Woolf's optimism, it does not necessarily follow that women will always resist fascism everywhere. De Grazia argues that, on the contrary, Italian women were particularly vulnerable to the seduction of the fascists because their liberal predecessors had so neglected women's demands for civil rights.[56] Women were attracted by the fascist promise of suffrage even when the promises resonated with hollowness. The relation of women to nationalism has evolved historically along a different path than the one taken by men. The conjunction of forces that produced the fascist male body may never find its female analogue, but as women accede to greater participation in the political sphere, in "the affairs of the nation," it becomes increasingly necessary to envisage and to watch for the possibility of fascism in a female form.

Mary Jean Green

The Bouboule Novels:
Constructing a French Fascist Woman

Women have no positive role to play in the French right-wing literature of
l'entre-deux-guerres. When they are not caricatured as the sterile incarnation
of a decadent order, they are castigated for their materialistic appetites and
their ability to flourish in serene indifference to the masculine suffering of the
Great War. In *Voyage au bout de la nuit* Louis-Ferdinand Céline sums up the
egotistical indifference of American-style capitalism in his erstwhile war
nurse Lola, while the women of Pierre Drieu la Rochelle, like praying man-
tises, seek to destroy the weakened male. Alternatively, these fictional women
sicken and die, like the madonna-like Pauline of Drieu's *Gilles*, mirroring the
fate of a mortally stricken France. The misogyny of right-wing political fiction of the 1930s goes beyond the personal idiosyncracies of individual writers: it spreads throughout the literary production of the interwar years, particularly in novels dealing with the war and its aftermath.

As is reflected in this fiction,[1] World War I produced a pervasive attitude of
hostility toward women, who were never subjected to the agony of the
trenches and were further perceived as using the war to gain their own independence while the men were off at the front. Mary Louise Roberts has argued that these widespread postwar attitudes expressed in gendered terms the
anxiety of a profoundly disrupted French society about its own future. In her
view, gender became "a discursive prism through which to envision the war's
effects.[2] She goes on to explain:

Debate concerning gender identity became a primary way to embrace, resist, or reconcile oneself to changes associated with the war. To make sense of these changes,
French men and women had to understand them on their own terms. Further, to make
these changes comprehensible, they focused on a set of images, issues, and power relationships that were both familiar and compelling. For many French men, it was simpler

to think about the dramatic shifts in their wives' behavior or in women's fashion than it was to seek to understand something as abstract as the fall of the franc or the decline of the middle class. Because gender issues were literally "close to home," they made the war's impact in some sense culturally intelligible. By debating issues of gender identity, the French came to terms with a postwar world that threatened to become unrecognizable to them.[3]

Women's voices were not dominant in this gender debate, and this was particularly true in the field of political fiction, which was left almost exclusively to men. While researching my own book on the response of French writers to the political events of the 1930s,[4] I was surprised and disappointed by my failure to discover texts by women who might, like their male colleagues, have used writing as a way of coming to terms with the overwhelming political issues of the day. Recognized women writers like Colette, although not by any means indifferent to politics, continued to explore their private fictional worlds, while women who would later reflect on the political meaning of the era, like Simone de Beauvoir and Clara Malraux, had not yet found their literary voice.

Only in the realm of popular literature is it possible to find a woman writer whose very titles assert the primacy of politics, in novels such as *Bouboule, dame de la IIIe République* (1931), *Bouboule chez les Croix de Feu* (1936), *Bouboule et le Front Populaire* (1937). Looking more closely, other volumes in the same series disclose a political content as well: *Bouboule à Genève* (1933) reveals itself to be a dissection of the League of Nations, while *Bouboule en Italie* (1933) affords an opportunity to observe Mussolini in action, and *Bouboule dans la tourmente* (1935) is centered on the riots of February 6, 1934. Even the first volume, *Bouboule, ou une Cure à Vichy* (published in 1927, well before the name of this provincial spa took on an ominous meaning), offers a commentary on the French political and financial corruption of the day.

The mysterious author of the series, who identifies herself only by the pseudonym of T. Trilby, is clearly a woman of the French Right, but I have been able to find little information on the real woman behind the name. Despite the fact that she published the seven novels of the Bouboule series with the major French publishing house of Flammarion—in addition to more than fifty other novels and twenty-four children's books—her publisher now claims to have no access to information about her.[5] All that we know of her is her real name, Thérèse Delhaye de Marnyhac (in some sources, Marniphac), strangely echoing, in form, that of her female protagonist, Béatrice ("Bouboule") Lagnat de Sérigny, suggesting potential parallels between author and character. Since the novels are written in the first person, there is no room for ironic distance between author and narrator, and it is evident that Trilby fully endorses the outspoken opinions of her character.

These opinions can be identified with the French Right of the late 1920s and 1930s, and, more specifically, with the positions of the Croix de Feu, of which Bouboule becomes a member in the last two volumes of the series. Thus, the Bouboule novels offer a unique opportunity to observe the construction of a right-wing woman of *l'entre-deux-guerres* in the hands of a politically engaged woman writer. Moreover, this vision of womanhood must have struck a responsive chord in some mainstream readership: although the editor has not made marketing information available, the fact that Flammarion published such a large number of Trilby's novels, including the seven in the Bouboule series, suggests they enjoyed some measure of popular success.

But I would like to go further and suggest that Bouboule is more than a reflection of vaguely right-wing ideas. In my reading, this literary figure represents an attempt to embody in a female protagonist the ideals of French fascism, much as writers like Robert Brasillach or Pierre Drieu la Rochelle had tried to do in the case of fascist men. By making this leap from the Croix de Feu to fascism, I am making a contentious move, since there is sharp disagreement over the applicability of the fascist label to the large, mainstream post–World War I veteran's movement. Many French authorities on fascism, from René Rémond to Pierre Milza, joined by non-French historians like Zeev Sternhell,[6] have excluded the Croix de Feu from their studies of fascism, on the grounds that it was merely a continuation of the conservative social and economic ideas of the traditional French Right. My own view of the Croix de Feu is more in line with that of Robert Soucy, who claims that such an attempt to exclude the Croix de Feu would "devalu[e] the *predominantly* conservative social and economic ends of Italian, German and French fascism."[7] Soucy prefers to emphasize the authoritarian nature of fascism and its opposition to political liberalism and Marxism, characteristics shared by the Croix de Feu. Moreover, he notes the reliance of the Croix de Feu on mass rallies and huge patriotic parades as a means of attracting supporters, a tactic having more in common with those of Italian and German fascists than with the practices of the traditional French Right. Another North American historian, William D. Irvine, who shares Soucy's view of the fascist character of the Croix de Feu, points out the significance of this controversy for our larger perception of modern French history:

Given its dominant role on the French right, it is a mattter of some consequence that most French historians insist that the Croix de Feu was not fascist. As Philippe Burrin has remarked: "If we exclude the leagues and especially the Croix de Feu, as all [*sic*] historians do, the [fascist] phenomenon becomes insignificant.". . . In the absence of a large formation like the Croix de Feu (and the Jeunesses Patriotes, which is also invariably excluded), one is drawn into the world of ephemeral political formations and cranky little magazines with a few hundred readers.[8]

If this large, mainstream veterans' movement is recognized as fascist, then fascism cannot be considered a foreign import, as most French historians have maintained. Rather, fascism would be revealed as a widespread indigenous phenomenon, deeply rooted in French right-wing thought.

It is true that Bouboule refrains from using the word *fascist* to characterize her political position, although she explicitly identifies herself with the Croix de Feu. This is not surprising, given her avowed disinterest in party politics. But the leader of the Croix de Feu himself, Colonel de La Rocque, also refused to claim his movement as fascist in the 1930s, perhaps in order to avoid identifying this group of highly patriotic veterans with movements and leaders perceived by many Frenchmen as foreign and opposed to the French system of government.[9] Despite Trilby's failure to adopt the term, however, it would not be an exaggeration to see in the evolving character of Bouboule an example, perhaps unique in French fiction, of the construction of a French fascist woman. Bouboule makes the political views she espouses abundantly clear, and they reflect many, but certainly not all, the concerns of the French Right in this period. Committed to the traditions of a rural France, she is strongly opposed to all traces of a threatening postwar "modernity," and her marriage, blending her own Auvergnat peasant blood into her husband's aristocratic family, unites the various strands of the old French conservative coalition. Bouboule's contempt for the chaos of the French parliamentary system is evident from the beginning of the series, and, as she admires the success of Mussolini in Italy, she yearns for a strong leader who would "rise up" (*surgir*) to solve the problems of France. While her nationalistic sentiments remain a constant, the threat of German aggression, which dominates the early volumes of the series, is increasingly replaced by a sense of menacing forces from within France itself, from both Marxist-led masses and the increasing presence of foreign immigrants (dismissively termed *métèques*). In this, she mirrors the evolution of the Croix de Feu and many other areas of the French Right.

These attitudes are the common currency of the French Right in this period. What is striking is the way in which these political positions are embedded in plot structures ostensibly concerned with events in the domestic sphere. It is evident that, in writing the Bouboule series, Trilby was faced with formidable literary and ideological problems. First, she was presenting material of an increasingly political nature in a form accessible and appealing to the mainstream women readers, housewives, and mothers, to whom the novels are obviously directed. A second but not unrelated problem derives from the nature of her ideology itself: she has framed a woman character primarily devoted to her role as wife and mother, committed to the traditional values of *la France profonde*, who is, at the same time, an active participant in political events at the national and even international level. How is a woman whose life is presumably consumed in service to others to become the active "hero" of her own story? The fascination of Trilby's novels lies in her literary solutions to these ideological dilemmas—which emerge as central to the position of women in fascist ideologies.

From the beginning of her series, Trilby attempted to reconcile her political interests with the presumed expectations of her readers by inscribing them in plots that center on romance and family relationships. In *Bouboule, ou une Cure à Vichy* (1927) Bouboule meets her husband, the handsome aristocratic Daniel de Sérigny (here named Cérilly). However, in the course of the novel her beloved father is talked into becoming a Senator and dies shortly after assuming office, presumably a victim of the noxious atmosphere of Paris and its corrupt parliamentary system. Having inherited the family estate in Auvergne, Bouboule heroically adopts an entire family of small children, left homeless by the imprisonment of their corrupt banker father, a situation that is surely an oblique commentary on the world of high finance. In this first novel of the series, political commentary is not foregrounded, but the ideological drift is unmistakable.

When, in *Bouboule, dame de la Troisième République* (1931), Daniel de Sérigny assumes the father's role as parliamentary representative of the region, Bouboule at age forty is again plunged into the Parisian political scene. Responding to the violent chaos of the Chamber of Deputies, she arranges for her husband to take boxing lessons, which prove eminently useful. As he battles German imperialism on the parliamentary scene, she wages war on the home front with the German baron who attempts to seduce her daughter Denise, in the end driving him out of the country at gunpoint.

Although Bouboule wins this battle with the Germans, she loses her daughter to the convent in the course of a family pilgrimage to Rome and the sources of European culture in *Bouboule en Italie* (1933). But all is not lost: she has an opportunity to see Mussolini and to admire his beneficent influence on the happy, industrious Italians. She has earlier had an opportunity to discover the beauty of traditional Japan, as she develops a strange but chaste extramarital friendship with a Japanese aristocrat while accompanying her husband on a mission to the ineffectual League of Nations in *Bouboule à Genève* (1933). The main plot in this novel revolves around her husband's attempts to marry off their remaining daughter, Claire, herself hopelessly in love with Bouboule's adopted son Jacques, who in turn suffers from unrequited love for Claire's older sister Denise, now forever beyond his reach. Happily for all, this romantic impasse is resolved when Jacques is killed in the February 6 riots of 1934 in *Bouboule dans la tourmente* (1935), freeing Claire to marry a nice young Croix de Feu section leader, which in turn liberates Bouboule from her constant preoccupation with her daughters' marriages and allows her to join the Croix de Feu herself.

In *Bouboule chez les Croix de Feu* (1936), politics clearly move out of their subordinate status to dominate the main plot, which could be characterized as a sort of political bedroom farce, as Bouboule and Daniel attempt to conceal from each other their membership in the Croix de Feu. In *Bouboule et le Front Populaire* (1937) all pretense of a nonpolitical plot is dropped. The birth of Claire's twins is subordinated to Bouboule's confrontation with the evil forces of the Popular Front on the streets of Paris and in the countryside, as hordes of politicians with Semitic noses invade her beloved Vichy, site of her first meeting with Daniel, and left-wing labor agitators threaten to corrupt the purity of the Auvergnat peasants. As is clear from the dates of publication, the novels mirror the development of current events, and the increasing dominance of politics in the series reflects the growing importance of politics in French life during the 1930s. The evolution of Bouboule from a character who is primarily wife and mother to a role of political activism extending beyond the home mirrors the increasing attempt to enroll women in fascist organizations like the Croix de Feu during this period and suggests an evolving concept of women's role in fascist ideology—a role fraught with contradictions, as was the case in Germany and Italy.

As I have argued, the interest of Bouboule as a fictional construct lies less in her explicitly stated political views than in the way these views are staged and embodied in a woman character. My use of the term "embodied" is not innocent, because Bouboule's body itself is constantly foregrounded by the writer. As her nickname ("little ball") suggests, Bouboule's figure is round, refusing to conform to the slim elegance of the Parisian fashion silhouette. She is constantly pointing to her plumpness in a way that is self-mocking but also self-affirming. Mealtimes are at the center of her world, and she is never happier than when the family is gathered for a copious teatime snack on the terrace overlooking the river on the Auvergne estate or in the comfortable Paris residence near the Bois de Boulogne. As a young country girl, Bouboule has expressed disdain for her mother's world of Parisian fashion, but as she goes on to assume the responsibilities of the wife of a government minister, she makes frequent visits to Parisian milliners and couturiers, under the tutelage of her fashion-conscious daughters. As she admits, maintaining a suitable French elegance is a patriotic duty, the necessary consequence of her nationalistic views. But even her daughters' fashion counseling cannot avoid the inevitable disaster, like the clown-like striped pajamas that send her into fits of self-mocking laughter on the overnight train to Rome.

Bouboule's rotundity could easily be dismissed as a foible of the author's (and perhaps a reflection of her own physical characteristics as well), if it were not for the prominence of woman's body shape in the discourse of gender in the interwar period. In fascist Italy, as described by Victoria de Grazia, the discussion of maternity focused on a set of opposing female models, one fat and the other thin: "Fascist propaganda manufactured two female images. One was the *donna-crisi*: she was cosmopolitan, urbane, skinny, hysterical, decadent, and sterile. The other was the *donna-madre*: she was national, rural, floridly robust, tranquil, and prolific."[10] In France, as Mary Louise Roberts has pointed out, anxiety about the destructive effects of change in the immediate postwar years was focused on the stereotype of *la femme moderne*, with her short skirts, bobbed hair, and slim, boyish figure. Freed from all traditional social constraints, she represented the sexually promiscuous woman who, as portrayed in war novels and films, had indulged in infidelity while her husband endured the hardships of the trenches. In her refusal of the soft roundness of the maternal form, she summed up French anxiety about the nation's declining birthrate, attributed in much of the public discourse of the active pro-natalist movement to women's selfish refusal to have children. As Roberts documents, medical authorities saw a clear connection between the new, slim body image and the declining birthrate: "In 1919, the natalist doctor François Fouveau de Courmelles claimed that the new styles had 'reduced' women 'to the state of eunuchs or sticks [*bâtons*], in which no supplementary being could find a place to lie or be nourished.' He dubbed postwar fashion 'the fashion of non-nursing . . . the fashion of non-motherhood.'"[11] Of course, this new standard of slimness imposed additional constraints on women in terms of dieting and corsets, and this may have been a factor in Trilby's violent defense of plumpness. But most commentators condemned the new body shape as a repudiation of women's traditional role, and many shared in Drieu la Rochelle's lament that, in the cultural decadence of the postwar world, French civilization "no longer has sexes."[12]

Bouboule confronts an example of a young flapper type in the figure of her daughters' friend Ginette, who smokes cigarettes, dances to jazz, and mixes up a mean *cocktail*. Interestingly enough, Ginette makes her first appearance at the center of a parliamentary reception in her parents' home; clearly, her "decadent" behavior is to be identified with the corruption of the parliamentary regime. The drink she mixes is fittingly dubbed a *cocktail ministre*, and when Bouboule accuses her of using it to poison them all, her commentary extends beyond the alcohol being served to encompass an entire political milieu. As is her general practice in these novels, Bouboule combats these threats to French stability by exercising her maternal skills: after chiding Ginette for her behavior, she takes the young woman to her bosom and turns her into an ally and confidante—although never allowing her to take her place in the ranks of good French mothers. This is a destiny apparently reserved for her own plump daughter Claire, a mirror-image of her mother. Ginette appears later on as an activist connected with the Camelots du Roi, the youth wing of the Action Française, whom Bouboule views as political allies.[13]

Bouboule's identity as a plump, nurturant figure is reiterated in her constant connection with the serving of food. Moreover, the food she prefers to serve, whether in Paris or in the country, is deeply rooted in her native Auvergne: "Voici le goûter: thé, toasts, beurre frais qui vient de chez nous, confiture et miel de Jenzat, fruits de notre Auvergne."[14] It is in Auvergne that Bouboule finds her sustenance, and it is here, in the French countryside, that she finds the healthy, life-giving (if calorie- and cholesterol-rich) *produits du terroir* with which she regales her family, just as France itself symbolically draws strength from its connection with the land and the peasantry. This association of the maternal role with the images of traditional French stability was, according to Roberts, a major factor in its importance:

> The image of the loving wife and mother provided a badly needed fiction of stability in a time of great turbulence and change . . . [French men and women] signaled their profound anxiety concerning the passing of cherished ideals and social practices. In the decade after the war, legislators, novelists, social reformers, journalists, and feminists of all political stripes invoked the importance of a domestic and maternal role for women. They demonstrated a strong urge to return to a prewar era of security—a world without violent change.[15]

If the sanctification of the maternal figure by men in the war could be seen as a yearning for the stability of the prewar world, in the universe of the Bouboule novels this world is represented by the Auvergne estate, a place of unchanging natural beauty and simple peasant traditions (which, however, will be challenged by the intrusions of the Popular Front).

The roundness of Bouboule's maternal form underlines her rejection of the life-denying thinness of the "modern woman" (at one point, she refers to these elegant fashion plates as "squelettes ambulants"[16]). However, natalist concerns, so prominent in the public discourse of the time, are hardly mentioned in the Bouboule novels, aside from a brief passage in which the Popular Front is accused of making it impossible for a young shopkeeper to have any children at all. Bouboule's own family is hardly a demographic model, since she only has two children, both of whom are daughters, and she seems unconcerned about having failed to produce sons for the army. As was the case with Italian fascists studied by Victoria de Grazia, the pro-natalist rhetoric of the political leadership seems to have had little effect on the traditional values and practices of the bourgeoisie.[17]

However, Trilby is concerned with constructing a spiritual model of motherhood, which seems almost independent of children actually borne. This in itself was wholly in accord with the discourse on women of the Croix de Feu. In the public ceremony that inaugurated the movement's *section féminine* in 1934, one of the principal speakers, a Protestant pastor, glorified women's role as mothers and even encouraged unmarried women to become "indirect mothers, mothers by divine right," by adopting one or several (orphaned) "children of France."[18] Such a practice of spiritual maternity is central to the Bouboule novels, especially the first, *Bouboule, ou une Cure à Vichy*. In a story focused on the courtship of Bouboule and her husband, Daniel, the obstacle to their otherwise foreordained marriage is provided by Bouboule's temporary adoption of an entire family of small children during their father's imprisonment. Initiating an important pattern of action in the series, Bouboule's sense of maternal devotion empowers her to undertake a form of independent feminine action that flies in the face of the social norms, as represented by her tradition-bound, social-climbing mother. Her mother's warning that the presence of the children will drive away the handsome, aristocratic Daniel, however, only gives him an opportunity to demonstrate his true strength of character. As she will later do in the case of Ginette, Bouboule is able to use the weapons of maternal nurturance to save the oldest son, Jacques, from his father's corruption, and in *Bouboule, dame de la IIIe République*, we find that Jacques has grown up to run his father's banking career and provide moral guidance for his father's life. Here, what might be viewed as a plot element belonging to the feminine sphere of private life takes on far greater importance against the background of the financial scandals of the last decades of the Third Republic. Clearly, Trilby has constructed a situation that allows a woman who confines herself to playing a socially sanctioned role within the family nevertheless to extend her action to the public sphere and take a hand in saving the country.

However, the implausibility of this form of action must soon have become apparent to Trilby herself: events showed that it would have taken more than a few good mothers to put an end to France's financial scandals. This is perhaps recognized in Trilby's unwillingness to realize a possible marriage between Jacques and Bouboule's older daughter, Denise. Never freed from the taint of his father's corruption, Jacques dies satisfyingly and heroically fighting for "l'honneur et la propreté" of France, a phrase that is repeated several times,[19] becoming a leitmotif of Bouboule's ideology. Jacques's fatal wound is inflicted in the street riots of February 6, 1934, which, as must be remembered, occurred in protest against the political and financial corruption exposed by the Stavisky affair, in which a clever con artist had seriously compromised a number of members of France's governing regime.

In *Bouboule, dame de la IIIe République* motherhood continues to be the empowering force in Bouboule's life, although here it leads to a scene of unexpected aggression. Forced to take action in order to save her daughter from abduction by a German baron, Bouboule is able to use her trusty revolver to defend both her family and her anti-German nationalism, hustling the baron out of the country even as her daughter prepares to elope. This culminating episode, with its melodramatic overtones, is jarring in its contrast to the otherwise calm domestic setting, and it is apparent that Trilby has gone to some lengths to provide her heroine with this occasion for action. Most noticeably, she constantly invents thin excuses to keep the facts from Bouboule's husband, who might more appropriately have dealt with the situation. The wild implausibility of the dénouement suggests a certain impatience on the part of the writer with her protagonist's confinement to a merely domestic role; she appears to be seeking a greater freedom of action for her heroine, one with clearer impact on the public sphere.

Bouboule is constantly asserting an independence of mind that jars with her stated ideals of feminine self-sacrifice and submission to authority, and she often rebels against the prevailing social norms for women of her class. She is critical of women's enslavement to fashion, although in the later novels she recognizes the importance of French elegance as a unique and important feature of national identity. She is a devoted mother, but she is openly unenthusiastic about having to assume the feminine role of hostess and promoter of her husband's political career. On the other hand, she is eager to assume managerial responsibility for the Auvergne estate, directing the work and managing the accounts with confidence and skill.

Constantly invoking the need for discipline and obedience, a favorite theme of the Croix de Feu,[20] Bouboule is nonetheless eager to assert her own independence from those in authority, whether in the nation or in her own family. In describing the activities of French right-wing groups, she singles out for admiration the audacious exploits of young women: the young Croix de Feu supporter who slaps a disrespectful passer-by, and her daughters' friend Ginette, who is arrested during an illegal protest with the Camelots du Roi. Far from encouraging feminine obedience to authority in this case, Bouboule seems to revel in the new self-assertiveness of the young fascist women: "Actuellement les femmes ont du cran, ce ne sont plus des brebis qui acceptent sans protester les décisions des hommes au pouvoir."[21] In the later novels of the series Bouboule herself frequently acts in defiance of her husband's wishes, although the implicit conflicts are inevitably resolved by the fact that she always acts in support of the right cause (and the cause of the Right), thus ultimately winning the approbation of her husband, although often after the fact.

As would be expected of a woman of her political stripe, Bouboule is openly hostile to feminism, and she is particularly opposed to women working outside the home. In *Bouboule dans la tourmente* Bouboule has a direct and hostile confrontation with a feminist, whom Trilby has appropriately dubbed Mme Braillard. On several occasions, however she expresses a backhanded approval of women's suffrage, on the grounds that women voters could not possibly do worse than what men have done in producing the current parliamentary regime. In her 1933 novel, *Bouboule en Italie*, she ends her criticism of a former government minister by articulating a rather surprising optimism about women's voting rights: "quand les femmes voteront et auront des pouvoirs égaux à ceux des hommes, il faudrait mettre à l'écart des types de ce genre."[22] Later in the same book she reminds her readers that, in a critical period of its history, France was saved by Joan of Arc, "une femme qui aurait bien mérité d'être électrice."[23] In several instances, these novels seem the work of a woman trying to break free of a stereotyped feminine role. Yet, because of her essentially conservative ideology, it is impossible to interpret Trilby's writing as a clever strategy of feminist subversion.

Throughout most of the seven novels, Bouboule sees motherhood as her primary form of identification, and it is in this role that she seeks justification for her independent actions—a definition of independence she sometimes carries to the point of eccentricity, as in the episode of her encounter at gunpoint with the German baron. Her privileging of the maternal role corresponds to its importance as a means of defining women's place in society in the ideologies of the postwar French Right, and indeed in the fascist ideologies prominent throughout Europe at this time. As Claudia Koonz[24] and Victoria de Grazia have extensively documented, motherhood constituted women's major mode of participation in the societal projects outlined by both Hitler and Mussolini, however different these projects might appear in other ways. In France, Mary Louise Roberts has explained the reasons why, particularly during the war and throughout the postwar era, motherhood was at the center of women's claim to a role in the state, since it offered the only occasion for a sacrifice equal to the *impôt de sang* (literally the blood tax) demanded of men in battle.[25]

Examining the issue in a larger context, Nancy Huston has found this gendered equivalency between childbirth and war to be "one of the rare constants of human culture," and she demonstrates the way in which the two activities have long been perceived to be mutually exclusive.[26] The force of this traditional polarization of roles may account for the profoundly ambivalent social attitudes observed by Margaret H. Darrow in her study of representations of the French war nurse in World War I, the only socially sanctioned form of women's wartime activity in France.[27] While the maternal caring role stood behind women's nursing activities, Darrow concludes that it nevertheless provided only insufficient justification for women's involvement in the masculine sphere of war, since the volunteer nurses were widely criticized and their contributions quickly forgotten after the war. These attitudes are reflected in Bouboule's hostility to the former nurses who dared to claim their status as veterans and their right to march alongside the Croix de Feu men in the parades of the postwar years.[28]

Yet, as the Bouboule series progresses, the demands of *haute bourgeoise* motherhood seem to provide insufficient occasions for the type of hands-on action Trilby prefers, and she gradually abandons motherhood as a motor of her plot. In the last two volumes, after Bouboule finally succeeds in marrying off her remaining daughter to a politically suitable husband, she plunges headlong into politics, joining the women's section of the Croix de Feu and participating in its activities. But, although Bouboule obviously yearns to take action in the public sphere in order to save an endangered France, the ideology of the Croix de Feu, with which she is concerned in these texts, presents her with a number of contradictions. At the center of *Bouboule chez les Croix de Feu* and *Bouboule et le Front Populaire* are Trilby's efforts to create a role for women in a paramilitary organization composed of male war veterans, an organization in which physical combat, from which women have traditionally been excluded, is seen as the sole arena of meaningful action.

The dilemma faced by Trilby was not unique, nor was it limited to the Croix de Feu. It was a problem faced throughout Europe by fascist women who had espoused the activist ideals of the movement but had found themselves, as women, excluded by the very ideology in which they professed to believe. As Victoria de Grazia has shown in the case of Italian fascism, this ideology of activism and motherhood contained dangerous contradictions for fascist women: "there were manifest tensions between the ideals of self-abnegating motherhood invoked by the dictatorship and its endorsement of social activism; between the pressure to be docile homebodies and the challenge to be the fit companions of elites."[29] As de Grazia goes on to document, the women who joined the Italian fascist movement with great enthusiasm in its early years were soon marginalized: "As the first groups of women joined the *fasci di combattimento* in 1920–21, fascist leaders argued that the piazza was no place for women. Women belonged in the back lines, engaged in assistance. The male hierarchy clearly regarded even this service as subordinate and auxiliary."[30]

In the original organization of the Croix de Feu, composed of veterans of the Great War, there was indeed little room for women, although the place given to women by the movement's monthly (later weekly) newspaper, *Le Flambeau*, evolves, from its first issue in 1929, to reflect the changing political realities of the 1930s. Despite Bouboule's disapproval of their presence in parades, their status as veterans did enable former nurses to participate in the Croix de Feu, and in September 1933 *Le Flambeau*, disputing a statement that few women possessed the *carte du combattant*, claimed 120 women as members of the movement.[31] Several articles in the early years of the paper's existence describe the wartime heroism of individual women nurses, prisoners-of-war, and *cantinières*. However, before the official establishment of a *section féminine* in 1934, women played a relatively minor role in *Le Flambeau*, although the content of the advertising indicates that women were assumed to be among the paper's readers: there is regular advertising for household appliances, perfume, and beauty salons, although much space is also taken up by publicity for radios, cars, and wines, in ads that are clearly aimed at male readers. Women were certainly targeted by the columns of recipes and household hints that appear sporadically in the newspaper, beginning in 1931. Ironically, these women's columns are generally entitled "Ce qu'une femme doit savoir," a name that echoes another rubric much in evidence in the paper, "Ce qu'il faut

savoir," a column concerned with informing the readership of issues and policies directly affecting veterans. Knowledge is thus neatly divided into gender-
determined spheres: while men must keep abreast of matters relating to war
and politics, women must know how to prepare dinner (preferably using traditional recipes) and knit small items of clothing. The implied message sums up
the rather limited Croix de Feu thinking on women at the time: with the exception of bona fide war veterans and, of course, the movement's revered heroine,
Joan of Arc, the place of women is not in politics, but in the home.

However, this concept of women's role in the Croix de Feu undergoes a
major change in 1934, with the official formation of the *section féminine* in the
wake of the February 6 riots. The reasons for this move are never explicitly
stated in *Le Flambeau*, but the women's group is formed at a time of acceler-
ated recruitment and rapidly growing membership, and it precedes by only a
few years the movement's forced transformation into a political party. According to figures cited by Robert Soucy, at the time of the February 6 riots the organization had 35,000 members, mainly war veterans. By August 1935 (over a
year after the creation of the *section féminine*) police estimated the membership had expanded sixfold, to 228,000 members, many of them nonveterans.
The formation of the women's group—the term "ladies' auxiliary" is perhaps
a more accurate translation—also coincides with a new emphasis on "social
questions," which begin to displace the movement's original concern with foreign aggression; as is also true in the Bouboule novels, after 1934 the Croix de
Feu seemed to perceive the threat to French cultural survival as coming less
from the Germans than from the indigenous French Left.

· · ·

The Croix de Feu leader, Colonel de La Rocque, set the policies for the
women's group, as he did for all other aspects of the movement. According to
his directives, women in the *section féminine* were expected to devote themselves exclusively to social action, organizing summer camps, soup kitchens,
and mother and child health services. Thus, women were excluded from the
central activities of the movement, the parades and demonstrations, which
were, in the turbulent 1930s, often accompanied by the threat of violence. In
Bouboule's own summation, the task that La Rocque set forth for women in
his movement is that of caring for the children of France: "penchez-vous in-
lassablement sur toutes les misères des enfants de France."[32] A full-page drawing in *Le Flambeau* of May 23, 1936, illustrates this activity by showing a
woman holding up a baby, a woman tending a sick child, and another woman
wearing a wide-brimmed hat who rather grimly supervises a boy digging in a
garden.

At least some of the Croix de Feu's new concern with social issues may
well have been inspired by the threat posed by the newly formed Popular

Front, the union of French communists and socialists precipitated by the February riots. As Bouboule revealingly explains, Croix de Feu women were expected to go off into the communist-dominated suburbs to bring about "national reconciliation" through their charitable deeds: "Il faut partir pour la Croisade Sainte, il faut aller dans la banlieue rouge apprendre à ceux qu'on dresse à nous haïr, que nous voulons leur bonheur."[33] Such social action was seen as an acceptable extension of women's primary role as mother, as the movement's discourse makes clear. However, the rather abstract nature of the Croix de Feu rhetoric of social action cannot help but give rise to some suspicion on the part of a skeptical reader. *Le Flambeau* often refers to these charitable projects in general terms, but the paper offers few concrete examples of successful social action (although at one point statistics are offered on the success of soup kitchens and the distribution of clothing).[34] Similarly, little in the way of effective social work is reported in the course of Bouboule's involvement with the women's group in *Bouboule chez les Croix de Feu*. In the one meeting of the *section féminine* Bouboule actually attends, the women are engaged in sewing unidentified items for a sale destined to benefit the Croix de Feu propaganda effort, hardly a project aimed at helping the poor.

In fact, even after the creation of the *section féminine,* women's position in the Croix de Feu remained marginal in this period, before being further reduced when the movement was dissolved in July of 1936 and subsequently reemerged as a political party.[35] The account of the ceremonies that inaugurated the *section féminine*—relegated to page 4 of *Le Flambeau* of April 1, 1934[36]—makes clear the paradoxical nature of the effort to create a place for women in this male-dominated milieu. The true nature of women's place in the movement is reflected in the very organization of the program. While it is the Colonel de La Rocque who sets the tone of this meeting, as in all gatherings of the Croix de Feu, it falls to the three main speakers—all of them men—to define the proper role of women in French life. They are not only men but clergymen, representatives of the three major French religious traditions—Protestant, Catholic, and Jewish.[37] Clearly, divine sanction must be invoked if women are to be enrolled in a political movement. The two women who are permitted to speak, presidents of the Paris sections of the Right and Left Bank, do so only briefly and apologetically: "Jamais je n'ai parlé en public," one of them explains.

The ceremonies themselves seem directed toward an inherently self-contradictory goal, asking women to participate in the public sphere of politics when their proper place, in the ideology of the very movement they are urged to support, is in the home. In fact, much of the public discourse seems designed to resolve or at least blur the edges of the dilemma. The issue is directly confronted in the opening paragraphs of the article in *Le Flambeau*, which justifies the political involvement of women by invoking the grave threat to French security. The idea that women have no place in politics ("La politique ne regarde pas les femmes") is fine for those who, erroneously, believe that all is well with France, claims the writer. Since this is evidently not the case, women have joined the veterans in their effort to save their country, but this, he concludes, cannot be considered politics ("il ne s'agit pas de politique").

As might be expected, the speeches stress the importance of women's place in the family and the sublime nature of the role of mother. The Protestant pastor takes advantage of the occasion to call for an increase in the French birthrate and compares those who object to new births ("objecteurs à la naissance") to the pacifist conscientious objectors ("objecteurs de conscience"), who also pose a grave threat to the survival of France. But in the context of this political gathering, it is not enough to urge women to stay home and take care of their children. As is suggested by the titles of the speeches—"La Femme au foyer," "La Femme dans la cité," "La Femme dans la nation"—the moral ideals of motherhood, Service and Sacrifice, must be extended to the whole of France. According to the pastor, France and humanity itself may be regarded as a mere extension of the domestic sphere: "ne donnez pas votre foyer comme le but suprême à l'existence de vos enfants . . . Prolongez-le, utilisez-le pour des fins qui le dépassent et le dépasseront toujours: pour la Patrie et pour l'Humanité toute entière." Both the rabbi and the priest echo this sentiment, citing biblical and historical examples of wives and daughters who worked alongside their men for the cause of peace and justice (perhaps significantly, mothers are not mentioned in this context of civic participation).

As the press accounts of these ceremonies make abundantly clear, the real place of women in the Croix de Feu is on the margins. Framed by male speakers, their role defined by masculine discourse, women in the Croix de Feu had little power to speak or act. Such a role runs counter to the personality of Trilby's protagonist, who clearly desires to speak and act in her own name. On one level, Bouboule is well aware of the marginalization of women in the movement, and Trilby structures an entire scene to represent this marginalization and inscribe Bouboule's acceptance of this aspect of women's "place." Agreeing with the men that women have no place on the battlefield, Bouboule concludes that women have no right to march with the veterans. Yet, not content to remain a mere onlooker, during the Croix de Feu parade on November 11, she walks along with them—on the sidewalk. She even manages to construct a role for herself, subordinate though it may be, in enforcing respect for the flag: "Je marche sur le trottoir avec les Croix de Feu, dans le défilé, il y a très peu de femmes, c'est préférable. Souhaitons que la prochaine fois il n'y en ait plus une, elles sont mieux dans la foule, promenant leur enthousiasme, et obligeant ceux qui oublient à saluer les drapeaux."[38]

In an earlier episode, also set during a parade, she admiringly describes a young woman Croix de Feu sympathizer who had physically attacked a hapless young cyclist disrespectfully attempting to cross the parade route. The woman tells the cyclist, "on ne passe pas," echoing the famous slogan of Verdun, which Trilby has recalled elsewhere in the volume. Although Bouboule is generally in favor of discipline and obedience to the leader, who wants women to confine their activities to charitable action, she resembles many of the young right-wing men of the era in her yearning for a good street fight. In *Bouboule dans la tourmente,* she longs to participate in the antiparliamentary riots of February 1934, but she follows her husband's orders by limiting her activities to caring for the wounded in a nearby restaurant, thereby mimicking the nursing role of women in the Great War. Bouboule also yearns to be among the students throwing rotten apples at a French law professor who is involved in the Ethiopian affair (which she refers to, in racist terms, as "l'affaire noire"):

Si j'étais déjà un membre des Croix de Feu je m'offrirais pour ce petit travail. Je me vois très bien attendant dans la cour de la Faculté le passage de ce triste professeur. J'aurais dans un sac, pour ne pas me faire remarquer, douze pommes, de mauvaise qualité, c'est tout ce qu'il mérite, et avec quel plaisir je bombarderais l'affreux bonhomme.[39]

But in *Bouboule chez les Croix de Feu* the nearest she comes to direct action is an unprovoked verbal assault on a group of women supporters of the Popular Front who have had the misfortune to sit near her in a tearoom. In sharp contrast to the nurturant maternal stereotype to which she usually attempts to conform, Bouboule does not hesitate to threaten the women with a violence worthy of the worst of fascist street gangs:

Croyez-moi, si vous avez vraiment les idées que vous défendiez tout à l'heure, évitez de les dire à haute voix comme vous venez de le faire, les Françaises ne le supporteront plus, et vous risqueriez un jour de recevoir quelque chose en pleine figure qui pourrait compromettre votre maquillage, l'arrangement de vos boucles et la situation de votre chapeau. Voilà ce que les femmes Croix de Feu sont capables de faire, vous êtes prévenue et je suis certaine que vous ne recommencerez pas.[40]

Bouboule justifies her threats on the grounds that such rich women ensconced in a luxurious *salon de thé* have no right to propagandize the masses (although she does not feel it necessary to justify her own right, as a rich estate owner who frequents the same tearoom, to speak for the same masses). While this type of action has little support from the official rhetoric of the *section féminine*, which she has quoted at some length, Trilby assures her readers that it is an acceptable part of the "propagande individuelle" expressly encouraged by Colonel de La Rocque. In the subsequent volume, *Bouboule et le Front Populaire*, Bouboule does not hesitate to enter directly into the realm of action, entirely abandoning all mention of the *section féminine*. Instead, she mobilizes her peasants to repel unionizing efforts on the part of the Popular Front and later manages to get herself arrested during a Croix de Feu demonstration.

While Bouboule explicitly states her agreement that women have no place in such activity, she nevertheless begins to play a more active role in the public sphere in the last two novels of the series. And as she does so, despite the earlier assertion of her role as mother, she gradually lays claim to a different identity. It is her success in placing her daughters in their own adult lives, Denise in the convent and Claire in her marriage, that frees her to participate in political activities in her own right, after years of watching her husband from the visitors' gallery of the Chamber of Deputies or the League of Nations. As Bouboule evolves from observer to participant, she begins to renounce her identity as mother in order to reclaim the status of daughter. This change in self-definition is clearly articulated when, as Bouboule formally joins the Croix de Feu, she is asked to state her name and profession. She responds by unexpectedly reverting to her maiden name, omitting her husband's surname on the grounds that she does not wish to compromise his parliamentary career as a member of the Radical Party (from which, unbeknownst to her, he has already resigned). Indeed, as related in the novel, the Croix de Feu has, in a sense, returned her to the status of daughter as a condition of entry. While men like her husband, Daniel, are assured membership by their status of veteran, women must obtain the endorsement of two members, whom Bouboule refers to as *parrains* [godfathers], while happily regarding herself as a *filleule* [goddaughter].

When Bouboule is asked to state her profession, she is momentarily puzzled. Not mother, she muses, since the departure of her daughters has put an end to her maternal duties. Instead, she decides, she is fundamentally a *fermière*, an identity meant to convey her attachment to the land and her identification with the rural workers (although readers may recognize that it merely identifes her as the owner of a large rural estate). The profession of *fermière* defines her not as mother or housewife but as the daughter of her father, whose work she has continued and from whom she has inherited the estate. Ironically, the role of wife does not seem central either to French right-wing ideology or to Bouboule's sense of empowerment; in fact, in her constant concern with Daniel's potential criticism of her independent opinions, the wifely role seems to be a constant impediment to action.

Now that she has symbolically reassumed the status of daughter and the independence of an unmarried woman, Bouboule feels empowered to attend political meetings and demonstrations on her own, often concealing her whereabouts from her husband, and even, in *Bouboule et le Front Populaire*, defying him by writing letters to the minister of the interior in her "own" name and getting herself arrested in a demonstration. As she returns to defend her Auvergne estate from the depredations of labor agitators, imported agents of the Popular Front, Bouboule performs what is certainly the most effective independent political act of her lifetime by personally confronting the labor organizers and convincing the peasants to complete the work of the harvest rather than going on strike. In gaining a voice with her tenant farmers, she again casts about for an appropriate form of her name and, once again, she feels unable to act in her role of wife and mother. Instead, she adopts the signature of "Votre Demoiselle," the name by which the peasants had known her as a child, when, as her father's daughter, she had participated in the running of the family estate. Ironically, this name, with its implied status of unmarried maiden, is reclaimed by Bouboule at the moment when she is about to become a grandmother. And, in fact, she chooses to privilege her new, political identity over her role as mother and grandmother: as her daughter's twins are born while Bouboule is out negotiating with the peasants and doing battle with the Popular Front.

Trilby's fictional reclamation of the power of agency seemingly possessed by the unmarried daughter oddly echoes, not the official discourse of the Croix de Feu, which consistently privileges the maternal role, but the reality of the roles women seem to have played in the movement. Indeed, before the creation of the *section féminine*, the only column in *Le Flambeau* that gave a place to women's names was that of "Fils et Filles des Croix de Feu," a title that, avoiding the gender neutrality of "Enfants," made a specific mention of women. And, in fact, Mlle Féraud, the general's daughter who maintained the archives for this group, goes on to become one of the first two leaders of the women's group. Leadership roles seem open to young, unmarried women, and a number of women whose names are preceded by the title of Mademoiselle play active roles in the *section féminine*, several of them going on to occupy the post of secretary general.

If unmarried women seem to play a significant role in the movement, the only woman whose character and philosophy of life are described in detail by *Le Flambeau* is, in fact, the unmarried daughter of the Croix de Feu leader Colonel de La Rocque. Nadine de La Rocque had been her father's close companion and colleague during the two years that preceded her illness and death at the age of twenty in August of 1934. In the articles that appear in *Le Flambeau* following her death,[41] every detail of her young life is held up as an example, passages from her letters and notebooks are cited with admiration, and she seems well on her way to canonization by the movement. Her anonymous but clearly female hagiographers present moving images of the scenes at her deathbed, describing her father kneeling for hours at her bedside, holding the hand of his dying daughter. Although Nadine's death is a consequence of a typhoid fever apparently unrelated to her work with the Croix de Feu, *Le Flambeau* nevertheless constructs her death as a martyrdom to France: "Tout pour la France . . . même cela, mon Dieu," murmurs La Rocque at her deathbed. Nadine's last words to her priest—"J'aime Jeanne d'Arc"—connect her to another young maiden who sacrificed her life to save France. Directly addressing Nadine's spirit, her biographer clarifies the analogy: "Vous, que vos camarades appelaient le 'chef de notre génération,' vous, dont le coeur battait pour un pays et un père également nobles. Vous, l'amie des travailleurs et des pauvres, vous vous êtes naturellement remise à la bergère qui sauva la France." Like Joan of Arc, Nadine is envisioned as an inspiration for the movement, her spirit going forth before the line of veterans, "étoile des Croix-de-Feu, sainte de nos Associations." A year after her death, another anonymous article in *Le Flambeau* reports that no day passes without flowers and pious visits to her tomb.

In many ways, these obituaries construct Nadine de La Rocque as an icon of the movement's ideals, and thus her qualities may not be those ascribed to an ordinary woman member. In her last illness, for example, she is attended by doctors and nurses representing all three of the major French religious faiths, and, while herself a member of the bourgeoisie, she wears a medal made for her by a worker and a "modest and virginal" garment given her by a working-class woman. Thus, she is said to embody a "fusion of religions and classes." In these accounts it is sometimes difficult to separate the symbolic from the real, but each of the characteristics attributed to Nadine has significance for the movement's view of an idealized female figure.

Not unexpectedly, Nadine subscribes to the charitable role assigned to women by the Croix de Feu. In a letter of October 1933, she writes, "Ne jamais s'occuper de soi-même, souffrir silencieusement, mais parler sa foi patriotique, l'affirmer partout et sans crainte, là est l'existence de mon père, là sera très humblement la mienne; j'irai sans cesse dans les maisons ouvrières, dans les familles pauvres, où je trouve déjà tant d'amitiés sincères et sans détours." In another letter, written a month earlier, she exhorts, "Je voudrais toujours servir, ne jamais paraître." Her personality, in the eyes of *Le Flambeau*, is characterized by a "radiant goodness." Yet, or in addition to these quintessentially feminine qualities, Nadine de La Rocque has other strengths, particularly a keen intelligence: "Tête d'enfant, cerveau d'homme," comments *Le Flambeau*. She is described as having attained the degree of "bachelière complète" at the age of sixteen, but having renounced further study in order to acquire the secretarial skills that would presumably make her useful to her father. Nevertheless, according to her admiring biographer, she continued to read widely in the fields of law, political economy, history, and philosophy. She was, the article assures us several times, *un chef*, a word full of meaning for this right-wing movement with its cult of the leader. A leader in her own right, she is capable of participating completely in the role of her father, and *Le Flambeau* speaks admiringly of "l'union spirituelle totale de notre chef et de sa fille . . . leurs existences fondues l'une dans l'autre." Thus, despite the official exhortation to women in the Croix de Feu to perform their maternal duty, the only woman chosen by the movement to exemplify its highest ideals of womanhood is an unmarried daughter. Like Joan of Arc, the only historical female figure consecrated by this veterans' group,[42] Nadine is a maiden, deemed worthy of direct participation in the spheres of action generally reserved for men.

Both the novels of Trilby and the newspaper of the Croix de Feu reveal a discourse of daughterhood that runs counter to the official idealization of the mother. As it seeks an exemplary female figure to offer as a model for its female followers, the Croix de Feu selects the martyred daughter of their leader, comparing her with the revered French maiden warrior, Joan of Arc. Similarly, as the fictional Bouboule seeks an acceptable feminine role that would allow her the possibility of effective action in support of her political beliefs, she tests the possibilities of the maternal role before discarding it in order to regain the freedom of action she had enjoyed as an unmarried woman empowered by her father and not yet restricted by her husband and children. In both cases, this unstated foregrounding of the daughter seems to undermine the explicit idealization of motherhood so important to fascist ideology.

Yet, there is a certain logic in the movement's choice of Nadine de La Rocque as her father's true female counterpart, as there is an inevitability in Bouboule's recognition of the freedom of action possessed by the unmarried woman. Their reasoning reproduces the cultural patterns traced by Nancy Huston that have traditionally refused participation in warfare, the sphere of masculine action, to married women and especially to mothers, as if, in Huston's words, "the act of giving life were incompatible with the act of dealing death."[43] Virgins, however, have had the power to overcome this cultural ban on women: from the legendary Amazons to the Walkyries to the Maid of Orleans, some virgins, in myth and history, have been able to participate in war. As Huston explains:

> When women do take part in the sacred, it is because they have either renounced motherhood or gone beyond it. As virgins, they have the right to carry the Holy Grail, or to enter a nunnery; among the Celts they could become magicians or prophetesses; among the Aztecs they could be sacrificed to the Sun God. As widows, they often "retrieve" their chastity and acquire new magical powers. But as mothers, they are inhabited by the ignominious forces of the natural world and must therefore be prevented from having anything to do with the spiritual.[44]

Since warfare was considered the primary activity of the Croix de Feu, it is to be expected, following Huston's cultural analogies, that only as maidens would women be admitted to full participation in the movement. This is an insight at which Trilby arrives implicitly by a process of elimination, as she explores the potential for action offered by fascist definitions of women's role. Caught between the urgent need to act on her political beliefs and the limitations those same beliefs placed on women's freedom of action, Bouboule unwittingly enacts in fiction the contradictions at the heart of the fascist feminine ideal.

Martine Guyot-Bender

Seducing Corinne: The Official Popular Press during the Occupation

Mass media offer easy avenues to disguise ideology through what looks like information.[1] This was the approach the French collaborationists took during the German Occupation of France, both in the unoccupied zone under the Vichy government and in the occupied zone under the direct supervision of the German authorities, when they took over the French press and created, with sizable Nazi financial support, a series of publications designed to propagate plans for a German-inspired new society.

As the Occupation progressed, many Parisian collaborationists increasingly distanced themselves from the Vichy government they considered too moderate. However, both groups were basically inspired by authoritarian social structures clearly influenced by fascism.[2] As Michèle Cointret-Labrousse indicates in *Vichy et le fascisme*, Vichy, at least in its early stages, differed from fascism in its strict definition insofar as it did not win its power by force nor succeed in imposing a single political party. Nevertheless, what she calls the regime's *tentation fasciste*, founded upon a long right-wing tradition in France, underlined its four years of existence.[3] This became particularly true after 1942 with the implementation of uncompromising anti-Semitic measures and later with the establishment of the militia. It is also clear that the overt nationalistic bases of the radical Parisian collaborationists showed irrefutable growing influences of fascism.

As historian Andrew Shennan states: "Paradoxically as it may seem, an immediate consequence of the defeat was the creation of a political atmosphere highly conducive to the rhetoric of renewal."[4] Indeed, in both zones, many newspapers advocated the official discourse on this national renewal. Geared to a predominantly male, politically aware, and consenting public, they explicitly laid out their agenda. Concurrently, another type of publication was

69

created to attract a presumably less political feminine audience that was equally needed for the success of this New France. The intention here was to sketch a favorable image of a new social order through enthusiastic and reassuring rhetoric that would shed an auspicious light on the National Revolution.

This was precisely what journalist and politician Jean Luchaire attempted to accomplish in *Toute la vie*, a women's magazine published weekly as a supplement to his collaborationist daily, *Les Temps nouveaux*. *Toute la vie* was published religiously each Tuesday, and in the later part of the Occupation every other Tuesday, from 1941 to 1944. Its goal was to gain women's support for the National Revolution by promulgating both trust in the continuum of French national identity and the need to restructure a society shaken by a former socialist government that was considered responsible for the 1940 political and military downfall.

For today's reader, *Toute la vie*'s thinly disguised message presents the distinct characteristics of an ideological propaganda difficult to accept. In fact, some contemporary observers even question whether it had any effect at all on the French population at the time.[5] However obvious, its soothing rhetoric and its univocal social and gender messages were, I argue, instrumental in anchoring pro-German and pro-Vichy feelings deeper in the minds of the population already predisposed to the ways of the occupying forces. The obscuring smoke screen *Toute la vie* created to cover the Nazis' activities in France and in Europe comforted marginal collaborationists in their indifference and thus dampened potential resistance to the invaders.

Evidence of such appeasing impact is found in *Ma Drôle de vie*, an autobiography by Jean Luchaire's own daughter, actress Corinne Luchaire, written as a response to the accusations made about her family's amicable rapport with the Nazi and Vichy officials during the Occupation. Such an enterprise, in 1948, was rather daring but was doomed to be overlooked. Understandably, *collabos*, even the marginal ones, were not too eager to publicize the details of their lives under the protection of the Nazis. However controversial *Ma Drôle de vie* is, in our own attempt to comprehend the ambiguities of the Occupation and the basis of passive collaboration, its candid recounting of the author's experiences between 1940 and 1945 documents quite clearly how the concerns of women presumed to be peace-oriented, such as those of Corinne Luchaire, served the propagation of fascistic social archetypes in France.

The following study focuses on the rhetoric and reception of *Toute la vie*. It is divided into two parts. The first part draws on Corinne Luchaire's autobiography. It examines how, kept out of the political arena, she and many women from equally privileged milieus, became easy targets and victims of simplistic nationalist propaganda. But, more importantly, I will suggest that these women's assumed values not only permitted but nourished the existence of such discourse. Indeed, *Toute la vie* and the National Revolution planners considered privileged women a malleable audience easy to secure by repeatedly reflecting their interests for peace and stability, and not by proposing social models radically different from the ones already accepted. In a second part, I will observe how, in fact, *Toute la vie* carefully synthesized these long-term aspirations into a new model of a society that would eventually confine women in their traditional roles and forever remove them from the political scene, hence from power. During the Occupation, as in many other crisis periods, women's political neutrality constituted a major asset for power-hungry political factions. Only the vision of normality could convince women of the productive foundations of the new regime.

Let me preface this study by making clear that neither *Toute la vie* nor *Ma Drôle de vie* brings any really new historical particulars to what is already known of the Occupation. The goal of this essay is therefore not to add historical facts to our body of knowledge. It is rather a case study, a close observation of one historical example of intensive social and gender construction. Reading *Toute la vie* and *Ma Drôle de vie* in light of each other, as I propose to do here, informs us both concerning on what premises gender-based social construction can (and, during the Occupation, did) draw, and concerning its reception and impact. The relationship of these two texts, and the study of the fundamental structures of Vichy propaganda that follows, point to the significance of social and political disengagement in the shaping of nationhood, and to the necessity of tranquility that was assumed to be women's most basic desire in the implementation of this revolution.

Targeting Political Neutrality

According to popular-culture observer Colin Mercer, popular publications are especially dependent on the consent of their readership and are more successful when they mirror rather than upset their readers' interests: These "disposable commodities par excellence . . . constitute either a preamble or a break in the routine of the day but not in the sense of an escape, more in the direction of setting a frame, a tissue of confirmation, beliefs and expectation."[6] With this assumption in mind, we will observe in *Ma Drôle de vie* two ways in which Corinne Luchaire found in *Toute la vie* the confirmation of her own social beliefs that comfort and prvileges were given. On the one hand, the actress's portrayal of her social milieu and of her own privileged adolescence defines the audience targeted by *Toute la vie*. The magazine continually celebrated values she considered essential to her survival: luxury, the easy life, simplicity, and peace. On the other hand, she is also the voice of a captive readership ignorant, by design or by choice, of Nazi cruelty. At no point does she distance herself from her own anecdotal history to measure the extent of what happened in

Europe between 1940 and 1945, nor does she evaluate her own, or even her family's, interaction with the Nazis. Clearly her indifference to the social turmoil made her (and other actresses) an obvious icon of positive collaboration, a model of good behavior. As for *Toute la vie*, she was everything at once: she inspired the magazine, read it, and was on occasion its subject. She and the magazine shared an identical lack of compassion and a visible self-contentment. Luchaire's egocentric ideas of politics clearly underscored her social choices.

Throughout *Ma Drôle de vie*, Luchaire asks the following embedded question: "what did I do wrong, what did my family do wrong, that led ultimately to my father's execution for treason at the Liberation?" There is, on the other hand, no trace of any *mea culpa* to be found in her text. Indeed, in 1948, when the impact of the Nazis in Europe was subject to public evaluation, when trials revealed the atrocities committed during the Occupation, Corinne was still oblivious to the implications of her family's relationship with the German embassy between 1940 and 1944.

The situation created by the Nazi invasion offered to the Luchaires, as to many ambitious individuals in France, the prospect of bright tomorrows. As Corinne clearly remembers, "From my earliest childhood, a ministerial crisis, for example, could upset our situation, make us give up plans, elevate or diminish my father's situation, and, consequently, our family's. A certain policy allowed us to have a well-furnished home, a brighter life, pleasant trips. A sudden reversal, on the contrary, forced us to move, to mend our dresses, to go on joyless vacations" (*DV*, 9).[7] Anticipating the benefits he could draw from the German takeover, such as the creation of an important newspaper "of which he had been dreaming long before the war" (*DV*, 139), Jean Luchaire made sure that he was on the right side of the political scene as soon as the Germans arrived in Paris, and immediately supported a policy of collaboration in both zones. He was obviously correct in his plans since, a few months later, he was able to launch the powerful and financially rewarding *Les Temps nouveaux* and later its easy-reading, light-hearted supplement, *Toute la vie*.

Following a general principle that "in reality, the vast majority of the French people . . . [was] apolitical,"[8] Otto Abetz, the German ambassador in Paris and close friend to the Luchaires, heartily encouraged the official press both to generate a message that would speak to the general public free of political jargon and to design a French-specific propaganda. Rather than stress the necessity of political involvement, *Toute la vie* envisioned a future society that would address and solve material concerns that were believed to matter more to homemakers. Consequently, it offered a mixture of fashion, cooking, and leisure articles typical of women's magazines like *Marie Claire*, published since 1936. It also addressed working women's concerns and gender issues previously found in *La Femme au travail*, another women's magazine published between 1936 and 1938, and designed primarily for career-minded women. Many of *Toute la vie*'s themes were especially attractive to upper-class professional women like Corinne Luchaire, who considered herself born for "simplicity and home" (*DV*, 8) and possessed "a furious taste for luxury" (*DV*, 27). Throughout its existence, portraits of healthy, beaming young women graced the front covers of *Toute la vie*, unequivocally reaffirming presumed feminine desires for security and happiness, while acknowledging their ingrained desire to be recognized publicly.

Toute la vie's scope drew directly on Corinne Luchaire's aspirations: "Very young, I was used to seeing sumptuous and delicate decor before my eyes, to consider that beautiful linen, neat clothes, fine fabrics were indispensable to me" (*DV*, 27). Amidst this luxury, the adolescent dreams resembled fairy tales which she liked to reenact in real life. For her, "the legend of the Handsome Knight still rests deep in the heart of the young woman who wants to be 'new look'" (*DV*, 10). *Toute la vie* offered similar visions of Prince Charming, dashing heroes, luxury, and also of traditional gender-based family values, often combined with the image of a dreamland come true. This "reality" bore little resemblance to the repressive state of affairs experienced daily by the majority of the population. It was no more than meticulous linguistic manipulation.

Luchaire's mimicking of the magazine's rhetoric in *Ma Drôle de vie* suggests her silent agreement with *Toute la vie*'s ideological agenda. The chapter titles that divide her autobiography contain both the apparent candidness and the sarcasm typical of the magazine's headlines. She uses military terminology to introduce vacuous social anecdotes, thus illustrating her disbelief in or indifference to the state of war and mocking its effect on the population. Titles such as "My Plot with Flandrin against England" (*DV*, 98) turned out to refer to a tennis match, while "Thunderclap . . . War in Deauville" (*DV*, 102) introduced a story of busy and competitive social life on the Normandy coast. These are obvious imitations of *Toute la vie*'s use of military terminology in the headlines of articles on elegance or social life: "Nachas Pacha Wants to Liberate Egypt" (*TV* 2/19/42), "Women's Mobilization" (*TV* 5/14/42), or "To the Order of Elegance" (*TV* 7/16/42). Similar plays on words were common in other popular publications of the time. *Actu*, the equivalent of *Toute la vie* in Marseilles, offered such sneering headlines as "Among the Little Worries of War, Mosquitoes Are Soldiers' Number One Enemy" (9/5/43), or "Corsets and Wasp Waists Launch an Offensive" (10/9/42). Subsequently, the world became for Luchaire a place where war and suffering were blatantly ignored or mocked, where ambiguity did not exist, and where words such as "happiness," "glory," and "luxury" coincided with reality. As she asserts in the first pages of her book, "life is reality . . . and this is the life I will reveal" (*DV*, 11). In 1948, *Ma Drôle de vie* still echoes, hence still implicitly defends, *Toute la vie*'s ethics.

Toute la vie regularly buffered the severe economic situation of the period. Tales of entertainers illustrated the cultural health of France. Stories of heroes in the occupied territory and on the war fronts symbolized French autonomy and strength. The magazine contained none of the alarming accusations characteristic of caustic publications like *Je suis partout, La Gerbe,* or *Au Pilori,* aimed at more politically aware audiences and resembling the propaganda published in Germany.[9] The depictions French women found in the pages of *Toute la vie* made no allusion to genocide or racism and hardly any reference to war or even to the German presence in France. The fear that Nazism had inspired before the invasion was utterly dismissed in peace-oriented rhetoric.

It is thus hardly surprising that, in the rare instances when Luchaire acknowledges the Germans, she does it in recognition of their *savoir vivre.* She remembers that upon hearing Pétain's announcement of the Armistice on the radio, the German officers who were staying in her hotel calmed her apprehension by their noticeable demonstration of respect as they stood up and saluted. The positive remarks that Luchaire had heard about these officers were confirmed when she "learnt from the maid that Germans were in the hotel, were settling in there, but that they were not doing any harm to anyone, that they paid for their drinks, and that they were dining around small tables without paying attention to the other clients of the hotel" (*DV,* 127). Germans were after all not the "big bad wolves" they had been presented as before the war. *Toute la vie*'s prepackaged ensemble was attuned to women's conceptualized sensitivity and appreciation of civility.

Even in the climate of the postwar years, Corinne's reminiscence of the Occupation in *Ma Drôle de vie* was still marked by nostalgia for a period that had treated her so well. In 1948, Abetz remained for her the incarnation of integrity and someone who was "sincerely francophile" (*DV,* 63). She remembers her delight upon receiving her first invitation to the German embassy: "I admit that I was nothing short of flattered. I had never been invited to an embassy for an official reception" (*DV,* 79). Luchaire's ostensible pride illustrates the role she was implicitly asked to play: a visible, consenting, neutral link in the Franco-German relationship. It was a role that gave her a taste of power.

In fact, her participation in these elegant social episodes that gave her the illusion of being transported back to the cheerful life of the prewar era had, in her eyes, no political implications. In her memory, Christmas 1940 remained "a wonderful celebration at the Bouffémont Castle, followed by a fancy-dress ball" that reminded her of "the nights out before the war during which, as a young beloved artist, [she was] attracting everyone's attention" (*DV,* 138). She was caught up in "a whirlwind of pleasure and easy life" (*TV,* 21), a type of entertaining life *Toute la vie* interpreted and depicted as a healthy sign of the nation's recovery. In participating in such events, Corinne, like many other artists, became a showcase for a new society in which she represented the uppermost tier of the hierarchy. Later, responding to the accusations of treason that targeted her continued luxurious life to the German sphere, she insists on the fact that she "never understood anything of politics" (*DV*, 127) and that the making of a new film interested her far more than "all these political stories" (*DV*, 65). The social side of the collaborationist milieu was so successful in disconnecting private and political life that, as late as 1948, Corinne Luchaire was still unwilling to admit her credulity.

Such obliviousness underscores *Toute la vie*'s obstinate characterization of France's past and future greatness, especially in the first two years of its existence. Women were consistently reassured of French independence and the imminent recovery of their country's glory. Paris remained a center of cultural and intellectual life, the provinces the cradle of tradition, and the French colonial empire an icon of the nation's former and future power. France's glorious past was depicted in articles ranging from the rediscovery of coats-of-arms (*TV*, 2/26/42) to the use of archives for the revival of "true French history" (*TV*, 1/29/42). It was complemented by visions of an equally glorious future that would derive from technological inventions such as three-dimensional cinema, and from fashion, a typically French-specific industry. Both industries would guarantee the traditional French leading role in the world. Indisputably, film and theater artists like Luchaire, hypnotized by a political regime that valued and financially supported their industry and interests, encouraged an impersonalized trust in the Franco-German collaboration. *Toute la vie* acted as a mediator between its fully consenting and sought-after audience, and a general public that was directly affected by the Nazi presence. Treated as an ally and an accomplice by her father, who "was fully dedicated to things he believed right" (*DV*, 31), she saw no need to question the role she played.

Throughout and after the Occupation, she remained the heroine of her own fairy tale, enjoying the idealized reflection of her life that *Toute la vie* mirrored back to her. The charm of such images was still vivid at the time she was writing *Ma Drôle de Vie,* when her only bitterness was directed toward the French resistors who, according to her, treated her severely at the Liberation, far worse than the Germans had during the four years of the Occupation. Indeed, her worst memory of the Occupation derives from her arrest by the resistors. She stayed in a prison cell, was addressed harshly by French officers, and was not provided enough milk for her baby. She seems never to have realized that her level of discomfort was utterly, even revoltingly, out of proportion to the years of severe restrictions in France and, above all, to the genocide.

Ma Drôle de vie's naive retelling of the actress's experience during the Occupation gives a rare insider's view of an individual blinded by the reflection of her own image. In spite of the relatively little impact it had on the population at large, *Toute la vie* accomplished a great deal by addressing and mirroring upper-class women's social ambitions. It maintained these women in and reassured them about the virtues of political innocence. Under the pretense of change and renewal, the society portrayed by *Toute la vie,* in which Corinne Luchaire was a star, consolidated women in glorified secondary roles free of politics. The National Revolution as it is portrayed in the magazine rested upon systematic compartmentalization of society according to values that had been condoned by women for centuries.

Revitalizing the Old Gender Order to Shape the New One

With the premise that description (what is) contains implicit prescription (what should be), *Toute la vie* represented the New France through unambiguous language, favoring portraits over analysis.[10] It combined simple dichotomies, which could be easily retained: new and former politics; youth and old age; Parisian and provincial lifestyles; allies and enemies; Western and Eastern cultures. Embedded in these dichotomies, which aimed at differentiating desirable and undesirable social types, lay the distinction between masculine and feminine natures, the familiar assumption that "'feminine' qualities [are] counterposed to 'masculine': women are labeled passive, men active; women are defined as emotional, men described as intellectual; women are assumed to be 'naturally' nurturing, men 'naturally' ambitious."[11]

"In the face of historical cataclysm, how does the difference between the sexes function?" asks a group of critics examining the issues of French women's history.[12] *Toute la vie* implicitly posed and answered the question by addressing men's and women's roles and making the interaction between them the centerpiece of its rhetoric. Because of its essentially female readership though, the magazine focused for the most part on women's place in French social transformation; it both reasserted their crucial role in the family unit, the basic social structure of the new nation, and opened for them new doors in the public sphere. Yet, while courting women's cooperation, the magazine also implied that women would eventually be restricted to supplementing men in the reconstruction and to playing supporting, rather than decisive, roles.

A first approach toward attracting women was to offer them the responsibility of what had typically been men's functions. Following a strategy founded upon Nazi ideology, in which "both men and women are considered only in terms of the contribution they could make to a powerful state," *Toute la vie* implied that social and familial responsibilities would ultimately be more equally shared.[13]

Indifferent to gender, communal structures for male and female youth were regularly promoted, particularly in the first year of the Occupation: "forward, in the struggle from which a new world will be born . . . Wholly at the marshal's command, French youth is fighting for its future" (*TV*, 8/7/41). Women were encouraged to practice sports (a discipline formerly restricted to men) as a way to ease psychological recovery after the fall of their nation to the Germans: "When a woman feels her country's foundation shaking, sport provides her with an invaluable moment of serenity, . . . a healthy relaxation. Moreover, exercise will bring her willpower, determination in her efforts, but without harming our friend's natural charm" (*TV*, 10/7/43). Sports was to counterbalance individualism, support order, and establish solid competitive and ceremonial spirit, all essential for the good morale of the nation. Personal fulfillment could be achieved in these communities of work and play where everyone, men and women, served the national good and was able to thrive through the cult of a healthy body and a well-structured society. On occasion, women were encouraged to take up typically masculine professions and were praised for their assumed natural adaptability and willingness to give up individual freedom for a higher national calling.

Although crucial for national recovery, the appearance of a more egalitarian society was nevertheless only exceptional.[14] Women, in *Toute la vie*'s vision, were but "helpers" in a men's society, and their temporary promotion would not translate to later competitiveness with men because:

woman's role is to transmit life and to inform the soul of the child and the man. Being a mother is an Occupation in itself, the most beautiful and the most difficult. Thus, boys and girls should not receive identical educations because girls do not always profit from studying, at the higher levels, disciplines which were designed only for young men. (*TV*, 3/19/42)

Toute la vie remained loyal to this gender essentialism and offered two clear *modi operandi*, one for each gender.

Indeed, rhetorical seduction of women came above all from a request to remain "women," to be faithful to the supposedly true nature of femininity, as a poem on the ideal French woman suggests: "Miss France . . . is simple, comely, and knows, as does a great lady, how to keep her natural charm" (7/6/42). Series of hyperbolic portraits classify women in broad categories based on geography, age, and social background, thereby absorbing individualism and individual choices into social group identity. Some of these groups, like the one Luchaire belonged to, were inspired by the public representation of upper-class French fashionable stereotypes. Others took their image from patriotic and hard-working lower-class women and bore a similarity to what Claudia Koonz calls "German feminism."[15]

Older women, previously ignored by women's magazines, were now being romanticized as links between generations, the keepers of tradition who would restore national and family values, as well as the virtue of self-denial. *Toute la vie* depicts them as provincial, physically and mentally strong, respected, hard-working, capable of perpetuating France's traditional professions and skills. Motherhood is similarly emphasized through such spokespersons as Mme Rollin, a member of a family advisory committee, who declares: "I do not envision a woman anywhere but in a family. She may well be a jurist, physician, lawyer or worker, but all these are still only activities on the side . . . I feel sorry for women who do not have babies (*TV*, 4/9/41). Moreover, for women who were not "blessed" with their own children, like a certain Mlle Allard, adoption became the correct patriotic and personal choice. As the adoptive mother of twenty-six young girls, she exemplified ultimate devotion to the natural vocation of motherhood as well as social responsibility toward the nation. Mlle Allard embodies the ideal larger-than-life mother whose self-denial is compensated by the satisfaction of raising—in the sense of forming, in the sense of educating purposefully—twenty-six *vraies Françaises*.

At the other extreme from such absolute dedication to the nation stand the mythical glamorous *Parisiennes*, including the young female actresses, "the ambassadors of the new European order" (*TV* 3/26/42), whose life depended upon unlimited luxury and pleasure. Through their busy social lives, the elegant balls they attended, and the sophisticated dresses they wore, movie stars exemplified the common people's dreams, thus illustrating the benefits to be gained from fully participating in the social order. When *Toute la vie* portrayed Corinne Luchaire, it was in ways that mirrored her adolescent fantasies of princesses and Prince Charmings. The account of her wedding is straight out of a fairy tale: "So, the wild little girl of *Jail Without Bars* (Corinne Luchaire's first movie) who used to climb up the trees to go bird-nesting has become the Countess Guy de Voisins Lavernière" (*TV*, 5/2/42). This desirable fate, obviously dramatically counter to the hardship the rest of the population was experiencing, could yet nourish in the less fortunate audience desires of similar destinies, and implicitly encouraged attitudes comparable to the ones illustrated by stars.

For women who, like most of the readership, did not fit into either of these extreme categories—that of the thoroughly dutiful, hard-working woman or that of the star entertainer—*Toute la vie* proposed a compromise: frivolity and fashion as national duties:

My first reaction was one of revolt against any idea of elegance or novelty. Yet, one evening, while I was crossing from one bank to the other and observing the Seine, I understood that it was normal to speak once again of elegance. It was impossible that life would not resume, that Paris would not continue with its tradition of elegance, the seduction of the arts and beauty. And, for us Parisians, after completing our duty, as mothers or in our profession, our role was to put on the costume, the adorable and ridiculous hat covered with flowers, birds, ribbons and feathers whose panache was indispensable to us. (*TV*, 8/7/41)

For the author of the article, fashion was a political statement, a patriotic attitude, an economic responsibility, as was the return of a flourishing social and cultural life. The transition to life under foreign occupation would be eased by overt optimism.

Such optimism could derive from the nonthreatening public attitude, especially at the beginning of the Occupation, of the Germans in Paris, whom Corinne Luchaire found courteous, chivalrous, and above all, respectful of French identity.[16] In fact, the very notion of barbarism, used before the war to describe the Nazis, was turned around to discredit enemy nations, such as the United States, England, and above all, the Soviets, who are described as "the only people among all others, who do not hesitate to mobilize young women to fight on the front" (*TV* 3/4/43). As such remarks suggest, rather than focusing on political incompatibilities to publicize the Bolshevik peril, *Toute la vie* focused on the "against nature" roles the Soviets attributed to women. Women were constantly informed of non-Allied men's uncivilized ways toward women. A simple rhetorical equation based on male-female relationships was established: allies of the Germans were well mannered and understood women's needs whereas political enemy nations had no respect for women's nature, thus were considered uncouth. Idealized models of men and of women served to establish trust in domestic politics and to denigrate political adversaries. Sarcasm and stereotypes of the enemy reinforced the feeling of comfort and security that the New France was offering women. This New France was a place where assumed feminine natures, be they maternal, professional, or frivolous, would be respected and enforced.

An equally reassuring and compartmentalizing discourse defined the roles of men, whose assumed sense of manhood and self-confidence had been shaken by the 1940 military defeat. The National Revolution aimed at redeeming men not only for their own sake but also in the eyes of women, so that the "natural" hierarchy of genders could be reestablished and, once again, respected. In *XY: De l'identité masculine*, Elizabeth Badinter reminds us that, over the centuries, men have used specific methods to make of the young boy a "real" man, and that initiation rites, homosexual pedagogy, and confrontation with peers have been used as means to "fabricate" men.[17] Similarly, a 1941 title claims: "Now, school will make men out of them," stressing that education, not aggression, could preserve and enhance masculine traits. *Toute la vie*'s vision of masculinity encompasses many such rites of passage, glorification of virility, of male exclusive friendship, as well as the neutralization of fatherhood. Yet, the magazine focuses on models of masculinity chosen in non-Western countries rather than in Germany, so as not to frighten the population with German role models. Models chosen in allied faraway and "exotic" lands somewhat universalized the discourse on masculinity and appealed to the equally mythical universal French woman. Images of Burmese soldiers (*TV*,

7/1/42), Filipino men (*TV*, 1/22/42), or men of Indian origin (*TV*, 2/5/42) out-numbered the more local German models while clearly resting on such features of Nazi Germany as the cult for healthy bodies, heroes, and hierarchy.

For political reasons however, such discourse on masculinity had to be nuanced. When applied to the enemy, these values became the very emblems of barbarism. Russian soldiers were described as assassins and vandals (*TV*, 4/30/42), while German soldiers in similar situations were depicted as patriots giving up their lives "to make their ideal triumph" (*TV*, 3/26/42). The dichotomy between Allied and non-Allied countries, between the "fit" and the "unfit," emphasized Germans' desirability in comparison with the enemy, thus pressing women into praising German and French men. Given the political inclination of *Toute la vie*, the very notions of enemy and ally were at stake: the ally was the caring, Francophile German, and the natural enemy of France was to be found in Britain or in the Soviet Union. That distinction in itself denotes an overt collaborationist attitude. By displaying examples of primitive or ridiculous ways in war, *Toute la vie* diminished the enemy's very manhood and deprived him of any possible leadership. Illustrations (usually out of focus) showed enemy men lying dead, or terrorized prisoners, while French and German soldiers were portrayed in well-defined, smiling group pictures.

At a time when only sporadic news from the front or from prisoner camps reached wives and mothers, *Toute la vie*'s coverage of the French men's situation outside the country sought to reduce hostility toward Germany. Sympathetic toward women's concerns, an article of August 8, 1941 reads: "Prisoners, our dearest worry. How they live, what they think, what they are expecting from us." While prisoners were pitied·as indirect victims of the former government, they were also seen as the forces out of which the French Renaissance would rise. Prison camps in Germany resembled initiation camps where prisoners would rediscover manhood and social truth. Series of pictures showed reassuring snapshots in which readers discovered the "universal man" at war or at work, comfortable and eager to accomplish his duties, attending to daily activities with a smile, with confidence, and sometimes, even with humor. The image of any specific missing brother, father, or son disappeared behind the universalized allegorical and indistinguishable image of the *soldat*.[18]

At home, younger males were encouraged to develop the skills needed to energize the country: physical strength, competitiveness, and communal effort were the qualities that would permit the physical reconstruction of the nation. Series of articles depicted groups of men accomplishing superhuman tasks, obviously enjoying the challenges of their mission, never involved in aggressive actions that could remind the readers of the state of war. These images were obviously patterned after that of the sixteen athletic, young, and joyous German soldiers all diving simultaneously, as though they were one man, off the deck of a ship stationed "in the golden light of the Far East" and "in the scorching sun of the tropics" (*TV*, 5/2/42). Team work, physical strength, and passion for communal well-being also characterized miners working in high altitudes, those men "for whom duty goes before personal life" (*TV*, 1/24/42).

Amid such groups of common soldiers and workers some heroes stand out, those exceptional individuals after whom every man should pattern his own life because "tomorrow's Europe will be a Europe of soldiers" (*TV*, 2/5/43). A unique German example, Captain Münchberg, a pilot of the Luftwaffe, can well serve as a prototype for such society. Beyond his sixty-two victories (at the age of only twenty-four), "every leisure moment he has is spent improving himself" (*TV*, 5/21/42). Captain Münchberg's example recalled the ultimate heroism that could both inspire men and make women hopeful for the future.

Leadership was not restricted to physically fit heroes. *Toute la vie* thus also repeatedly promoted the paternal figures of the Vichy government whose common sense and wisdom were as impressive as younger heroes' brilliant actions. The men in Vichy were praised for their mental strength, their concern for the population, and their appeasing effect on the nation. Although only few pictures of Pétain appeared in *Toute la vie*, those that did appear were reassuring. The marshal was usually portrayed walking peacefully on the estate of the Château du Parc, in a reflective mood and in complete serenity. Rural background and sensitivity to human nature were stressed in order to make him the ideal individual for uniting the country, as a verbal portrait in honor of his eighty-sixth birthday illustrates: "The human qualities inherited from his peasant background, political experience, friendship for the working world . . . a man of reconciliation, firm, intransigent, merciless toward traitors, understanding" (*TV*, 4/30/42). Every feature, including the absence of explicit references to his collaboration with the conditions of the Armistice, aimed at reassuring readers. He represented all the traditional human values put forward by the National Revolution. He was the embodiment of the metaphorical father that France had lacked since the 1789 Revolution. Pétain seemed, after a century and a half of social republican turmoil, to reincarnate the monarchical presence that would attract universal support and respect for himself and, above all, stability for the nation, that very stability for which women were believed to yearn.

The reestablishment of trust in male leadership through hero or father types completed the portrayal of desirable female positions and supported the general social definition of the New France. Only a clear definition of both groups could lead to the national renewal. Gender differentiation was by no means accessory to the national goal. It was its very core. "Travail, Famille, Patrie," Vichy's infamous and superficially encompassing motto, carried different undertones for women than for men. But it did not grow out of a vacuum. It grew out of a global preexisting belief in such gender division, which was itself perpetrated not only by men's flattery and superficial respect of women but by many women who became active agents in developing and maintaining it.

This examination of *Ma Drôle de vie* and *Toute la vie* has suggested the centrality of women's concerns in Vichy's political propaganda. Using social fantasy, the magazine provided a reassuring vision of "life after the war" that was thought to monopolize the attention of upper-class women as depicted in *Ma Drôle de vie*. To address women's concern about comfort, independence, and peace at home, the magazine downplayed the German presence and glorified ancestral French gender identity. Series of portraits suggested to women of different social conditions the roles they were to play in the new society as well as the unfailing respect that was due the male population, which, by nature, was the true leading force of the nation. Women were not ignored but rather honored—in ways that would obviously benefit male power. Because of the drop in male leadership caused by the defeat, it was crucial that women be both courted as an interim force within the nation and reminded that ultimately only male supervision could save the nation. Corinne Luchaire indicates that these values were acceptable to her. *Toute la vie*'s apolitical rhetoric indicates that women were easier to convince by means of nonaggressive fairy-tale-like social reporting rather than by constructed political discourse. They were drawn into politics through an externalization of their assumed desires, through promises that their wishes for stability would come true. The purpose was to construct a new reality free of social turmoil, with the prospect of an unquestionably optimistic future. It was assumed that women would respond to this kind of perspective better than to a blatant defense of the political and economic benefits of a fascist-oriented government. *Toute la vie*'s prescriptive methods did not attempt to "explain" the social benefits of the new regime: its rhetoric remains at a superficial level at all times.

Ma Drôle de vie exemplifies the success of *Toute la vie*'s message. It confirms that the ideology of the time, based on socialist, national authority (*Toute la vie* advocated social duty, confirmed the conservation of French integrity, and admitted no ambiguity), was indeed accepted as such because of the unproblematic picture of normality it propagated. Corinne, never questioning flattery, became the agent of a male-dominated political system that knew how to use socially ingrained attitudes to perpetuate its power.

Elizabeth A. Houlding

"L'Envers de la guerre": The Occupation of Violette Leduc

> At night I dreamed that the war was over, that the people with real ability had returned, that I was scurrying like a mangy dog to the refuge of an unemployment bureau. I would wake up soaked with sweat, convince myself with a stammering voice that it was a nightmare, then fall asleep again.[1]

Nightmarish images of the liberation of France from Nazi occupation recur frequently in Violette Leduc's autobiographical work, *La Bâtarde* (1964). At no point in this work does Leduc take part in her country's euphoric anticipation of Allied victory over the German occupying forces. Rather, for Violette Leduc, the liberation of France portends a dysphoric return to unemployment, despair, shame, and submission to those more able than herself. Who, we might ask, or what kind of woman would dread the end of Nazi domination and of history's most horrific international conflict? And, perhaps more scandalously, who would admit to such a thing in writing?

One might initially speculate that Leduc's fear of freedom is not entirely unusual, that it might, in fact, simply mirror the "articulation of female dread" identified by Susan Gubar in her important study of British women's literary responses to World War II.[2] Gubar defines this fear on the part of British women as an apprehension that "male vulnerability in wartime would result in violence against women" (230). Violette Leduc is of course French and not British; however, national differences matter little here since Leduc's specific and entirely personal fear is not fear of a backlash by men against women for taking their place during wartime, but is more like terror at the prospect of the community as a whole reverting to "normal" after a time of "gender disorder." This fear of the consequences of a social backlash in which the masculine attempts to reassert itself would seem at least partly, however, to fit Leduc's near-despairing anxiety at the thought of a return a to prewar social order. According to Joan W. Scott, the return of peace does have the effect of spinning hard-won, often tenuous gains back in on themselves: "War is the ultimate disorder; peace thus implies a return to 'traditional' gender relationships, the familiar and natural order of families, men in public roles, women at home, and so on."[3] In Leduc's case, the gains at stake are her hard-won profits in the worlds of publishing and black-marketeering during the Occupation. Her fear of losing these becomes tangible in *La Bâtarde*, where her identification with other women and with socially defined gender roles is shot through with ambivalence. Whereas Gubar argues that "the literature women wrote about World War II needs to be understood as a documentation of women's sense that the war was a blitz on them," one can, in Leduc's case, offer a parallel but distinct revision of this interpretation by arguing that Leduc's autobiographical representation of the Occupation depicts the war as a blitz on herself alone. It remains uncomfortably but undeniably clear throughout *La Bâtarde* that Leduc prospered materially and socially under the conditions of "gender disorder" provoked by five years of war, national anxiety, and foreign occupation. As an example of French women's lives during wartime, Leduc resembles less the model wives of prisoners-of-war, the "women who wait" recently studied by Sarah Fishman, than the "outlaw" women into whose experience Miranda Pollard has called for further investigation, women whose tales offer marginal and "less respectable" narratives of Occupied France.[4]

La Bâtarde's representation of the war years is structured by a series of personal and intellectual moments, mostly concerning femininity, gender roles (especially the role of gender as manifested by Occupation discourse and activity), and discontent, which together elaborate a view of the effects of the Occupation on an "outlaw" French woman and her text. To be sure, Leduc provides an extreme example of the crisis in the social "place" and the self-definition of women during the Occupation. Her illegitimacy, psychological instability, class affiliations, and above all her bisexuality all come into play in her search for a stance that will most effectively distance her from the postwar desire for quiescence. But the fact that Leduc *is* unrepresentative, an "outlaw" to a prescribed concept of femininity as well as to social legitimacy, is conversely what makes *La Bâtarde* so important to a fuller understanding of the textual memory of the Occupation. Just as Leduc felt drawn to what she termed the "underside of the war"—"l'envers de la guerre," her text tells the story of the underside of gender relations of the time.[5]

In an argument related to that of Joan W. Scott, Denise Riley has claimed that "war throws gender into sharp relief."[6] Although the war between France and Germany officially ended in June 1940, certainly such a highlighting of gender systems obtained in occupied France. Vichy discourse surrounding the defeat is fraught with an anxious harking back to a distant past in which France had not yet fallen prey to the feminizing influences of the Third Republic. The National Revolution was described by Pétain as "a strongly human and virile reaction to a feminized republic, a republic of women and homosexuals."[7] Yet dedicated women were precisely what Pétain needed to launch this conservative social vision, since only they could bear the many French children desired by the grandfatherly leader. In the case of Violette Leduc, it is worth noting that there is no room in the discourse of Pétain's new nation for the woman who is *also* a homosexual ("une république de femmes *ou* d'invertis"). Vichy's aim was to shape the potentially troublesome "femme" into the warmer "épouse" and "mère."[8]

In her study of social policy concerning women in wartime and postwar Britain, Riley makes the following crucial observation: "Women *when named as a sex* by the formulations of social policy cannot escape being the incarnation of gender as strange or temporary workers; nor can they escape being seen as hovering on the edge of maternity" (260). If we apply Riley's remarks to the equally appropriate context of occupied France, we can argue that it would be virtually impossible not to recognize oneself *as* a woman under such extreme conditions, impossible to avoid what Riley terms "gendered self-consciousness."[9] If women are "the incarnation of gender," they are not subjects but signifiers within the social project. For Violette Leduc, bastard, bisexual, black-marketeer, the imposition of gendered self-consciousness represented both the greatest release of power and the most oppressive, nightmarish ambiguity.

Born in 1907, Violette Leduc arrived at the war years as an unmarried woman of mediocre health, with an unfinished high-school education, several badly ended love affairs (mostly, but not exclusively, with women), unresolved conflicts with her mother, and massive insecurities: in short, having successfully completed and passed through none of the traditional stages of a French woman's life of her generation. Leduc's particular brand of marginality was accompanied by a heightened awareness of the "norm," of the appropriate way of living a woman's life, of the ways of being and becoming a *jeune fille rangée*—Simone de Beauvoir's phrase for her own bourgeois Catholic upbringing. Leduc was constantly aware of her failure to follow the appropriate life plot. This pain of the *jeune fille dérangée*[10] acts as the ongoing leitmotif of her work: the pain of forever being the unacknowledged offspring of an illegitimate union, of bearing what she describes as an unforgivably ugly face from day to day, of her inability to establish satisfying relationships with others.

The product of a brief liaison between a young housemaid and the ne'er-do-well son in whose parents' household her mother, Berthe, worked, Leduc never received her legitimate name of the father or the kind affection of her mother. As the daughter of an abandoned, impoverished, and resentful woman,

Leduc soon grew aware of the illegitimacy she eventually declared in the title of the work in question, a title that also bears the mark of gender in the English edition, *La Bâtarde*.[11] When *La Bâtarde* was published by Gallimard in 1964, it was accompanied by an important preface written by Simone de Beauvoir, literary protector, advisor, and friend of the less well-known Leduc. (Beauvoir was one of Gallimard's most distinguished authors by this point and was of course engaged in the writing of her own extremely successful autobiographical project.[12]) In introducing Leduc's first specifically autobiographical work to the reader, Beauvoir focused on Leduc's obsessive style and personality, and on what she termed her "scrupulous honesty" (xxiii) in telling the story of an unusual life.

Beauvoir also pointed out that Leduc did not hesitate to discuss in her work those topics that continually engaged her, regardless of their appropriateness as literary material for a woman of her generation. For example, Leduc in no way limited herself to a typically prescribed feminine *pudeur* (or modesty) when it came to revealing her obsessions with money, sexuality, psychological stability, and her physical appearance. On the other hand, this intensely personal writer remained, perhaps necessarily, disengaged from more public or ethical concerns, such as, for instance, the global historical significance of the war. I quote Beauvoir's preface here:

[A]nything that does not touch her personally leaves her indifferent. She calls the Germans "the enemy" in order to make it clear that this borrowed notion has remained quite foreign to her. She does not owe allegiance to any camp. She has no sense of the universal, no sense of simultaneity; she is there where she is, with the weight of her past upon her shoulders. (xxiii)

In regard to the Occupation, then, we might well ask what it means to read the work of a writer who has, according to Beauvoir, "no sense of the universal." For Leduc is surely more than an existential author. Dealing with the political crisis of a country to which her own affiliations were inherently ambiguous, and feeling that she had been assigned at birth the role of "public enemy" within a society that now no longer knew who exactly the enemy was, Leduc filters this literal crisis of the nation through her own inescapable self.

That self, however, was hardly the most stable or trustworthy medium. Critics in general agree that Leduc never succeeded in creating a literary persona other than her troubled biographical self, a point with which Leduc concurred during an interview: "I told the story of my life as it happened, my books, my mistakes, my despair, in short, my life as a failed writer."[13] Although Leduc is not alone among women writers in suffering this critical fate, in her work the problem is perhaps more acute. Leduc's case, with its particular mix of ego and anomie, poses an interesting question in the problematics

of autobiography and literary self-representation, namely, how does a fla-
grantly self-centered woman write about the outside world in her autobiographical work?[14] And more specifically, how does the historical event that
was the Occupation enter Leduc's life and her text? It is her status as a witness, and the value of her testimony, that are at stake in these questions of
Leduc's relationship to the universal.

In fact, the years of the Occupation are crucial to the development of both
Leduc and *La Bâtarde*. The fact that Leduc chose to end her book with the
closing moments of the Occupation of France in 1944 should not be overlooked; it is perhaps the most simple but also the most telling example of an
important historical and textual coincidence. The co-termineity of the book
and the Occupation may at first seem surprising in a writer as obsessed by self
and closed to the greater field of international politics and affairs, but *La Bâtarde* weaves life story and history together in ways that have previously been
disregarded, but that are very telling in the larger context of the literary representation of the war years.

Like Beauvoir, Isabelle de Courtivron interprets Leduc's insistence upon
italicizing the term "the enemy" to refer to the Germans within her work as
symptomatic of Leduc's inability to identify with the social crisis around her.
De Courtivron summarizes her view of Leduc's representation of the war in
this way:

Violette's reactions to the war are devoid of value judgment. The Germans, whom she
feels obliged to label "the enemy," are invisible in her account. The tragedies she witnesses are told in a detached manner, exhibiting the same lack of concern with which
Violette will later allude to the deportation of her Jewish neighbors. The world's cata-
strophes do not seem to affect her except insofar as they interfere with the course of her
private world. An occasional allusion to the progression of the war, gleaned from dialogues of people who surround her, is the only marker of real time and events.[15]

Leduc's detachment from what is generally termed the "political" cannot be
denied. There is no attempt made in the narrative of *La Bâtarde* to look back at
the war years and analyze the politico-historical significance of events.

Yet I would argue that Leduc does indeed represent the Occupation. Indeed,
to embrace the opposite point of view and focus on Leduc's subjectivity tends
to deny the historical context and political content of Leduc's wartime text
(and of women's texts in general). It is to do a disservice to all works of this
period. To view Leduc's writing as apolitical in nature is to overlook precisely
that which is historical and political about this work; it is to support the interpretation of women's writing as limited to the realm of the personal. To write
that "the Germans are invisible" in Leduc's account, as though this were an un-
fortunate oversight on her part but one that bears confessing, is simply not to
see where the Germans are in the text.

Leduc's refusal to comment directly upon the Germans or upon Nazi ideology does not mean they have no bearing in and on her text. The Germans are not invisible; like all aspects of the war and the Occupation, their presence is a fact, one with which Leduc copes in life and in language. But the war itself and the German "enemy" enter the text through an extremely partial, discontinuous discourse, through the men in Leduc's own life, and through the details of her daily life, as is the case with many other women of the time. The fragmented manner in which Leduc represents wartime and the intersections of the war and the Germans with her own life calls not for dismissal but rather for what I have termed a reading "between the lines."[16] To call for such internal reconstruction does not set us free to proffer our own version of what Leduc leaves unsaid by glossing her infelicities or supplementing her lack of political commentary. It is rather a reading that takes into account the indirectness of many women's experience of history, exemplified here by the oft-noted "fragmentary" nature of Leduc's narrative. In this way, we can account not only for the larger moments of international combat, the declarations of war, and the signing of peace treaties but also for the details of daily life, the private negotiation of food rationing, and the sexual politics of military occupation.

If Leduc does purposefully distance herself from the war through such tactics as the italicization of charged elements of public discourse or her refusal to include "value judgments" in her narrative of the time, these strategies tell us something important about the degree of Leduc's social alienation, and also about our expectations as readers of these wartime texts. Could it be that, unless War is represented monolithically, we tend to think that it is not present at all? Leduc's overriding concern with herself complicates, but certainly does not erase, her relationship to "real time and events." Given the critical commentary we have seen remarking upon Leduc's idiosyncrasies and limitations as an observer of her time, one might even be tempted to retitle her work *La Bâtarde or How Not To Write An Occupation Memoir.*[17]

We have already reached the midpoint of Leduc's six-hundred-page narrative when the possibility of war with Germany enters the text. Half of the book (or three hundred pages) is then devoted to the five years of World War II, a telling proportion in a story recounting the first thirty-seven years of Leduc's life. (The first half of *La Bâtarde* is an account of Leduc's unhappy childhood, adolescence, failed studies, and lesbian initiation, up to the age of thirty-two.) Immediately before the war, Leduc worked as a Girl Friday for Denise Batcheff, a film impresario. Leduc was constantly delighted by the contact with the bright lights of the Parisian artistic world this job afforded her. In addition to Maurice Sachs, by whose sophisticated banter and flirtatious attention she is attracted, Leduc mentions the office visits of Jean Gabin, Michèle Morgan, Jacques Prévert, and Robert Bresson, among others.

These were the early months of Leduc's friendship and fascination with

Maurice Sachs, a writer and notorious member of the Parisian artistic world. Her frustrated love for Sachs was the first in a series of Leduc's attachments to homosexual men, Jean Genet among them. Although little known to today's readers, Maurice Sachs was a highly visible figure in Parisian literary circles between the two World Wars.[18] Through his association with Cocteau's "Boeuf sur le Toit" group in the 1920s, Sachs became known for his scandalous behavior, debauchery, and extravagance. Despite his sexual adventures and shady financial affairs, Sachs (who had been raised by his nonpracticing Jewish mother) underwent a very public conversion to Catholicism under the guidance of the Catholic intellectual Jacques Maritain and his wife Raïsa, with Jean Cocteau as his "godfather." His newfound piety and desire to become a priest ended in failure, however, when Sachs returned to his old ways and fell in love with a young man while on vacation at Juan-les-Pins. (Like Leduc, Sachs was also married for a brief time.) While Sachs adored celebrated writers such as Cocteau and Gide, Leduc was equally flattered by his attention and came to adore this profoundly dishonest and misogynistic character.

Shortly before the outbreak of war in 1939, Gabriel Mercier, an old friend of Leduc's and a potential lover, resurfaced after an absence of many years. At this point, Leduc's life seemed just about "complete." It was this precarious "almost" that the possibility of war threatened to destroy:

I don't want the war to interrupt a new love affair and a new friendship. I had been a failure in everything: studies, piano, examinations, relationships, sleep, health, holidays, tranquillity of mind, gaiety, happiness, security, application at work. Now I was winning; I almost had a job, almost a lover, almost a friend with a position in Parisian society. They couldn't declare war, they couldn't take all that away from me. I shall never cease to insist on the terror of insecurity instilled into me as a child. One must always have a few sous in one's purse. The war would push me into the gutter. (289)

A failure at each and every duty of the daughters of her generation, Leduc feared that just as she was getting her feet on the ground, the war would sweep away all stability by removing both men, the friend (Sachs) and the lover (Gabriel), from her side. Like many of her counterparts, including Simone de Beauvoir, Leduc's reaction when faced with the invasion of her private life by such things as history and war was to echo those common questions of selfish impatience: Why now, and why me?

As predicted, Leduc's job did indeed disappear with the declaration of war in September 1939. The men in her life received their postings (Sachs was sent to Caen as an interpreter, and Gabriel was assigned work as an office clerk), while Leduc found herself in Paris without a job, worried about money and her financial future. With both men away in the military, Leduc was concerned about their well-being and dutifully wrote both of them letters. Sachs did not remain in the military long, however, as he was discharged for "unacceptable sexual behavior" and soon returned to Paris.[19] Due to his complicated medical history, Gabriel was soon judged too weak to be sent to the front and was returned to Paris to take a job in the records department of the War Office.

As literary or indeed as memoir material, Leduc's relationships with Sachs and Gabriel are problematic. Clearly, neither of these men can serve as a traditional war hero. Indeed, in a conventional war narrative, the soldier's story should provide the plot. However, for a brief time at least, Gabriel's status as a soldier does propel Leduc's life story along a more conservative path. For, within weeks of the declaration of war between France and Germany, the lack of social stability drives Leduc to a previously unconsidered extreme: she announces a desire for the security of marriage to Gabriel, no matter how unorthodox their relationship has been up to this point. Therefore, what becomes important during the war and the Occupation is Leduc's surprising turn, after the two most serious lesbian relationships of her life, toward a visible heterosexual relationship and toward public acceptability.

· · ·

When war invades women's private lives, even a life as unorthodox as Leduc's, the pressures brought to bear immediately center upon "a woman's place" in society. Leduc knew that as the legitimate bride of a French soldier she would be entitled to financial support from the state. And this woman wanted to be a bride as soon as possible: "Why weren't we both Americans? I longed for a runaway marriage like the heroine of a Western" (293). For the unmarried daughter of an unmarried mother, it was marriage above all that would place Leduc, for the first time in her life, in a legitimate position in society:

My husband would be a soldier, I would be able to draw the allowance made to soldier's wives, I would have someone to love, and I would be saved . . . I had been in exile, and now I had come home again . . . My fourth finger feels uneasy, the poor thing needs a ring around it. You shall have your wedding ring, I promise you. It will shine, and when my marriage is glowing on my hand I shall know how to make the most of it. (293)

Exiled as a woman, repatriated as a wife, Leduc's legitimation proved, however, just as alienating as her original bastard state. Leduc does not make it entirely clear to her reader whether in fact she did benefit financially from becoming a war bride. Shortly after the wedding, Gabriel writes to tell her that she will not be able to draw an allowance from the army, but no reasons are given for this in the text, nor do we know if this was perhaps only a temporary delay due to French bureaucracy. From this point on, though, Leduc complains that her husband is an unsatisfactory provider: "The cards were down: Gabriel was not going to give me anything" (297). Within the convention of marriage,

Leduc quickly finds herself in a familiar state of sexual frustration and financial uneasiness.

Simply stated, Leduc's feelings about sexual involvement with Gabriel were extremely conflicted. Gabriel's interest in Leduc appears to have been grounded more in friendship than in physical passion, with Leduc often dressing in masculine attire and adopting the role of Gabriel's "bonhomme." On their wedding night, when Gabriel declared, "Nothing is changed, you will be free, I shall be free" (296), Leduc was wounded by his indifference: "I admit it: I wanted to be attractive to Gabriel" (167). The chapter immediately following the euphoric wedding band passage opens with this evocative description: "It was an old marriage that smelt of napthalene" (294). Leduc's disappointment in marriage is perhaps predictable. Because of her marginality and lack of physical beauty, Leduc never felt that she could play the parts available to women of her time. Certainly she knew that her relationship with Gabriel did not conform to current heterosexual norms. Nonetheless, Leduc was no sooner in the marriage than she grew nostalgic for the life of the single woman, alone and independent. Pulled in both directions, Leduc wanted to have her wedding cake and eat it too.

. . .

In writing of this first winter of war and marriage, Leduc's representations of wartime experience center in great part on moments of gendered activity, moments that are grounded in Frenchwomen's experience of the time: waiting in line with other Parisian housewives for rationed food; waiting for letters from absent men; worrying about food and supplies. Leduc offers the following passage as an example of feminine conversation carried on to pass the time while waiting in line for vegetables. For both Leduc and the other women present, these exchanges constitute a veritable "orgy of platitudes" in which everyone participates. "All is not lost," one of the strong-minded ones whispered in my ear. 'All is not lost,' I would say to one weaker than myself. The enemy, our troops" (321). Leduc finds her place within the circularity of this exchange; she talks to the other women, commiserates, and for once she speaks the right language: "I chatted. I put myself in the others' shoes . . . I wanted to please them" (321). Leduc realizes that this sharing of common experience is largely a matter of manipulating the right vocabulary:

So I talked: parcels to be packed for prisoners, letters received, letters sent, the advances, the defeats of our enemies, a ray of hope, relatives in the country, relatives going short themselves in order to send a piece of bacon. Repetitions, twice-told tales, lamentations, threats. I imitated the other housewives. (321)

Leduc takes satisfaction in her role as one of this group of women. She is eager to please and to identify with others, to get outside of herself by placing herself "in their shoes," or "in their skin," as expressed by the original French. Here at last is her link to Frenchness and to femininity, for as a newlywed she too has an enlisted husband and household worries. The identification with each other and with the nation comes through the domestic elements of their lives, literally through the home(front) which is their "lieu commun."

While these clichés place the speaker in a circuit of conversation, with the oppositional phrase "the enemy, our troops" functioning as a crucial password, it is not clear from Leduc's written account that information is actually exchanged. These words may prove to be merely skin deep, just another "formule de politesse" so beloved by the French, that is, a superficial means of establishing verbal contact that allows speakers to steer well clear of the unwelcome awkwardness of the private. What does appear to be essential here is the exclusionary rhetoric of "us" versus "them." While able to enter into this network of public exchange, Leduc is, however, unable to forget the conditions under which she personally enters the war: "This new vocabulary did nothing to help me in my war against Gabriel, nothing to prevent us from humiliating each other all the time. My defeat had merely coincided with the outbreak of war" (321). Leduc's private battles with her husband, Gabriel, with marriage, and with desire are not forgotten in the midst of war with Germany. But neither is the private seen to eclipse the public. The imagery here is one of mirroring and coincidence rather than exclusion. The war provides new ways for Leduc to visualize and articulate her domestic conflicts, by shifting her temporarily "outside" of herself, even by means of a seemingly trivial chat with other women about letters, packing string, and parcels.

While participating in these feminine exchanges in what she terms "good faith," Leduc admits in writing that she is "neutral" at best and, moreover, that she secretly desires the dramatic upheaval of the war for the personal opportunities an unstable environment may afford her:

> But in fact I was sincerely neutral. And what is more, I was hoping for world-wide disaster, I was hoping that when everyone in Paris had fled I would be promoted in their absence. I wanted bombs and mortar shells to shatter my past failures. The war would get me out of the rut I was in. (. . .) I was living in one squalid room; but all those luxury apartments with their signs "To Let"—they also belonged to me now. I breathed more freely in a Paris without people. (321–22)

Although the "world-wide disaster" of war means exodus for many, it augurs liberation for Leduc, from her past, from social conventions and restraints, and, finally, from herself.

The structure of the confessional relationship with the reader that Leduc constructs in her text recalls very strongly a "window scene" in which de Courtivron locates the apotheosis of Leduc's obsessive relationship with her mentor Simone de Beauvoir. As de Courtivron notes in an analysis of *L'Affamée*

(1948), a surrealistic account of Leduc's obsessive attachment to Beauvoir, Leduc's problem with "others," namely, her "failure to establish enduring relationships with other human beings," is one of miscalculated distance and skewed perception.[20] Conscious of this problem, Leduc herself creates a metaphor of binoculars, a device de Courtivron finds especially appropriate for describing Leduc's project of looking: "Binoculars cut you off from people by bringing you close to them. You close in on what's happening far from you but without participating in it."[21] Indeed, de Courtivron argues that the sole moment in *L'Affamée* during which Leduc manages to achieve the perfect distance from "Madame" (the Beauvoir figure), her constant object of observation, occurs when Leduc stands outside a café window and gazes in to watch Beauvoir as she reads peacefully on her own: "Separated by a glass pane, they are apart yet near."[22] Leduc's binocular gaze brings her relentlessly close to her objects of study, only to disappoint and disorient her when removed. Leduc's texts serve, then, as a window between herself and others. Through her texts, she manages to put herself into circulation, while guarding a self-protective distance.

In the moves between proximity and distance, Leduc establishes a cautious relationship with an imaginary "nous." Within the context of the Occupation, however, the stakes of proximity and distance are particularly meaningful. As a marginal member of French bourgeois society, Leduc often identifies *in writing* with victims of persecution under the Occupation, only to undermine this closeness through her acknowledged failure to make the slightest gesture of support to aid her Jewish neighbors, and through her profiteering on the black-market.

A telling example of Leduc's simultaneous identification with and distance from her "subjects" is found in her references to a young Jewish neighbor, Esther. This young girl, with whom Leduc does not appear to have a personal relationship, is referred to as her "friend on the other side of a windowpane" (320). Esther's second-floor room is directly across the courtyard from that of Violette and Gabriel. From their windows, Esther and Leduc serve as silent spectators of the other's life: "The visits we paid each other through our windowpanes were more real than any spoken greeting. I would appear, she would rush to see me; or she would be there, and I would hurtle to watch her" (321). Leduc observes Esther and comments upon her grace and beauty. In Leduc's terms, they know each other well: "Ours was a public idyll. We had nothing to say to one another, nothing to confide, nothing to offer" (321). Both women are trapped within the lives they lead inside their respective rooms, Esther by the war, Leduc by her marriage. The actual terms of this relationship remain, however, undefined and entirely one-sided. Do the women truly have "nothing to say to one another" because their profound similarity and intimacy transcend speech? Or is it that Leduc is most comfortable with a relationship that remains unconsummated, seen through a window, or italicized, as it were?

When Gabriel announces that the Nazis have arrested Esther's father, Leduc admits that, at this point in her life, she cannot be seen as unlucky. Illegitimate daughters with failed professional and emotional lives remain insignificant and relatively secure citizens of occupied Paris:

I didn't dare cry out that we were two monsters of indifference safe by our fireside. On my Aryan maiden's helmet there perched a parrot that would keep croaking: how lucky that we're not Jews, how lucky that we're not Jewish at this moment. (339)

Leduc takes a measure of pleasure in exposing her own indifference, cowardice, and anti-Semitism at this time: "Having been suppressed, reduced to zero at birth by members of the wealthy classes, I was by no means unhappy, now we were at war, to see the rich being forced to escape into the Unoccupied Zone" (339).

Leduc calls Esther into her narrative at different moments, much as the unnamed Jewish girl punctuates segments of Marguerite Duras's *La Douleur*.[23] As the Occupation progresses, Esther's family members are arrested; Esther herself is taken away in the middle of the night by the Germans:

Next morning I was told that the enemy had come at five in the morning and taken Esther away. The neighbours had to tear the gas-pipe out of her mother's hands by brute force. Mme Lita and Mme Keller went out shopping as usual, with their yellow stars sewn on their bodices. They didn't dare mention Esther's disappearance. (352)

In this instance, the reader finds no ironic quotation marks around the words "the enemy," a choice we might attribute to Leduc's professed affection for Esther, and to her tendency to identify with victims rather than oppressors. However, each of these Jewish women, Esther, Mme Lita, and Mme Keller, remains forever silent in Leduc's text. The reader is left to wonder whether Mme Lita and Mme Keller did not dare mention the disappearance of Esther to Leduc in particular, or whether they chose, for their own reasons, not to communicate with their neighbor. And Leduc further clouds her identification with Esther by confessing that on the night of Esther's arrest she had been awakened by shouts and screams and had selfishly gone back to sleep "so as to escape the nightmare of a woman who was suffering" (352). Leduc had done nothing to intervene. In a disturbing admission, Leduc reveals to the reader that her nightmares of the period are conditioned not by fears of the present but by that future time at which the war and her good fortune will end: "At night I dreamed that the war was over, that the people with real ability had returned, that I was scurrying like a mangy dog to the refuge of an unemployment bureau. I would wake up soaked with sweat, convince myself with a stammering voice that it was a nightmare, then fall asleep again" (339).[24] Although one would in no way wish to defend Leduc—in fact, one could argue that she literally begs to be condemned by the reader for her cowardice and complicity with the Nazis and Vichy—it seems important to point out that here again, as in the representation of the Parisian housewives doing their marketing, the relationship with Esther is initially idealized (however offensively) as one of mirroring, harmony, and intimacy. Leduc's attraction to Esther and subsequent break with her suggest something quite different than the total "detachment" mentioned by de Courtivron. It is in no way the case that Jews or Germans are missing from Leduc's narrative; it is, rather, that Leduc refuses to describe her responses to Nazism and Vichy policy in more heroic, and thus, more readable, or more palatable terms of resistance.

The most striking examples of Leduc's simultaneous distance from and investment in femininity and the lifestyle of the good French housewife occur during her marriage to Gabriel and her active work life—a life that encompassed both licit and illicit forms of labor. Although worried about money, Leduc was never better employed than during the war years and the Occupation. Because of the exodus from Paris in the early months of the Occupation, there was a great shortage in the publishing business, and with the help of Maurice Sachs, Leduc was asked to write several short pieces for a women's magazine (311).[25] All the while she hid her marriage, her married name, and her much coveted wedding band from Sachs and her employers so that she would appear to be a "self-sufficient woman": "Invincible celibacy, I had hidden my wedding ring in my handbag before going into the magazine office . . . A self-sufficient woman must be single . . ." (312). The tension between the illegitimate daughter and the disappointed wife is now complicated by an additional, less conventional role, that of the outwardly single woman, the woman who writes.

For her second assignment, rather than "fiction," Leduc is asked to write several editorial articles, a kind of self-help column and morale booster for women separated by the war from the men they love. In her attempts to reproduce kernels of "common sense" about women's daily lives, Leduc's distance from the categories of "woman" and "wife" becomes painfully, and hilariously, clear. Blocked in the writing of these self-help columns, Leduc remarks of her female audience: "I had to inspire them with good humour, strength of mind, energy and health. Using the materials of their day-to-day existence I was supposed to provide a firm foundation for the women on the home front . . . My double life began" (323–24). In her narrative of this tension, Leduc brilliantly stages the contrast between the model life of the cheery French housewife and her own inability to live up to the apparently simple advice she is dispensing. As Judith Butler has observed, "[t]he injunction to *be* a given gender takes place through discursive routes: to be a good mother, to be a heterosexually desirable object, to be a fit worker, in sum, to signify a multiplicity of guarantees in response to a variety of different demands all at once."[26] The following cropped passage will serve as an example of Leduc's cutting analysis of the multiple binds of gender and identity during a time of war:

> I wrote several editorials.
>
> Get up early, I told my readers. I used to get up at eleven, screaming for Gabriel's sex inside me . . . I like begging, I like asking for things, being given things, getting something for nothing. Oh God, yes, oh God how magnificent it was, my mendicancy as I lay weeping on Gabriel's bare feet in front of the sink . . .
>
> And, above all, get out on the right side of the bed, I told my readers.
>
> I didn't give a damn about the right side of the bed. Exhausted by my privations, I collapsed limply on our divan. My tear-spattered hair rained down on my cheeks . . . Gabriel gave way because he couldn't kill me. Then he tore himself away from the room . . .
>
> Don't waste time: see that you're in a good temper when you get up. Put on your boxing gloves and face your everyday routine, Mesdames, Mesdemoiselles. Your difficulties will fly away, I told my readers.
>
> If I got up at the same time as Gabriel it was to argue about the two francs for the electricity, the three francs for the gas, the one franc for the coal, the hundred francs for the rent . . . Bizarre rivals in rapacity. We both lied about our earnings . . .
>
> Strength of mind above all else. Tend your nerves as though they were a precious garden. A sound mind in a sound body, the Greeks used to say. Not a moment to lose, breathe in breathe out, window wide open as soon as you get up, I told my readers. (326–27)

Not surprisingly, Leduc goes on to explain that she wrote only a few editorial articles for women and that they were not accepted for publication because she lacked the appropriate point of view: "What I did was meaningless, abortive, rejected. I couldn't see things through the readers' eyes" (331). In spite of this disclaimer concerning her unacceptable "way of seeing," Leduc indeed knew the appropriate clichés for the occasion. In this reader's eyes, this extended and willfully graphic passage represents a virtuoso redeployment on Leduc's part of the insipid discourses of femininity so prevalent in women's publications during the war. By obsessively dwelling on her failures, Leduc discloses the performative nature of gender and places herself and her readers soundly inside the gap between publicly constructed discourses of femininity and our private struggles with these received models. Indeed, Leduc makes clear to her reader that wherever she is located, the act of being a "woman" (a good mother, a good wife, a fit worker) lies, necessarily, somewhere else.

As a writer for fashion magazines and "la page féminine" of newspapers, Leduc was working in a woman's world. At the same time, she found that she was perceived as a woman more than ever before in her movements through occupied Paris. This was an extremely new and charged situation for Leduc, as she had not previously experienced such attention paid to the fact of her sex.

Under the gaze of police enforcing the curfew, Leduc tries to make her way home one night after covering a cabaret act for a magazine. Desperate to get home to Gabriel, Leduc is allowed to pass without the required "ausweis," simply by virtue of being (dressed like) a woman. The French police officers on patrol warn her, nonetheless, that the clicking of her high-heeled shoes will make it more difficult for her to pass through the streets unnoticed:

"You can try your luck if you want," he said, "but it's dangerous. All that way in those heels . . ."
"They make a noise," I said miserably.
"I'll bet they do," he replied. "Ah, women, women . . ." (346)

Interestingly, many women of the Resistance linked their ability to outsmart the Occupation forces to their manipulation of the prevailing stereotypes of femininity. In order to conceal illicit documents or material, women often hid them in one of the many feminine accessories typical of the time—shopping bags, hand bags, sewing bags, cosmetic bags, baby carriages, even in tubes of lipstick.[27] Leduc drew heavily and eagerly on these stereotypes during her black-market days in order to avoid arrest. After making it past the street patrol on this occasion, Leduc repeats the phrase "les femmes, les femmes" to herself like a mantric password to ward off danger as she runs through the unlit streets in her high heels toward her husband and home.

It was, however, in order to escape from the utterly real disappointments of domestic life with Gabriel that Leduc turned to the other principal male figure in her life at the time, Maurice Sachs. When Leduc first met Sachs, he moved within a world of writers, artists, and intellectuals but was not yet known as a writer himself. During the 1930s, Sachs worked for a time as a reader for the Gallimard publishing house. Yet, throughout his life, Sachs was drawn to illicit financial deals, and during the war this criminal activity escalated with his involvement in the trading of black-market jewelry and the trafficking of Jewish refugees into the Unoccupied Zone. For a time, Sachs also served as an informer for the Gestapo, but he was soon compromised on both sides of the law and opted to flee Paris in the fall of 1942. Leduc had separated from Gabriel by this time, and she chose to accompany Sachs in his flight to Normandy.

During their stay in the small town of Anceins, Sachs completed his autobiography *Le Sabbat* (1946) and brought about Leduc's "coming to writing"[28] by encouraging her to record her childhood memories. In Leduc's version of this pivotal episode, Sachs, exasperated by her incessant talk and complaints, turned to her and said: "Your unhappy childhood is beginning to bore me to distraction. This afternoon you will take your basket, a pen, and an exercise book, and you will go and sit under an apple tree. Then you will write down all the things you tell me" (403–404). And in fact, vexed but obedient, Leduc began to write the childhood memories that became her first book, *L'Asphyxie*

(1946).[29] By subsequently abandoning Leduc in Normandy—to the world of fabulation and self-recreation, if you will—Sachs also set the conditions for Leduc's finally taking herself in hand, although not in the predictable way she had encouraged other women to do in her editorials. Only after Sachs's departure did Leduc wholeheartedly undertake the black-market dealing at which she proved to be extremely successful.

· · ·

After mysteriously volunteering for work in a German factory in November 1942, Sachs disappeared while there and was presumed dead in 1945.[30] From Germany, Sachs made a desperate and perverse request of Leduc that clearly "named her as a sex" and, more precisely, as the mother of his (nonexistent) child. Here, too, we have only Leduc's version of his note to interpret:

My love,
You tell me that you are pregnant and that things are going badly for you.
Would you like me to come and see you, would you feel better if I were by your side? Please answer. I kiss you my darling.
Maurice   (437)

Leduc's initial reaction was euphoric: "The miracle had taken place. I had a homosexual at my feet" (437). Although she immediately recognized the letter's urgent undertones and Sachs's wish to return to France, Leduc was tempted by the thought that there may be some truth to Sachs's vows of tenderness, and easily procured from her doctor a medical certificate verifying a (false) pregnancy. She never sent it.

Leduc explains to the reader her anger at Sachs's knowing manipulation of wartime policies and of her affections in this way: "'My love,' a mockery. 'My darling,' a mockery . . . There was no doubt that to Maurice my heart and his sperm were mere commodities of trade. I threw the certificate into the fire" (438). In later letters, Sachs claimed to have "found a way around his difficulties" and to bear Leduc no grudge. In the postwar years, Leduc remained haunted by her decision, by her refusal to indulge Sachs's physical and psychological requests, and by her failure, quite possibly, to save his life. It was, of course, not Leduc's heart that Sachs desired.[31]

Significantly, an earlier rejection of Vichy's powerful maternal model had also marked the end of Leduc's marriage to Gabriel. Having become pregnant, Leduc did not want to carry the pregnancy to term, and she informed Gabriel of her "visits to the so-called midwives" (356). Although Gabriel was by now living separately from Leduc, he offered to help her raise the child. After weeks of waiting for the mysterious procedures of the "so-called midwives" to take effect, Leduc finally aborted in the fifth month of pregnancy. As those who have seen Claude Chabrol's affecting film *Une Affaire de femmes* (1989) are aware, abortion was considered an illegal procedure under Vichy law, punishable by death as a form of treason against the French State.[32] After this final abortion attempt, an infection caused Leduc to fall gravely ill; she entered a clinic for treatment, and upon her release, spent several months convalescing at her mother's home (357).

La Bâtarde closes in 1944 with the depiction of Leduc's euphoria during a long walk from Paris back to the village in Normandy, in which she feels at home with her black-market colleagues:

> I reflect: my wealth and beauty in the paths of Normandy lay in the efforts I made. I kept going until I had what I wanted: I was existing at last. I was succeeding, and my courage led me astray. I toiled and I forgot myself. (468)

Finally a "self-sufficient woman," she has found her place in this village and in this "profession," just as she will find her place in the autobiographical text whose writing she has now begun. In transporting food into Paris to wealthy acquaintances of Sachs, Leduc experienced moments of personal danger and triumph. She is, paradoxically, most at peace when in motion, most successful and socially integrated when purposefully living in the margins and able to "forget herself." In her determination to enter into public circulation, both as a black-market dealer and as a writer, Leduc did not choose the most common routes. During the Occupation, this marginal woman proves that she is a survivor, although in ways that are much less heroic than we might wish. Leduc is eventually at her best during these years, productive, successful, and momentarily content.

Leduc chose to delay representation of the end of the war and the Liberation until the second volume of her autobiography, La Folie en tête (1970). We read there that, just as she had feared, the Liberation was a dysphoric and disturbing experience. Obsessed by fears of bankruptcy, Leduc was arrested in Normandy during the last winter of the war and taken in for questioning concerning her black-market trafficking. During her interrogation, she discovered that her notoriety among the local police had earned her the criminal name of "Paris-Beurre."[33] In turn, the police wanted Leduc to reveal the names of the farmers who acted as her suppliers during the Occupation. Rather than risk further punishment herself, Leduc chose to denounce the very individuals whom she had come to consider her allies. The end of the war signaled, then, the end of Leduc's positive associations with her friends in Normandy, and the end of her financial success and happiness. As France moved toward the postwar era, Leduc was thrown back into alienation and despair, caught between liberated Paris and a Normandy village whose inhabitants would no longer tolerate her presence: "Paris had been liberated, but I hadn't been liberated from my lust for profit . . . Paris had been liberated, and I was torn between a village in Normandy that no longer wanted anything to do with me and a city in which I had no wish to rot."[34] Unable to imagine a persona for herself in a world seeking to restore gender and social relations to a semblance of prewar order, Leduc surrenders to the anomie that had governed her life before the Occupation.

Although *La Bâtarde* was itself the object of great scandal and critical attention at the time of its publication in 1964, in recent years it had fallen out of print altogether. It has now been reissued by Gallimard.[35] Recognized as a work of great literary merit by many, *La Bâtarde* was considered as a candidate for the Goncourt and Fémina prizes but was rejected by both juries. The reason given for this by the Goncourt jury was that since the book was not, after all, a novel, it was not a legitimate contender for the prize. (Questions of genre, however, did not prevent Marguerite Duras's "autobiographical novel" *L'Amant* from receiving the Goncourt Prize twenty years later, in 1984.)

Often dismissed as a sordid lesbian exposé, it is worth considering to what extent *La Bâtarde*'s representation of the Occupation disclosed perhaps even more dangerous aspects of a woman's participation in social life. Although marginal, lesbianism holds its attractions as a literary subject. However, Leduc's blatant confession in *La Bâtarde* of complacency, hypocrisy, anti-Semitism, political inaction, greed, and black-market collaboration during the Occupation move the work into extremely volatile territory. What is more, *La Bâtarde*'s euphoric ending can be seen as daring to recast the narrative of a failed life in the form of a collaborator's wartime success story. Clearly, there are deeply troubling aspects of this work that have remained closeted, although Leduc defiantly placed them in plain sight. Dealing with a moment that was and was not a war, produced by a writer who felt that she was and was not a woman, Leduc's *La Bâtarde* offers today's readers a strangely legitimate way of looking at the still controversial, unclassifiable war years in France.

Andrea Loselle

The Historical Nullification of Paul Morand's Gendered Eugenics

The many histories and literary accounts covering the German Occupation
and the immediate postwar years in France frequently refer to the writers and
journalists who were prosecuted under the Liberation purge. Their words were
charged as deeds at the same time that a good many nonverbal acts—notably
those discreetly perpetrated by French financial backers of the Nazi war machine—were not prosecuted.[1] Whereas attention is generally paid to the more
blatantly notorious writers who stood trial for their collaborationist statements
such as Céline, Brasillach, Rebatet, and Maurras, little mention is made of
those writers, who in spite of clear adherence to France's policy of collaboration with Nazi Germany, escaped this intensive postwar period of retributive
bloodletting. Understanding why some writers survived relatively unscathed
can, however, be equally instructive in the on-going project to disentangle the
real events and facts of the Occupation from the myths and mystifications generated by France's postwar effort to forget Vichy's actual collaborationist
policies. Since the early 1970s a good deal of this repressed history has come
to light—including the forgotten pasts of such figures as Maurice Blanchot
and Paul de Man—but there is to my knowledge only one text, Henry
Rousso's *The Vichy Syndrome*, that pauses for several pages on the fate of one
lesser-known writer, Paul Morand, and the scandal surrounding his candidacy
for a coveted chair at the Académie Française. Unlike those writers mentioned
above, Morand neither was showcased immediately after the war in the purge
trials nor has he been belatedly featured in narrative reconstructions of a secret
past recently come to light. Yet, his political position both in his writings and
in his other profession as a diplomat was—and remains—an open secret. This
very transparency constitutes a certain blind spot in the history of the Occupation. As we will see later on, this fact, brought out in Rousso's brief treatment,
made Morand an ambiguous figure in the fragile politics of the postwar years,

triggering a question that, in the interest of maintaining peace within the Academy, was repressed: how did Morand escape prosecution?

In this essay I address how this escape is traceable to the author's gender politics. My aim in examining his gender politics is to uncover the persistent representation of a masculinist ideology under threat of erasure by the feminine. I argue in a series of close readings from the author's short stories and essays that this ever-present threat is linked to the manner in which Morand fails to become a historical subject in most histories of the collaboration. Of course, it would be only fair to mention that part of the reason he barely figures in the numerous literary histories of collaborationist writers is that he was neither "notorious" nor "great" enough as a writer. This is also true of the scant attention given to the work he performed in his many posts as a career diplomat, a profession to which he himself seems to have attached an importance secondary to that of his writing. The history of his literary and diplomatic acts is nonetheless worth a closer look because it discloses a pattern in the reception of this figure—a pattern of consistent repression of certain features of his life and work that reflects and draws attention to a larger pattern of postwar repression of gendered historical continuities.

Morand launched his literary career in 1921 with a series of three female portraits gathered under the title *Tendres Stocks*. The preface that Marcel Proust generously provided not only guaranteed the success of this book but also helped pave the way for the regular publication of his other works. Up until his death in 1976, Morand would write an impressive number of novels, short stories, essays, and travel accounts in which the themes of modern speed and travel appeared with such consistency that they are today almost all that readers remember of him. These themes are central to Morand's work, as they are linked to another theme also popular during the period of his own popularity as a writer: the relationship of speed to fashion. Technical inventions that made speed an important theme in the twenties figure in Morand's work in ways that highlight both what the latest trends were and the writer's lifelong obsession with keeping up with the latest trends. Trends accelerate in direct proportion to the greater efficiency and speed of twentieth-century inventions. Morand was concerned with how innovations trickle down from their so-called more serious applications in art, science, and politics to their fashionable, often kitsch, manifestations in clothes, interior design, alternative life-styles, changing social roles, and sexual mores. These latter manifestations of the culture of speed explain, in part, Morand's preference for women characters, for as inconstant "creatures of fashion" they wear on the surface the trends whose more serious effects presumably take place further below the surface in men (who thus always figure in Morand's fictions as introspective narrators or protagonists). The effect of the same trends on the male is the loss of physical, psychological, and racial vigor. In Morand's narratives the male, his strength sapped by the culture of speed and fashion, frequently succumbs to the corruption of the female and her taste for simulation and perversion.

This persistent view of the woman as always already corrupted by twentieth-century modernity has occasionally sparked the offhand dismissal of the author as misogynist. But the complexity of his misogyny, namely the connection made between capitalist modernity and women's liberation, never manages to come to light because of one overriding flaw perceived in his work: its single-minded superficiality. Indeed, Brasillach wittily characterized Morand's tenacious "will to be superficial" as "prêt-à-penser" (a play on *ready-to-wear* using the verb *to think*).[2] And Paul de Man in a 1941 review of Morand's novel *The Man in a Hurry* for *Le Soir (volé)* instructed his Belgian readers not to waste their time speculating about why French authors do not entertain more serious topics at this important time in history: "This is all very inoffensive and it is inappropriate on this occasion to heave disenchanted sighs over French frivolity, which still delights in such mediocrities at a time when one ought to have more serious worries."[3] This self-indulgent, picturesque novel that is mere entertainment literature, de Man tells us, should not be taken to be representative of all French literary work. This generalized judgment of his work persists today in offhand critical comments and asides such as that made by the contemporary historian and sociologist of speed Paul Virilio, who imputes by omission that even Morand's nonfictional texts on speed amount to no more than mere "literature": "Not many writers have touched on speed. There is of course Paul Morand, some Kerouac, but that's literature."[4]

What de Man did not sense in 1941 was the degree to which Morand did take frivolity very seriously as a pervasive feature of French society. Frivolity precisely was not and could not be inflected by the seriousness of the historic event of war. Present in Morand's work primarily as a by-product of his focus on speed and fashion, frivolity can also be read as a symptom of modernity's particular temporality. As de Man himself would much later observe: "Fashion (mode) can sometimes be only what remains of modernity after the impulse has subsided, as soon—and this can be almost at once—as it has changed from being an incandescent point in time into a reproducible cliché."[5] Fashion did not stop during the war, as French propaganda film clips demonstrate. Hardships and shortages were optimistically glossed over by highlighting French ingenuity in the service of the on-going demand for new fashions: complex hats made of newspaper, women's suits woven from poodle fur, simulated (painted on) hose, and new, more simplified, yet always stylish, coiffures.[6] Morand's superficiality is clearly linked to this process of fashionable reproduction, a process that is explicitly gendered and that, because it is feminine, does not generate a serious narrative. Masculine control of the narrative (the serious) is nullified by the feminine, a modern force that trivializes by reducing the real to simulation. In other words, Morand's predilection for—indeed, commitment to—ready-made thought would indicate that the thematic acceleration of modernity in his literary and nonfictional treatment of women and trendy fashions annihilates the sense of "rupture" associated with the historical moment of war (another kind of incandescence), requiring more serious thought. The distinction between masculine incandescence (invention) and feminine fashion (imitation) in Morand's work is, in fact, forever on the point of collapse, war or no war. This threat was certainly behind Sartre's 1947 reading of Morand's work, which he faulted for destroying traditions and history.

Sartre comes close to detecting the temporal mechanisms that allow Morand to escape his own "historical situation."[7] Notions such as an "incandescent point in time" and a "historical situation" are always articulated in relation to difference (from other cultures, groups, women, etc.). When historical difference is gender-coded it implicitly maintains a present social order between the men who have ideas, invent, and interpret and the women who consume, reproduce, and "wear" those ideas. In giving to the writer, for example, the role of "making history" (praxis), Sartre predictably genders the difference between writer and reader as one in which "[the public] is an inert mass in which the idea will take shape [*prendre corps*] . . . [T]he relationship of the author to the reader is analogous to that of the male to the female . . ."[8] Here the analogy is biologized: the writer impregnates his feminine public with his idea, which is in turn reproduced as a body (*prendre corps*). Morand was obviously thought to be on the receiving end of history since to him were attributed the will to superficiality and the motive to escape his historical situation. He is more representative of a presumed feminine ahistoricality than— to cite another of Sartre's famous pronouncements from "Qu'est-ce qu'un collaborateur?"—of the feminized male or homosexual collaborator. This latter judgment on fascist collaborators was, as David Carroll points out, "generalized [by Sartre] from a limited number of references in the work of noted fascist collaborators, and from a limited number of cases of homosexuals who had collaborated . . ."[9] Notwithstanding the fact that these cases conveniently served to underscore the "weakness" of the collaborator before a stronger foreign enemy vis-à-vis the heroism of Resistance fighters, the charge was a crucial one for Sartre because, as an imputed sign of deviance, it marked and intensified the difference between the past as "inversion" and disorder and the present as a return to order. In assigning this specific difference to the collaborators, Sartre performs an historicizing act whereby "[d]iachrony ('point of departure')," as Sande Cohen writes in *Historical Culture*, "must negate memory in order to move forward."[10]

Morand's books filled with "tinsel, glass jewelry, pretty foreign names,"[11] however, make no difference; they merely mark time in their seeming indifference to their historical situation. Sartre's criticisms of Morand were revealingly made not on the basis of what he had to say about French culture but on that of his treatment of other cultures, and his tendency to blur the difference between—to use Sartre's example—European and Arab cultures. That example Sartre pulled, in fact, from his own memory to dramatize what he considered to be a typical Morandesque technique of cultural conflation: a veiled Muslim woman on a bicycle, an arresting sight for Sartre, who recognizes in the apparent contradiction (dynamic Western invention vs. passive "Oriental" tradition) not his own underlying Western male Orientalist perception but the annihilating effects of an abstract, capitalist universalism.[12] More important, the sight disrupts the process by which diachrony is generated, that point of departure marked by difference, because Morand's sin had been in not insisting that the woman and the bicycle are two discontinuous, mutually exclusive things. However, the memory that Sartre negates and replaces with his "real" gender-coded memory is that Morand had established another point of departure dating from long before the end of World War II: a negative view of the post–World War I liberation of women in capitalist modernity. Morand's gendered discourse registers the perception of a historical derealization of masculinist identity in French culture. What Morand had to say then about France both before and during the Occupation—and he wrote as much about his own country as he did about others—constitutes a blind spot in Sartre's reading.

What is it about this writer that makes Sartre reach back into his own memory for a Muslim woman, an absolute other, but not the dozens of French women characters in page after page of Morand's fiction? Sartre's blindness to these characters seems simultaneously to render Morand historically invisible. Both writers, however, clearly use a similar gender coding, one that incidentally made Morand's explicitly racist, pro-German ideas—a full-blown, gendered eugenics—remarkably undeserving of mention in Sartre's reading. The difference between the two writers is, of course, a matter of stress. The male wins in Sartre's work, imposing order on the chaos Morand has apparently made of other cultures. The male in Morand's work is constantly threatened by social disorders thought to be caused by women. In a sense, he gave capitalist modernity the feminine gender. One suspects in the end that the repeated charge of superficiality stubbornly arrogates to Morand's work the features of a presumed femininity because his gendered discourse belies a historical displacement of masculine identity as historicity. History, Morand might have said, is no longer written in the name of this identity but in that of its derealization.

The dismissive assertions of his willful triviality aside, the soul of Morand's literary work is profoundly masculinist. It seems at first assimilable to the specific virile ideology of fascism that colored the thinking of other collaborationist writers. Yet, unlike those who during the Occupation opted for membership in fascism's warrior class, Morand remained the superficial, fashionable elitist he was always considered to be. At the same time he consistently attacked France for its lack of virility, citing as evidence of this lack the degeneracy of its women. France, he thought, was not "man enough," because not even the beneficial effects of collaboration with a presumably more virile nation could reverse a decline that had, in his mind, been taking place for a long time prior to the Occupation. For Morand, the cause of France's surrender in 1940 was not simply that its male population had been diminished by World War I, as the "official" excuse proclaimed, but it was this fact combined with a capitalist modernity in which liberated women had undermined the very fabric of French culture, that made the German invasion an inevitable good.

In a short essay written in 1944, Morand, of course, did blame the Occupation on French youth's failure to carry out their *raison d'être*, procreation. Without a million babies per year, he predicted, "we will remain alone faced with our sterility."[13] But as this and other statements in his essays and narratives written before, during, and after this period repeatedly suggest, men were becoming increasingly enfeebled in direct proportion to the number of women who were eschewing their childbearing responsibilities either to lead decadent life-styles or to compete for jobs in professions once the exclusive domain of men. While Morand's 1944 statement was targeted at the official reason for France's surrender, it also spoke into an older, more deeply ingrained discourse on the nature of men. This political discourse drew on late-nineteenth-century medical findings concerning the national birthrate, the so-called "masculinity" index, procreation, heredity, degeneration, and family, as Robert Nye's excellent history, *Masculinity and Male Codes of Honor in Modern France*, demonstrates with great clarity. The "masculinity" index was, for example, the ratio of male to female births. "Contemporary readers," writes Nye, "may be amused to see these numbers referred to habitually as the 'masculinity' index, as though these declines [in male births] reflected somehow on the maleness of male progenitors. But that was precisely what *was* believed." Instead of sparking a reevaluation of masculinist ideas, the social changes brought on by, for example, the employment of women during World War I only intensified the examination of masculinity: "From the late 1860s well into the twentieth century, the shock of military defeat, the fear of depopulation, and the corrosive effects of the gender revolution focused medical and scientific attention as never before on the bodies and masculine qualities of men."[14] Thus Morand's persistent focus on the liberated woman, depicted in so many of his novels and short stories as both the corrupted and the corrupting sex, did not cause his readers to question his politics, which were well within the lines of traditional social thought. In the context of that very masculinist thought, that which had made the collaboration between Nazi Germany and France not an exceptional catastrophe but an altogether logical outcome, was France's growing effeminacy.

It is necessary to emphasize here Morand's lasting belief that World War I was not a victory for France but a defeat, for his masculinist background also links the wartime mutilation and decimation of France's male population to the postwar invasion of French territory by other races. Indeed, as we will see, this older masculinist ideology is typically linked to racial doctrines; the stronger the male population, the purer the race. But lacking adequate male representation, France's invasion will come at the hands of women characters both foreign and domestic. Nowhere is this clearer than in one short story written early in Morand's career, in 1925. "Mme Fredda" opens with a male protagonist's pessimistic reflection on France's then current state of vigor. A metaphorical body, France is "this living anecdote, absolutely new in history, of a country fallen victim to the pleasures that it knew how to create for itself and to universal lust."[15] On this body are traceable the skin diseases and oozing sores passed on by foreign invaders: "pale baldness of Russian exiles; English uric acid; periodic eczema of Italian emigration; suspect spots of Romanian origin; colonies of American boils; Levantine pus, and other germs incubated between the skin and the flesh of nations" (1:420). These rhetorically polemical diseases recited by Morand's character Daniel, a journalist for the conservative opposition, comprise a list of simple stereotypes. Indeed, English uric acid is not even a disease, a sure sign that all these metaphorical lesions and sores proceed out of enduring stereotypes of the time. Uric acid stands for the French notion of the English phlegmatic temperament, pale baldness for the White Russians exiled by the Revolution, and suspect spots of Romanian origin for, perhaps, those people whose "real" origin was thought to be suspect, Jewish political refugees. Paris becomes a vast pleasure center saturated with expatriates, refugees, tourists, emigrants, and the exiled, thus reducing France's historic standing (masculine victory on the battlefield) to mere anecdote. In retrospect, World War I General von Kluck did not lose in the battle at the Marne after all: "'Von Kluck won,' Daniel said to himself, 'Paris is surrounded and captured'" (1:420). This defeat can only mean that France lacks the vigor found apparently in the Nordic races, which incites Daniel to appeal in his articles for a refortification of his country's anemic, feminized blood with an injection of "Germanic or Anglo-Saxon globules full of courage and honor . . ." (1:420).

In this story, the protagonist meets one foreign invader, Mme Fredda, a Dutch horticulturist who specializes in tulip "super cultures." Her ostensible purpose in visiting France is to sell her fancy hybrids, but in her free time she is no less a dupe of the artificial pleasures of Paris than is the average tourist. Over dinner she displays her purchases of the day to Daniel: "false pearls from the rue de Rivoli, curious books from the Palais-Royale, perfume, Gallic gags—fake snot made of glass, and flatulent candies—in short, everything a foreigner could desire in Paris" (1:423). These souvenirs stress the artificiality of not only Mme Fredda but also French culture right down to Gallic gags that simulate unseemly physical distresses. The anecdotal national body that launches this narrative has even been reduced to replicating the symptoms of its degeneracy as commodities. As it turns out, Daniel himself is destined to become nothing more than a racial souvenir. The real motive behind Mme Fredda's visit is to spend a night with "un vrai Français" or "real" Frenchman, an elusive animal that she has spent most of her day tracking down. Daniel meets her standards of authenticity and, by the close of the story, faces the inevitability of becoming one more derealized addition to her collection of fake articles because France is "New Europe"'s corruptible, passive woman who "never knew how to say no" (1:423).

The racist principles of Germanic or Anglo-Saxon courage and honor evoked by the protagonist are clearly set in contrast to the negative connotations of fashionable trends and kitsch souvenirs, which are ultimately harbingers of an emasculation perpetrated by a foreign professional woman. Mme Fredda's role is overdetermined, as her business in tulip hybrids is, in a sense, crossing races. The interest of this story, however, lies more in the late-nineteenth-century masculinist ideology that Morand's readers during the 1920s might easily have recognized. Daniel is a conservative journalist whose particular talent is polemical prose. Having in the story reached middle age, he looks nostalgically back on his youthful journalistic sparring during the Belle Epoque when his words were capable of sparking his readers' reaction. In the postwar years, however, he "continued to lash people on the spot, each morning, with whipping words that frightened no one, so thick everyone's skin had become" (1:420). Daniel harks back to a type of journalistic masculinity that came into being when editors were compelled to encourage journalists to own up to their words by signing their names to their articles—editors were otherwise held responsible for unsigned articles. "Besides," writes Nye, "there was something suspect, even feminine, in anonymity."[16] The act of signing one's article meant courageously defending one's words, which led in the late nineteenth century to a high incidence of duels between journalists and those whose reputations had been impugned by them in print. "It thus seems to have been the case that if a journalist was willing to back up his words with his sword, he could write virtually whatever he wished, no matter how scurrilous or unsubstantiated it might be. More cautious men were obliged to bring their prose into alignment with their confidence in their skills on the dueling ground. This may be the reason that the boldest and most venomous journalists of the era were also the most frequent duelers."[17] If the strength of one's words was a reflection of masculine courage coextensive with one's expertise with the sword, Daniel's frustration at no longer being able to make his authorial sword pierce his victim's skin argues that his masculinity has correspondingly been vitiated by those he lashes "on the spot," since they no longer challenge him to defend his words. He is among the last of a dying breed, a historical strain of virile (= virulent) journalist known to have espoused extreme political ideas both on paper and on the dueling ground.[18] Indeed, his polemical, stereotyped diseases juxtaposed to Nordic honor and courage are reminders of the malignant journalism of Edouard Drumont, author of *La France juive* and also "a seasoned polemicist and dueler" remembered for the saying, "[b]ehind every signature one expects to find a chest."[19] That list of skin diseases—a quotation, in fact, from an article that he had penned the morning of his encounter with Mme Fredda—furthermore reflects the full extent of a blemished masculinity behind which one will not find Daniel's chest, the virulence of his prose not capable of conversion into an active battle against a passive yet more virulent form of feminizing foreign invasion. While he says "no" in his journalism he cannot say "no" to Mme Fredda, who instead offers him an ample chest that refuses to be "brought within reason." Daniel belongs to a new "generation *disarmed* by flowers" (1:423; emphasis added). His words, in failing thus to translate into deeds, amount to moral impotency. The cause of that nullification of the manly word is feminine sexual and racial corruption.

In 1928, Morand wrote for *Candide* a series of predictions for the year 1958. These predictions elaborated on the trends he had observed since the close of World War I: "Development of eugenics and beauty. Syphilitics, epileptics, and alcoholics sterilized. Many countries will be alcohol free. In certain lands in northern and eastern Europe, same sex marriage will be legal, in those of the south, customs [*les moeurs*] that go against nature will be punished with the most severe penalties. Men will have the right to dress as women, and women as men. Most women will wear pants. Many men will wear, at home at least, a dress. There will be women diplomats, lawyers, soldiers, bank managers, ministers."[20] The first set of predictions is straightforward and has positive connotations in typical racialist, social thought (the eradication of social degenerates); it introduces, however, a subsequent set of mainly negative predictions, for Morand, concerning homosexuality, geographical customs, cross-dressing, and gender equality. All of these latter predictions imply a fear of indistinction and homogenization, another type of social degeneracy that threatens not only to annihilate the difference between the sexes but also to reverse customs commonly thought to distinguish northern from southern European countries. Morand reverses the received opinion that sexual mores are more relaxed in the warmer southern regions than in the colder, hence more "virtuous," northern regions. Readers familiar with Gobineau's racial doctrines would easily recognize the implications of sexual homogenization in the northern countries, whose so-called purer Nordic ancestry was thought to be superior to the mixed racial ancestry of the south. In this seemingly bizarre exchange of cultural mores, one detects the traditional notion that homosexuality and gender equality "invert" the natural order of society. In this text as in "Mme Fredda," Morand's geographical *imaginaire* is ideologically slanted toward the north. To it are attributed strong masculine qualities that safeguard the difference between the sexes (hence maintain social order), whereas the south is essentially polymorphous and effeminate. To opt for the perversion and social degeneracy of the south is to sacrifice masculinist virtues. The message in these predictions is that this degradation in France has already begun, as the following reading of a story written five years earlier demonstrates.

The more the woman seeks equality in the public sphere, the more likely she is to be sexually deviant. Confronted by female homosexuality (one of Morand's favorite themes during the interwar years), the male is canceled out in both the public and private spheres in "La Nuit de Babylone." "Rue Royale. My car crosses another car, which slows down and revs up. Diverted I look over. Inside there are three persons. In the middle a young man, handsome as an actor; across his chest, he is holding two women who are kissing each other . . . I could have taken this as one of the thousands of insane spectacles that Paris has to offer, that is, amuse myself—men generally do that saying as they laugh: *'No man's land'* . . ." (1:241). The spectacle of two women locked in a passionate embrace eliminates the handsome, decadent man in the middle. The actor simile leads us to suspect that his masculinity is derealized as a filmic ideal, a notion further underscored by the car as *the* twentieth-century vehicle of a theme central in the representation of modernity: a sight seen in passing. The narrator, as this passage suggests, is disconcerted by this spectacle, not being able to laugh it off, as he would ordinarily do in the safe company of men. He has been isolated from that male bonding experience because the public spectacle reminds him of his own private dilemma. He suspects that a woman has seduced his lover, Denyse. His lover is everything he desires, softness and passivity, while the female interloper, Laurence, physically repulses him with her convictions, her severity, her gray hair, her sensible heels, and her decidedly unfashionable "somber cape, decorated with palms and the Legion of Honor . . ." (1:247). A respected doctor, her professional rectitude contrasts with Denyse's static, horizontal position in the story. Luxuriating in her bed, the lover is the very model of pure receptivity, admired by the narrator for her ability "to spend hours doing nothing, not speaking, not thinking" (1:245). Her agreeable simple-mindedness unfortunately makes her all too vulnerable to the vertical, abhorrently phallic Laurence. As the narrator reflects, Denyse's natural impulse is to offer herself to any admirer, male or female. This generosity is a symptom of her inherent corruptibility, but she cannot, of course, be blamed for her natural weaknesses. It is Laurence who creates a no-man's-land not just because she is a woman but because her professional identity competes with the narrator's male identity. A suspected lesbian vested with the potent signs (palms, the Legion of Honor) of a predominantly male order, she is thought to behave like a man by actively seeking women as her lovers. She is the source of perversion, a figure commonly pointed to as a symptom of postwar decadence, feared by men because she was "the aggressive seducer of other women, the ruthless, perverted competitor of the male suitor. She became man's enemy . . ."[21] Just as the Paris spectacle points to the narrative blurring of the public and private, Laurence blurs the same boundary as the threat of unnatural nondifferentiation. Since the narrator is beset by doubt concerning whether Laurence has in fact seduced Denyse, the narrator is himself placed in a no-man's-land of undecidablity, the boundaries separating the public from the private spheres, male and female, having been breached. He is like the derealized actor who cannot act and is instead turned into a helpless spectator of a "secret understanding, those rituals whereby two women recognize or are drawn to one another . . ." (1:247). Interestingly, this story is one of the few in which Morand gives his narrator his own profession—that of a disaffected diplomat. As the title of the story implies, the diplomat finds no differences to negotiate in this Parisian Babylon because anything goes.

Morand's gender code operates by a series of mutually destructive exchanges. Indeed, the threat of nondifferention informs most of his work by means of a structure that is characteristically chiastic: "The movies teach us two types," he writes, "the first is the very pale woman . . . who is the bleached negress, the exotic washed in pearl-white creaminess, and the second, with very black, sunburnt skin is the Swedish woman after her sunbath" (1:633). Unlike Sartre, who differentiates the male and female by transcendent hierarchies that are instances of noncommunication (male writer vs. female reader; present, male liberator vs. past, homosexual collaborator; European male versus exotic, colonial, female other), Morand remains fixed on the rapidly evolving collapse of hierarchies brought about by gender equality and current fashions that invert, for example, once identifiable and stable pigmentations that inform traditional racialist thought. Sartre sets up walls that historicize, that constantly enact difference, and thereby establish closure. Morand's code is forever open to shifts and reversals that make his female characters obsessive manifestations of the "same," a disorder that threatens to be communicated to the male, like an infectious disease, and against which he seems to be powerless.

Jumping ahead to the Occupation, one finds similar statements privileging masculine, Nordic supremacy in a collection of short essays written over the course of this period and published under the title *Excursions immobiles* in 1944. If "the world has progressed [a été] faster than its imagination,"[22] then it is up to writers like Morand to rid the public of degraded stereotypes and create a new "exoticism" that is at once authentic and virile, as in Daniel's desire for an injection of Nordic blood full of courage and honor. Morand insists that some revised ready-made thought will come in handy in the resurrection of France's true *ancestors*.[23] Always the trendsetter, Morand criticizes his public, which dares "admit that it prefers the sought after matador, the traditional English Lord to the great invisible Jews who lead the world; the comitadji to the Iron Guard, the carnation to the bomb, spahis to corporate leaders, the jousting of grand dukes [*tournée des grands-ducs*] to the raids [*coups de mains*] of the Frankish corps."[24] These juxtaposed stereotypes play upon such popular commonplaces of the time as the notion that Jews control the world financial market while they privilege the bomb, Romania's Iron Guard, and France's occupier, the Nazis, who in typical racist discourse are the Franks, conquerors of Gaul, France's legendary ancestors and aristocrats. Juxtaposed to these contrasting figures of anonymous Jewish world control and Frankish prowess are the outmoded matador, jousting dukes, and the effete English gentleman on his Grand Tour (perhaps the postrevolutionary, decadent version: the macaroni in his fashionably tight waistcoat). Morand explicitly constructs a masculinist politics that proceeds from standardized types, both past and present. The public has not kept up with the latest stereotypes and has consequently lost sight of its racial ancestors. Thus, though a *tournée* is a bygone ritual, a volley between aristocratic equals, the Frankish *coup de main*, a sudden raid establishing military superiority, indicates that the Germans are racially superior to France's aristocratic peers because "*la tournée des grands-ducs*" is also an idiomatic expression meaning a spree on the town. France's aristocratic descendants no longer joust; they debauch themselves. Finally, if the public prefers the flower to the bomb, it is not because it values peace over war, but because it prefers a degenerate, essentially effeminate, outmoded exoticism to a present reality, the Occupation. That reality is a chance, Morand clearly argues, to renew France's ancestors.

One can read in this appeal for renewal a code word for collaboration, but the basic content of the message is not new. The effeminate carnation juxtaposed to the virile bomb repeats the 1925 image of Daniel disarmed of his sword-like pen by tulips. What seems to have changed in the texts examined here is the temporal framing of Morand's static theme of effeminate degeneracy: from defeatist nostalgia ("Mme Fredda") to negative predictions based on a perceived decadence in the present (lesbianism and gender equality in the 1928 predictions and "La Nuit de Babylone") to a present opportunity (hope) to recuperate a past manliness (ancestors) for the future. The progression is, however, less indicative of the historical circumstances of each text's pronouncements than of an ever present drive to keep up with changes so rapid that the past becomes the resurrection of mere stereotypes and the present increasingly unreal as it devolves into passing trends, fashions, simulations, and kitsch. That present is an excess of the present replicating, outmoding, and remaindering itself in the form of stereotypes. Morand's "hope" for a renewal of ancestors by means of stereotypes is thus no different from Daniel's becoming Mme Fredda's *anecdotal*, racial souvenir. It is in the evocation of these souvenirs that the desire for authenticity (i.e., masculinity coupled with Nordic racial doctrine) is caught up in a self-canceling process in which the past is recollected in the stereotype, a stereotype that, because it is just that, reflects a minimalist form of survival within the temporality of fashion or keeping up with the trends: "Not-being-out-of-style is presence as it is suspended . . ."[25] This predicament is precisely what lies behind Morand's fear of racial and gender homogenization, for it points to a narrative degree zero of the uncontrastable. Without difference and discontinuity, "narration is reduced to zero-temporality, a textual state inconceivable in the historian's economy of the code of telling."[26] This all too conceivable temporal predicament in his writing is also reflected in his failure to have become a historical presence in the postwar narrative reconstructions of the collaboration. In turning to the events behind Morand's escape from history, one finds in them confirmations of the repression of the story of Morand's march toward zero-temporality.

As the preceding pages have suggested, Morand remained very active as a writer during the Occupation, publishing novels, essays, travel accounts, and articles for newspapers including collaborationist papers such as the Milice organ *Combats*. In these writings numerous pro-German as well as anti-Semitic statements appeared with the same regularity as before. It was therefore not surprising that when the Comité National des Ecrivains formed shortly before the end of the Occupation to draw up its famous blacklist of compromised writers and intellectuals, Morand's name figured on the list. Composed mainly of writers belonging to the Resistance, this committee, of which Sartre was also a member, had assigned itself the task of gathering evidence and information for future use by Liberation authorities. Yet, curiously, when the committee published its final list, in October, two months after the Liberation of Paris, Morand's name was not on it. The reasons remain a mystery, but it may have been, in part, this omission that saved Morand from arrest, the committee's role having been a key influence in the near single-minded prosecution of writers under de Gaulle's postwar government. Morand also wisely left France for Switzerland to live in exile for a number of years (an exile that did not, however, prevent him from making regular visits to Paris). Yet here it is also tempting to analogize the disappearance of his name to Daniel's compromised signature in "Mme Fredda," the potency of Morand's signature perhaps having been deemed not enough. Omission is tantamount to the cancellation of authorial, masculinist principles of difference that turned Morand's writing against him as if it were a reflection on his own effeminacy and not words considered to be deeds.

If Morand narrowly evaded prosecution for his verbal acts, then perhaps his diplomatic activities deserved a closer look, since he had been employed by the Vichy Ministry of Foreign Affairs and had also served under Pierre Laval, Prime Minister of Occupied France. As a diplomat and a member of elite, upper-middle-class society, Morand was a familiar figure on the Vichy and Paris scenes, socializing actively with writers and intellectuals such as Abel Bonnard and Ernst Jünger, and with top collaborators and Nazi officials, notably Laval's chief of staff, Jean Jardin, and German Ambassador Otto Abetz, both of whom, according to accounts, were on very friendly terms with the writer-diplomat.[27] But his service record during this period in particular reveals an intriguing series of fumbles that, if they suggest that Morand was a less than adept diplomat more inclined to socializing than negotiating and thus not worth putting on trial, also reveal that he played an important, if ambiguous, symbolic role in what Rousso has called the Franco-French War, which began with the signing of the French armistice and lingered well into the first decades after the Occupation.[28]

Morand happened to be stationed in London at the time of the Nazi invasion of France. In communication with both the newly designated Vichy government and the armies that had fled to England, he was in the unique position of being able to choose sides. He predictably rejected appeals from General de Gaulle and Jean Monnet, a prominent businessman at the time, to join the exiled Free French forces. At the same time, however, he disobeyed explicit orders from Vichy to remain at his post and maintain diplomatic relations with England and France when, as the Nazis initiated bombardments over London, he abandoned his office just one month after the armistice to return to France. After a circuitous voyage through Portugal and Spain, he arrived in Vichy with a report in hand, sternly blaming General de Gaulle and Jean Monnet for botching England's relations with France. Morand was met with a cool reception. Ordered not to return to London, he was quietly dismissed by Minister of Foreign Affairs Paul Baudouin, who in his diary held Morand personally responsible for severing Vichy's only diplomatic tie with London.

Morand's continued presence in London had been considered important, to say the least, to Vichy's interests. Although it would be pointless to speculate whether he might have changed the course of a rapidly escalating Franco-French conflict, this act haunts the arguments for and against his election to the Academy almost two decades later. Because he was stationed in London, Morand had an open choice; whereas those in France who either did choose, wished to choose, or would have chosen in retrospect to join the Free French could not make such a choice without considerable risk. The contrast highlights the fact that he had clearly decided to join Vichy with the paradoxical result of having his choice annulled on the official level by his Ministry. Yet this, like his literary form of masculinist nullification, also permits Morand to be perceived as someone who acts against himself. He affirms his choice by dis-affirming it.

Morand took advantage of his dismissal to write, among other things, a col-orful account of his eventful trip from London to Vichy. Pierre Laval eventu-ally reinstated him in 1942 and named him president of a committee whose function was to review and censor films according to Nazi regulations and Vichy's moral standards represented by the regime's motto: "Travail, Famille, Patrie." Again Morand canceled himself out by having to censor himself when one member of his own committee denounced him for a screenplay adaptation of Zola's *Nana*, which he had been writing in his spare time. Pétain personally wrote to Morand, rebuking him for not upholding Vichy's strict standards of morality, and ordered him to abandon at once any thought of submitting his screenplay for production.

That Morand would have entertained the hope that his screenplay could pass detection by his own committee bespeaks perhaps an overweening confi-dence in his position as president. It is, however, both interesting and pre-dictable that he chose *Nana* in the first place. *Nana* was Zola's criticism of the Second Empire represented in the systematic destruction of men by a female character's excessive sexual appetite, a criticism that could easily have been taken at that time to be an underhanded swipe at France's "emasculation" by the enemy occupier. As we have already seen, Morand was not, of course, ac-cusing collaborators as a specific group of prostituting themselves to the enemy, an accusation that recalls Sartre's retrospective, homophobic catego-rization of them as feminized males in "Qu'est-ce qu'un collaborateur?" He was accusing them of not being better collaborators with the Nazis. Occupa-tion or no Occupation, it was France as a whole that was the problem. The pe-riod covering the publication of Zola's *Nana* in 1880 and its reappearance in 1942 as a screenplay reiterates what the roots and continuity of Morand's thinking were. As Charles Bernheimer has written, *Nana* "implies that, once perverted by desire, any woman, whatever her class background, will embrace prostitution as her natural mode and spread the virus of her degenerate infec-tion."[29] Yet Morand uses *Nana* not to stress the natural corruptibility of women—a given that by itself would, for him, require no proof—but the ef-feminacy of French males in contrast to the Frankish corps. That fact meant that he had impugned Vichy's standards of morality as mere wishful thinking. Morality, an important feature of Pétain's regime, had to be a face-saving morality, in light of France's surrender, that is, a question of keeping intact the nation's honor as the National Revolution, which as a social order guaranteed the separation of the sexes. It is worth noting that under this regime laws were passed early on to restrict homosexual behavior (1941) and, as a remedy to un-employment, to permit employers to dismiss female employees with salary-earning husbands (1940).[30] What makes Morand's project interesting is that he chose another author's novel, and in doing so sought to "update" its content by means of the twentieth-century genre of film, a genre that accords well with Morand's own perceptions about the acceleration of modernity. That acceleration is also perceptible in who Nana is: a full-blown *femme fatale*, and a character unlike any of Morand's prior, more limited manifestations of feminine pathology. She devours men in an entropic narrative that signifies complete degradation.

In the end, the cause of this minor scandal over Morand's project may lie in the fact that Laval chose, so to speak, the wrong "writer." Well known for the "licentious" or, rather, "titillating" themes (lesbianism being the major one[31]) of a large number of his fictional works, Morand was obviously not picked to head the committee because of this feature of his literary reputation. Accounts attribute his selection to a text he wrote back in 1934, *France la doulce*, an attack on the so-called Jewish control of the cinema. He was a safe choice for the task of rubber-stamping pro-German, racist propaganda. As a censor during a time when anti-Semitism was officialized in the collaborationist laws forbidding Jews from most professions and denying them access to public places, Morand did not have to give much thought, if he gave any, to the moral values communicated in, for example, the notorious documentary "Le Péril Juif," which opened in theaters on April 6, 1943.

Morand's eleventh-hour omission from the blacklist and his two self-cancellations during the Occupation have obscured the picture of him as much as they probably aided him in escaping charges of collaboration. A foregone bungler as a diplomat and a "superficial" writer, he failed to become a historical subject because these discrete omissions, nullifications, and censorings do not "make history." Instead, they add up to a series of zeros. And yet the acceleration of "Nana" names a symptomatic part of his work's temporal mechanisms that came between a past overlooked by Laval and a present censored by Pétain. It was that fear again of zero-temporality which took him one more step on the path of the trends he always strove to keep up with. This time he pushed his gendered message a little too far beyond the then current, acceptable trends, and in the name of public morality (the present) it was censored. As an Oxford-trained elitist who believed in the virtues of "good breeding," Morand was overall never extreme enough; he was thoroughly mainstream, using a surviving nineteenth-century masculinist ideology that no one questioned. But "Nana" is a significant blip in Morand's superficial record and represents an advance in his work. It reappears once more in another (also forgotten) form in 1958, the year he submitted his nomination to the Académie Française. This event constitutes the single instance in which Morand's past activities managed to trigger public debate.

Split into two camps of Resistance and Pétainist intellectuals, this bastion of France's most illustrious minds was also a microcosm of the country's political divisions. As Rousso relates, while Morand could count on the support of the latter camp, the former would oppose him with the well-known fact of his collaborationist activities in his other career as a diplomat.[32] Morand's potential inclusion under the sacred cupola triggered a heated debate within the Academy that set into relief "the failure of the purge to establish a clear definition of the crimes and misdemeanors of collaboration. The Pétainists capitalized on this failure: why should Morand be excluded when he was not found guilty of violating any law?"[33] Letters of protest and support were written and published, and a petition against his election drawn up and circulated. Short just one vote of the nineteen required, Morand failed in this round as well as in a second round when he stood for election again the following year and was forced to withdraw his candidacy because President de Gaulle formally opposed him on the grounds that, as his opponents had already argued the year before, he would unnecessarily spark partisan hatreds within the Academy. There is a striking irony in this exceptional circumstance in which a French president intervenes in the Academy's election process, it having been Morand himself who, during a brief moment in 1940, found himself straddling the two conflicting sides and considered de Gaulle to have been at the root of this lingering civil war. In seeking to gain entry twice, at a time when the reigning politics of both the country and the Academy were to maintain a conciliatory harmony between opposing sides all too susceptible to sudden flare-ups of memories and past grievances, Morand showed no small amount of optimism and perseverance, if not plain impudence. Indeed, these were finally rewarded nine years later in October 1968. At long last—for he had been trying to gain entry since 1939—he assumed his place by filling the chair of a member who had firmly opposed him in 1958, an ironic twist of fate indicating that his past in the wake of May 1968 was no longer a relevant factor in his consideration.

More than a decade later Morand was opposed not on the basis of his writings but on that of his political involvement. The emphasis on his political past was no doubt partly due to the fact that he symbolically recalled the inception of France's later postwar political divisions and repressions, thus making the past present and diverting all attention away from his literary work. In fact, his opponents stressed in a letter to the Academy's director that they did "not question the candidate's literary credentials."[34] Thus concealed in Rousso's history of Morand's failed 1958 election is that the deciding vote of his first attempt *was* a judgment made on the basis of his literature. Furthermore, as in the case of the *Nana* screenplay, it was not his literary *past* that guided this last-minute deciding vote of a member, who initially was in favor of Morand, but once again his literary *present*. Someone had discretely passed this Academy member a copy of Morand's 1954 novel *Hécate et ses chiens* with its more salacious passages underlined.[35] Attended by her hellhounds, the Greek goddess Hecate haunts the crossroads here of a swing vote based on a standard of morality, a contemporary repression unlike the other repressions Rousso discusses, because if the earlier rejections sought to prevent the past from interfering with the present, the current one amounts to a reversal by accepting Morand's past literature but taking exception to his present work. By 1954, little had, of course, changed in Morand's attitude toward women. They are still the cause of social evil, the subject of this postwar novel being a woman who preys on children for sexual pleasure and—for no narrative by Morand would be complete without it—destroys the men in her life. The ideas that inform this narrative derive directly from eugenicist Havelock Ellis's turn-of-the-century masculinist theories on sexual deviance in women, a body of work that one might have thought, as the narrator in the novel says about his memory, was "rendered more distant by the acceleration of history" (2:390, 435; see note 20). That source, however, remained stable and present. What changed was the nature of the deviancy. While there are numerous short stories and novels about female homosexuality and promiscuity in Morand's earlier work, reinforcing over and over the threat of exclusion of masculine order, pedophilia represents an advance on the scale of feminine sexual pathology; it is criminally deviant. In escalating his masculinist principles to this point, Morand seemed to have outdone himself again, but only for the present, for it is generally the pattern of works that are considered licentious in the present to enjoy in later years poetic license. The nature of Morand's crime in the eyes of the Academy member who switched his vote was made in response to a notion of moral, social order thought to be static. The public would not, of course, remain fixed to that order but would sooner or later catch up with Morand. Although he would never see it, a film version of *Hécate et ses chiens* was made in 1979 (2:1062).

.   .   .

In this writer's case, moral judgment and censorship were enacted by the same tacit gender politics—this most clearly in the cases of Sartre and Pétain—on which Morand based his to call to attend to the destabilization of the "natural" difference between male and female. It was therefore used to support both a politics of collaboration and a Resistance-associated disengagement from the past. Returning to Sartre's criticism of this author's tendency to blur difference by means of an abstract, capitalist universalism, Morand's ruse was precisely to *capitalize* on trends as the mutations under which the same tired masculinist ideas were to be recycled again and again without ever regaining their former potency. In doing so, he also contested Sartre's gendered historicism in subjecting it to the acceleration of change.

Andrew Hewitt

Sleeping with the Enemy: Genet and the Fantasy of Homo-Fascism

Sometimes crude and anecdotal, sometimes subtle and theoretical—the ideological linkage of homosexuality to fascism has a long, if less than illustrious, history.[1] From the earliest days of Hitler's regime, conflating the political, historical, and moral decadence of the bourgeoisie with a homosexual
fascination with power formed a cornerstone of leftist analysis. In the writings of Adorno, for example—for whom "totalitarianism and homosexuality
belong together"[2]—such linkages would be traced both through the mechanisms of narcissism (social and individual) and through an effeminization that
marks for him the demise of the rational political subject. Through films such
as *The Damned* and *The Conformist*, meanwhile, the linkage permeates a popular culture that has long understood decadence as effeminization and effeminization as homosexuality.

It is not difficult to imagine the stakes of such a linkage in the political
realm: fascism is thereby pathologized sexually, while homosexuality is like-
wise stigmatized politically. The defeat of fascism feeds the fantasy of returning to a political and sexual normalcy. I do not even undertake here to refute
the linkage in any historical or political sense; for I am interested instead in
the leverage that this linkage provides in the aesthetic realm, and only subsequently—by way of Benjamin's analysis of fascism as the "aestheticization of
politics"—in what it might actually reveal about the "nature" of fascism. Even
if the conflation is purely ideological (is ideology ever pure?) and tells us
nothing about fascism per se, it at least reveals something about the ways in
which we have tried—culturally and theoretically—to understand fascism.
Since the linkage is so common, and operates at so many different levels of
cultural "analysis," it might not surprise us to encounter—in an essay luridly
titled "Genet: Dandy of the Lower Depths"—the following analysis: "The
Nazis built their movement by attracting men just like Genet. He would have

119

been at home in the SA which was, among other things, a cult of decadent homosexual toughs and aesthetes."[3] Overlooking, if it is possible, the strangely trivialized "other things" that the SA represented, and making the leap of imagination that would allow us to characterize them as "aesthetes," does this assessment have anything to say to us? The invocation of Genet as a "dandy" clearly suggests an aesthetic pedigree for fascism—the pedigree, indeed, of aestheticism itself. From other writings by Benjamin—who of course coined the term "aestheticization" in his essay on "The Work of Art in the Age of Mechanical Reproduction"—we can infer that such a pedigree was the one he too had in mind.[4] If the argument is crude in its generality—its application to "men just like Genet" euphemistically invoking again the linkage of homosexuality and fascism—it might perhaps prove more useful to us in its elaboration. The author of the article goes on to outline the terms that frame our consideration of the question of Genet and "fascism" here:

> Genet remains true to his own vision. He is attracted sensually and aesthetically—are they not intimately related?—to the Nazis because they are strong and because they do not hesitate to carry through the logic of their vision. He finds joy and pleasure in torture. Above all, it is murder that Genet adores. Murder is the final test of one's commitment to the aesthetic. (367)

I wish to focus on this conflation of the sensual and the aesthetic—"are they not intimately related?"—as a way of understanding and undoing the conflation of homosexuality and fascism. I contend that this relation between the sensual and the aesthetic must be central to any linkage of political ideology and sexual desire. Historically, it was only the development of an autonomous discourse of taste that dissociated the sensual from the aesthetic (by recasting aesthetic taste as the operation of *judgment*). Part and parcel of this desensualization of the aesthetic, however, is the stigmatizing of the sensual as the operation of *interest* in a faculty of judgment that should be dis-interested. To introduce—in the manner of the passage just cited—the category of (homosexual) desire into the aesthetic realm is to violate the pretensions of aesthetic judgment to suprasensual disinterestedness. This would be the point where homosexual camp and kitsch become inextricable: the preaesthetic, sensual desire of the homosexual uncovering the interest and desire at the basis of all aesthetic judgment; and the category of disinterest condemning any attempt to glorify (homosexual) desire as aesthetically disinterested. What Genet threatens—for the author of this passage—is not simply a slip into irrationality but a recognition of the "interests" at play in all aesthetic judgment. In short, the introduction of desire into aesthetic judgment in turn facilitates the introduction of aesthetics into political judgments. I seek to question this logic of escalation; to see in the insistence of desire as interest a *resistance* to aestheticization. What I hope to develop in this essay is a new typology of aestheticization that takes into account the role of desire in the construction of political fantasies.

Sartre, whose analysis of Genet forms the basis of this essay, occasionally moves beyond the abstractions of theory to argue that Genet's social vision "found a perfect image . . . in Darnand's militia, which was both criminal and military."[5] What Genet desires is an *image* of the political, and works such as *Funeral Rites* would certainly seem to justify Sartre's assessment. If biographical evidence of any Nazi sympathies on Genet's part is scant, these literary proclivities nevertheless remain troubling. Where aestheticization is at issue even the distinction between fiction and reality—aesthetics and politics—must be called into question. In an interview given many years after the occupation—and cited in Edmund White's *Genet: A Biography*—Genet would explain: "Look, when Hitler gave a thrashing to the French, oh, yes! I was happy, I was happy with this attack. The French had been cowards."[6] Pushed on the political implications of this pleasure, and the reality of the Shoah, Genet would reply only that "First, in truth, I didn't know about that. But it was a question of France, it wasn't a question of the German people or the Jewish people, or of the Communist people who could be massacred by Hitler. It was a question of the punishment given by the German army to the French army" (White, 162). Any protofascist sympathies in Genet's pronouncements emerge not as substantive ideology but in the absence of any such substance. Aestheticization would be precisely the displacement of political calculus by a solipsistic concern with the "pleasure" that a political intervention might yield.

But what relation does this "aesthetic" pleasure bear to the "sensual"? Whereas, for the author of the article quoted earlier, the possibility of fascism consisted precisely in the possible slippage from the aesthetic into the sensual, I would argue that the opposite is the case. It is precisely the sexual motivation of Genet's sympathies that obliges us to rethink both his work and our own understanding of "aestheticization" beyond the parameters of a Kantian aesthetics of disinterest. "In the 1940s," Edmund White tells us in his biography of Genet, "he wrote out daydreams about the Nazi soldiers and even had an affair with one of them, but aside from these strictly erotic feelings his only enthusiasm for the Germans derived from his pleasure at seeing them defeat and humiliate the French, his sworn enemies" (559). White further cites Jean-Pierre Lacloche's assertion that "Genet was as bad a fighter as he was a thief. He consoled himself by sleeping with Black American soldiers, just as during the war he'd slept with blond Germans" (261). These citations—instances of Genet's "sleeping with the enemy"—have more than a biographical or anecdotal importance. I am particularly struck by the indifference of Genet's sexual attractions and the play of homo- and hetero- they suggest: Black Americans and Blond Germans. Black skin and black shirts: Americans and Germans.

Different from each other yet united in their difference to "France," these figures oblige us to rethink the play of homo- and hetero- in Genet's desire. Are we to insist on the heterogeneity of a homosexual attraction to the other? Or on the homogenizing effects of a desire that seems to efface difference within the other in the slippage from black skins to black shirts? Is the uniform-ity of Genet's desire for the German an aesthetic paradigm for understanding a desire for black American soldiers; or does the sensuality of a desire for (black) skin undercut the desire for the uni-form? At what point does an insistence on the heterogeneity of partners revert to a homogenizing of alterity, and at what point does Genet's homo-sexuality in fact depend on alternative markers of difference and hetero-geneity such as race?[7] In other words, is an ontology of difference not always ultimately self-defeating? And would the black skins and black shirts provide precisely the "image" of this reified indifference? These are not questions that I will address directly here: I wish merely to indicate the persistence of a distinction (heuristic, perhaps) between the aesthetic (as a formalizing impulse toward homogeneity; black skins, black shirts) and the sensual (heterogeneous and negative in its choice of—non-French—sexual partners). I wish to ask: What does it mean to sleep with the enemy?

What can Edmund White mean, indeed, when he seeks to isolate certain sympathies as "strictly erotic"? For Genet's erotic fantasies seem anything but strict: they are transgressive to the extent that they transgress the very realm of the sexual itself. Genet's "transgressive sexuality" should be understood not simply as a transgression *within* the sexual—that is, as a violation of certain historical or biologized sexual norms or mores—but as a transgression of the sexual. The transgression marks a spilling out of erotic energies into realms of social, political, and cultural life that would not ordinarily seem susceptible to a libidinal analysis. Such a sexuality would transgress not just moral or normative values but epistemological structures as well, calling into question the very categories through which we seek to construct, understand, and at the same time delimit the sexual. Now, this radical or epistemological transgression by no means entails transgression in the more limited and strictly politicized sense. A sexuality that encroaches—or transgresses—on the terrain of political and social analysis by no means necessarily functions transgressively as a politics: Genet's sexual and political indifference would be proof of that. We should resist simplifying homologies in which transgressive sexualities translate necessarily into transgressive or subversive politics. For at the radical level, a transgressive sexuality (like aestheticization) de-differentiates the discourses across which such homologies would function. In other words: we cannot posit a parallelism of sex and politics, because we are no longer sure that they are not one and the same thing.

The obvious place to start this inquiry into the relation of the sexual and the political in Genet would be Sartre's monumental study of *Saint-Genet*, but I wish to start more modestly; with his short essay "Qu'est-ce qu'un collabora-teur?" In this essay it is a sexual rather than a political economy that, from the first, informs Sartre's analysis of collaboration. Considering the writings of French collaborators in a way that eschews traditional class analysis, Sartre feels compelled to acknowledge in their works "strange metaphors presenting France's relations with Germany as a sexual union, in which France plays the woman's role" (58).[8] In this tropology, he argues "there is a curious mixture of masochism and homosexuality. Indeed, the Parisian homosexual milieu yielded a number of brilliant recruits" (58). While it would certainly overstate the case to argue that Sartre sees any causal link between homosexuality and collaboration, homosexuality provides for him a social and psychical environ-ment in which collaborationist tendencies might thrive.

While Sartre considers the desire to be raped by Germany to be a homosex-ual fantasy, it retains in its very structure a dyadic, gendered heterosexuality. For the Frenchman to imagine himself a woman raped by Germany is to imag-ine a specifically heterosexual scene: effeminization—though taken by Sartre as indicative of homosexual desire—instead marks a desire for heterosexual order. Fantasies of effeminization, then, serve an ambiguous social and ideo-logical function, inscribing within the heterosexual order a homosexual im-pulse; the "homosexual" and narcissistic desire of the heterosexual in extremis for the retention (in however compromised a form) of the structure of hetero-sexuality. As we shall see, Sartre subsequently refers in this regard to the phe-nomenon of "prehomosexuality." The impetus behind this fantasy lies not in homosexuality but in the need of a heterosexualized political iconography to account for mutations in the world political order. In fact, though Sartre differ-entiates between homosexuality and masochism, the "homosexual" twist in this fantasy lies in the collaborator's casting of himself as the feminine victim in the heterosexual dyad. The fantasy, in other words, effeminizes France in order to avoid the fantasy of a homosexual coupling, and attests to the fact that the heterosexual order carries an imperative force greater than any attachment to masculinity as an identity-formation. Gender (as masculinity) is surren-dered in order that the machine of en-gendering may persist—as rape.

Sartre further focuses in this most suggestive small essay on the definitional distinctions between fascism, conservatism, and collaborationism. What fi-nally distinguishes the fascist mentality, for Sartre, will be a certain historical sensibility: "realism." "The collaborator is touched by that intellectual malady known as historicism," (52) Sartre writes, and this charge of "realism" forms the cornerstone of his analysis. Fed with an ill-prepared Hegelianism he can barely digest, the collaborator—a realist—believes only in progress, in the judgment of facts from the perspective of the future. Adducing reason from being, he seeks to justify everything in the name of historical necessity. To this extent, of course, "realism" would be highly unrealistic in its assumption of an ongoing ontological revelation in and through history. In its reliance on "the facts," it does violence to them by rendering them merely emblematic of a transcendent historical meaning. At first sight, we might think that Genet—who according to Sartre "lives outside history, in parentheses" (*SG*, 5)—would offer the very opposite of such historicism. If anything, his social vision is reactionary in a more traditional, conservative sense: "at most, he regrets that there is no longer an aristocracy in France and that class justice is not more ruthless" (55). But, oddly enough, it is precisely as a realist—that most loaded of terms—that Sartre will analyze Genet: "As a *realist*, he wants to win or lose in *this* world. Rimbaud wanted to change life, and Marx to change society. Genet does not want to change anything at all. Do not count on him to criticize institutions. He needs them, as Prometheus needs his vulture" (55). Sartre's presentation here necessarily raises the question of betrayal as an ethical and sexual necessity. Bersani's recent presentation of Genet as "The Gay Outlaw" has focused on this question, and Sartre, no less than Bersani, understands betrayal as the condition of homosexual desire (at least in its "passive" form).[9] It is, perhaps, some measure of the ground separating Bersani from Sartre that he will counter Sartre's analysis of protofascist historical "realism" with the recognition that "the Nazism of *Funeral Rites* is not a 'cause'; it is the apocalyptic appearance in history of an impulse to erase history"(12).

Clearly, Sartre will understand betrayal in a very different way from Bersani. For all his presentation of the passive homosexual's ascesis, he cannot help seeing betrayal dialectically, as that which links the homosexual (negatively) to the order he transgresses—"as Prometheus needs his vulture." Bersani, meanwhile, radicalizes betrayal as the "potential for erasing cultural relationality itself." This radicalized evil (though Bersani does not invoke Kant's notion of radical evil as such) would move beyond "the apparent dependence of evil on social definitions of the good" and consists in a "turning away from the entire theater of good and evil and its transgressions, that is, a kind of metatransgressive *dépassement* of the field of transgressive possibility itself" (9). Clearly, Sartre's dialectical reading of Genet's transgression is inadequate, but I would like to suggest in what follows an alternative reading of Bersani's "turning away," by invoking Sartre's notion of "communion" as a form of social relation that is not purely relative.

Though Bersani's reading of Genet is a necessary antidote to Sartre's, I would like to suggest that he confuses relationality and relativity; that his rejection of a limited "relative" reading of Genet's evil blinds him to new and important forms of social relation created by the very "metatransgressive" act of "turning away." Second, I would suggest that Bersani—for all his luxurious and seductive presentations of the sexual acts (primarily rimming) that constitute Genet's betrayal—is led by his feeling that "the aesthetic frequently arrests the erotic by monumentalizing fantasmatic moments" (9) into an ethical reading at times no less gestural and asensual than Sartre's. Rejecting the elements of "ethical kitsch" in certain readings of *Funeral Rites*, Bersani will reject them as a mere "straining toward *literary* originality," less important than his own disavowed ontology "of betrayal inscribed within homosexual love itself" (7). What I wish to bear in mind, in stressing the importance of the sensual as a moment of "interest" that is political, erotic, and writerly, is something Bersani himself reminds us of: namely, that "betrayal's place in an ethical reflection disappears in the immediacy of an 'erotic exaltation'" (6). The act of writing—as a moment of exaltation—will be the excessive product of Genet's ascesis and should not be too readily dismissed.

Genet scrambles the neatly defined terms of Sartre's essay on collaboration. His historically parenthetical existence might, instead, offer a model of the kind of historical sensibility Sartre has in mind when he speaks of "realism"— a sensibility that brackets history in all its worldliness for History as a structuring principle. At least in Sartre's presentation he is conservative—the quotation above points out his dialectical dependence on precisely the conventions and institutions he flouts—and yet he is a realist: that is, at least potentially, an ideological collaborator.

Genet's confused position articulates some of the difficulties in Sartre's apparently neat analysis. As a bourgeois ideological phenomenon, realism's commitment to progress faces certain aporias: most notably, the objectively reactionary position of the bourgeoisie as a class in post-1848 Europe. Realism is the futurism of those with no historical future and conceives of a progress from which the possibility of a proletarian revolution must be banished. The collapse of collaborationist ideological positions back into a form of feudalizing conservatism exemplifies the aporetic position of a class faced with irreconcilable intellectual and historical imperatives: to think, and not to think, its own demise. Consequently, Sartre's essay is riddled with the political terminology of feudalism. While the collaborator is not a conservative, he does seek to reinstate "a rigorous feudal order" (58); "a new system in which all relations are singular, from person to person" (57). Furthermore, in the "feudal bond between suzerain and vassal" France acquires the role of "Hitler's liege" (56). Suggested here is a second model for understanding France's relation to Germany from the collaborator's perspective: the feudal relation. Tropes of feudalism come to shape not only Sartre's understanding of bourgeois reaction, however, but also the social fantasies unleashed by homosexuality. This model by no means stands in opposition to or displaces the trope of effeminization: after all, Sartre will argue, "there is a definite sexual component in the collaborator's feudal ties to his master" (58).

Within this system, homosexuality frames the (im)possibility of a bourgeois realism. It is in this sense that we might consider Sartre's assertion that "whether or not he has occasion to manifest himself as such, the collaborator is the enemy that democratic societies harbor at their breast" (60). It is the equivocation I wish to stress here: the collaborator is a closet democrat and vice-versa—"qu'il ait ou non l'occasion de se manifester comme tel." It is precisely this function of manifestation, I argue, that Genet's writing performs. The homosexual manifests and eroticizes the homo-social bond on which society depends. Contrary to the tradition linking aestheticism with homosexuality, however—positing a slippage from depoliticized aestheticism to a fascistic aestheticization—we need to question the function of desire in this eroticization. What the erotic—or what I categorized earlier as "the sensual"—forecloses is the possibility of a social sublation, in which social order becomes totalitarian through internalization. For where the specific and sexual instantiation of the social is desired—as body—we have materiality and interest rather than a disinterested aestheticism. This, precisely, would seem to be the political threat posed by the homosexual: the eroticization not of the male object of desire but of the social connection itself. Or, as Sartre will put it in *Saint-Genet*: "the homosexual attempt can be regarded, despite everything, as an effort to enter into communication with other men" (136). Homosexuality functions as a continuation—and yet as a perversion—of social communication.

It is this relationship between communication and collaboration that we might fruitfully pursue. Despite foregrounding the question of (social) communication in examining homosexuality, Sartre will insist that homosexual relations are strictly nonreciprocal. Linking the criminal milieu to that of homosexuals, Sartre observes that "the same absence of reciprocity can be observed among homosexuals . . . Here too the ban that is cast on certain men by society has destroyed all possibility of reciprocity among them" (41 n.). The communication at work in homosexuality—the principle that every social order must carry at its breast—is not, then, communicative in any traditional sense. Betrayal is the principal mode of interaction: communication will not be understood as a process of mutual self-disclosure or intersubjective discourse. The homosexual fetishizes communication, so to speak; empties it of substance and takes the very principle of social relationality itself as the object of desire. I desire not the other man but my very relation to him. In this sense, then, desire is not just for the body of the other but for the empty place he occupies within the social relation. This is, we might say, a structural desire. We are caught, then, between two models of homosexual desire: one—the most obviously "interested"—reducing social relations to a carnal desire for bodies; the other subjecting bodies to a homo-social desire for relations. Might these possibilities—the homosexual and the homo-social—be mapped against the iconography of Genet's collaborations, as, respectively, the desire for black skins and the desire for black shirts?

Sartre will term Genet's mode of communication—or manifestation—a *communion*, and this notion of communion is crucial to his analysis of Genet. As we shall see, these terms—communication and communion—are subsequently triangulated by a third, politicizing term: community. Honing our original question, we may ask: What is the relationship between communication, communion, and community in the phenomenology of homosexuality developed by Sartre? And how does this nexus of terms enable an analysis of fascism? Before turning to *Saint-Genet* for a substantive analysis, however, we should take note of what it means to analyze a life in writing—a life that has become communication. For the homosexuality Sartre confronts in Genet is one that has already passed into the text, and this relationship between sexuality and textuality is itself one we must examine. I would argue that Sartre's notion of a homosexual communion corresponds more closely to his notion of writing than to any everyday notion of communication. We might approach the questions of homosexuality and writing by way of the phenomenon of theft, to which they are inevitably linked for Sartre. "As a thief," Sartre writes, "Genet served the established order; as a poet of theft, he destroys it . . . The inexpiable act consists not in doing Evil but in manifesting it" (493–94). The question of conservatism; raised in the collaboration essay is reposed here. The thief is a conservative; the writer is not. We need to clarify the political and aesthetic significance of these statements before proceeding with the analysis of any text—Genet's or Sartre's.

For all his citation of Kant on radical evil, Sartre essentially adheres to an Enlightenment (that is to say, early Kantian) notion of evil as lack ("Evil is the Other. The Other than Being, the Other than Good, the Other than self" (35). Evil is the lack in Being and therefore itself lacks Being. Thus, when Sartre writes of the evildoer—of Genet as an evildoer, for example—we need to understand such "evildoing" in terms of the dichotomy of Being and Doing. From the perspective of an essentialism, Doing would be the action that marks the incompletion of—or movement toward—Being. Doing would be a Doing *toward* Being. Strictly speaking, such action lacks a subject, for it emanates from the lack (of Being) in the subject. Genet's ethical project—as Sartre reconstructs it—is to think and perform Doing as a mode of Being. As Sartre points out, Being is the "essential which proves inessential" whereas Doing is the "inessential which proves essential." The real evildoer, then, would be one who refrains from the "doing" of evil in order to arrive at its essence or manifestation. In other words: "the inexpiable act consists not in doing Evil, but in manifesting it." It is as a writer that Genet is truly evil, as a writer that he manifests. At the same time, however, it is writing (and, therefore, evil) that absolves Genet of the task of collaboration with the existing social order. For the thief—or the pederast—"serves the established order" by negating its rules. Such criminals collaborate with an essentialism on which the fiction of social order is built. The homosexual and thief are evildoers, anchoring evil in the realm of Doing: their *acts* are evil. But by confining evil to acts, however, they reinforce its inessentiality: they posit evil in the realm of action rather than ontologically, as a mode of Being. It is not a question, then, of opposing the "evildoer" to the "good-doer" (that we must needs recur to a neologism in the latter case is significant), for evil remains of the order of Doing, where good is the condition of Being. It is not, perhaps, irrelevant that much of the fascination of the homosexual centers on one prurient question: What exactly do they do? For what they do, in fact, is Doing. As a writer, however,—as one who manifests—Genet refuses merely to do. "Genet's undertaking," Sartre insists, "constantly shifts from essentialism to existentialism" (120).

As a writer—and Genet wants nothing more than to be a writer—the homosexual enters the realm of Being with his nefarious Doings. The Being of homosexuality and theft would consist finally and irrefutably only in their writing. Evil—from the perspective of an essentialist philosophy and sociology—cannot appear: it is, indeed, that which prevents the Good from appearing. Genet, like all children, knows this: "to the child who steals and the child who masturbates, to exist is *to be seen by adults*, and since these secret activities take place in solitude, they *do not exist*"(15). To make evil appear would be the ultimate overturning of this philosophical as well as social order. This is the key to Sartre's notion of manifestation: the thief must be caught—the homosexual must be read. Sartre is dealing, then, not with homosexuality but with the writing of homosexuality. In this sense, we might say that communion is the Being of communication—and it is a communion with language that Genet the writer desires: "Writing is a religious act, a rite suggestive of Black Mass" (504).[10] This idea of communication as communion is, it must be noted, a recurrent and popular ideological component of cultural Rightism, partaking as it does of an implicit dichotomy of *Gemeinschaft* and *Gesellschaft*. *Gesellschaft* would be the society in which language is communication—that is, a society that moves toward its self-recognition, the manifestation of its Being (a society of *Doing*, in which language is the paradigm of action); whereas *Gemeinschaft* would be a community in which language is itself the marker of homogeneity, a communion—a community, that is, in which language is always already the expression of Unity (a society of *Being*). Necessarily, then, the question of communication and communion raises questions of community—questions directly relevant to the political assessment of Genet's work.

I have already stated that Sartre eschews traditional class analysis in this work, but the sociological leverage that such categories might provide is something he nevertheless depends on. For example, he misconstrues the social situation of Genet's foster parents—who were craftsmen rather than, as he assumes, agricultural laborers—in order to make a specifically political point:

Yet it was the urban masses, bourgeois culture and, above all, the bureaucracy that, from a distance, exercised an attraction on him and that facilitated his effort to liberate himself. In a purely agricultural society, he would have been irremediably lost. His conversion is not even conceivable if one does not imagine an incipient disintegration in the small village community which brought him up and then banished him. (52)

Sartre does not present Genet as a product of the agricultural classes, but rather as the bearer of an urban principle of progress transplanted into it—he is the alien from the city whose very presence sounds the death-knell of agrarian community. In other words, Genet will not be linked to any nostalgic *völkisch* ideology of community. His nostalgic communion will be inflected differently. In Sartre's presentation, Genet's rebellion might be seen not as a rebellion *against* but somehow as a rebellion *into* society. Communication would not be that which takes place within a discourse-community but rather the linguistic communion that inaugurates one. Marginalization from the agricultural community propels Genet into the heart of a new petty bourgeois bureaucratic order.

Is this not, indeed, the order that *fosters* him in every sense of the word? For all his opposition to bourgeois institutions, Genet lives the rise of the clerical petty bourgeoisie—traditionally, the class of *fascism*—as his revenge on the agricultural class. Again, Sartre observes:

As a product of both the naive substantialism of rural areas and the rationalism of cities, does he not belong to two groups at the same time? As an anonymous ward of the National Foundling Society, he adopts the point of view of the universal, autonomous subject in order to consider the particular figure of little Jean Genet, adopted child of Morvan peasants. (62)

Genet's social position is ambiguous: on the one hand he seeks a notion of community that opposes society (as a purely pragmatic and linguistically action-oriented *Gesellschaft*) but not in the name of a reactionary *völkisch* community represented by the peasantry. What Genet will seek, then, is a social order linking community with the rejection of community. This social split within Genet—he is Self and Other, peasant and State super-subject—clearly informs his erotic positionality as understood by Sartre.

Before reconstructing any social model adequate to Genet's political imaginary, we must pass by way of the erotic. For it is essentially as an erotic—as well as a linguistic—order that Genet thinks community. The models Sartre develops to explain Genet's sexuality serve also to explain his social and political ideology. What I wish to retrace now is the libidinal path that leads from homoerotic desire to a (potentially collaborative) feudalism in Genet's work; for, as Sartre insisted, "there is a definite sexual component in the collaborator's ties to his master" (58). In working toward this model of feudalism, we will necessarily pass through Sartre's theories of effeminization, thereby closing the circle of the essay on collaboration.

Let us first examine the ways in which Genet's sexuality approximates and distances itself from feminine desire in Sartre's presentation. The linkage of homosexuality to femininity in Sartre's analysis derives from a premise elaborated with reference to Simone de Beauvoir: "Simone de Beauvoir has pointed out that feminine sexuality derives its chief characteristics from the fact that woman is an object to the other and to herself before being a subject" (37). It seems pointless to criticize Sartre for sexism or homophobia in making such assumptions about women and, subsequently, homosexuals—for the point is to recognize the operation of the ideological in the everyday. (The phobic aspects of this presentation are perhaps nowhere better articulated than in Sartre's account (cited in note 10) of what it means to be sodomized as a reader of Genet.) At issue, then, would be the extent to which women and homosexuals themselves buy into a phallocentric order that necessarily marginalizes them. Are we all phallic subjects who must view our difference—gender or sexuality in this case—as a cleavage, or are we sexual, gendered subjects whose relationship to the phallic norm will necessarily be critical and ironic? If, in other words, "I is another," is the Other the norm we *cannot* be or the margin we *must not* be? Sartre never truly resolves this question, shuttling between the two possibilities, as if woman's orbit around a phallic norm or the homosexual's marginality to heterosexual society were themselves determinant of an ontological alterity (nonidentity, the negation of Being). In the crudest of terms, this is, of course, a projection: Sartre, the heterosexual male cognizant of and sympathetic to the alterity of the other—an alterity he takes as objective rather than as the result his subjective perspective.

That Sartre's account should—for all its weaknesses—prove so compelling derives from the fact that his presentation of homosexual desire in fact serves to theorize the ex-orbitancy of all desire. Like the collaborator, the homosexual serves as that which all men carry within themselves. Woman and the homosexual indeed *are* their own objects, but not by dint of their being objects of the social gaze. In fact, Sartre's whole presentation will turn on this fact—on his tracing the ruses whereby Genet "steals" the Being of his sexual partner by incorporating it into the body that was to have been an object. In a nutshell, the operation of Genet's desire is an attempt to *be* the other—or rather, to be *by virtue of* the other. If Being is elsewhere, I acquire it by incorporating the other, by becoming the subject who sees myself and makes myself an object. In other words, this is a narcissism fixated on Narcissus as subject—rather than as object—of desire. I desire not an object of desire but the subject of desire: and in desiring I constantly reaffirm the nullity of my Being. My desire is a performative contradiction.

Sartre will conclude from the perspective of effeminization-theory that "in his very depths, Genet is first an object—and an object to others. It is too early to speak of his homosexuality, but we can at least indicate its origin . . . One can expect that Genet, who is the object par excellence, *will make himself an object* in sexual relations and that his eroticism will bear a resemblance to feminine eroticism" (37). Sartre's methodological problems are clear: he wishes to characterize a certain psychical structure—self-objectification—as homosexual, even though his whole presentation depends on the assertion (which Genet refutes) that homosexuality will only subsequently be "chosen." It is to this extent that homosexuality equates the work of collaboration—that relation to the other inherent in the very desire of the subject or of society to close about itself. Prehomosexuality seems to be the precondition of heterosexuality. Thus, Sartre writes, "Genet seeks to *realize* his being and knows that he cannot achieve this result unaided. He therefore resorts to the mediation of others. This means that he makes of his objectivity for others the *essential* and of his reality-for-himself the inessential. What he desires is to be manipulated passively by the Other so as to become an object in his own eyes. Any man who places his truth in his Being-for-the-Other finds himself in a situation that I have called prehomosexual. And this is the case, for example, of many actors, even if they enjoy sleeping only with women" (81).[11]

The invocation of the presumably heterosexual actor is important here, for at times Sartre inadvertently slips into essentialist reveries of a Being that would not be actorly or mimetic. Nevertheless, Genet's "attempt to realize his being" in desire surely is the attempt to manifest Being through writing or communion. And this, finally, is the paradox of all self-enclosing Being. Being is defined—in distinction to the Evil—by its ability to appear. Yet if it needs to appear in order to be, its very dependence on appearing inscribes within it a mimetic moment that rejoins the opposite term of (mere) appearance as a Doing. The ideological work of the homosexual is as a collaborator within the very heart of Being: he forces the recognition that Being must appear and therefore can never subsist in itself. If appearance might be thought as the self-performance, as the action or Doing, of Being, Genet's writerly manifestation is instead the unthinkable Being of Doing—it manifests the performativity of all Being. It reveals the performance of Being as a *theatrical* performance—as mimetic—thereby questioning the self-presence and self-sufficiency of a Being. It works within and against ontology.

Sartre's attempt to present Genet's "passivity" in this scenario of manipulation will also be self-defeating. "No-one is more active," Sartre will concede, "than this homosexual who is called a passive homosexual" (112). Clearly the sexually laden terms of passive and active are being ascribed to the very operations of desire rather than to its instantiations: passive homosexuality is defined with respect to the subject's relation to desire rather than through specific sexual practices. Nevertheless, as we shall see, the slippage from this abstraction to the presentation of specific practices is key to Sartre's argument. Thus, it will be central to his presentation that "having been caught stealing *from behind*, his back opens when he steals; it is with his back that he awaits human gazes and catastrophe" (80). In other words, being caught in the act of theft is likened to a sexual passivity, a form of negative Althusserian interpellation, taking place behind the back of the subject. It is by way of sodomy that society interpellates, by way of a sexual objectification that it sends its subjects out to disrupt the idyll of a peasant *Gemeinschaft*. Sartre's observation obliges us, I think, to reconsider Bersani's refiguring of betrayal as a "*turning away* from the entire theater of good and its transgressions" (my emphasis), for the very act of turning invites a sexual and social violation. To turn one's back on society, as Genet does, is a profoundly ambiguous act: it symbolizes both rejection and a coquettish desire to be sodomized from behind, to be named—to "be" a homosexual. Turning one's back on society, far from inaugurating a realm of solitude that would be purely and ontologically nonrelational, is the precondition of all social and sexual placement: one manifests one's desire for social order—and communication—by turning one's back on it. "Sexually," Sartre explains, "Genet is first of all a raped child. This first rape was the gaze of the other who took him by surprise, penetrated him, transformed him forever into an object. Let there be no misunderstanding: I am not saying that his original crisis *resembles* a rape, I say that it *is* one" (79). But Genet will be vociferous in rejecting Sartre's grounding notion that society makes of him a criminal and that he "becomes" homosexual in response, as an embrace of that fate. He was asking for it.

This taking from behind also marks an important distinction between the homosexual and woman; between gender and sexuality as modes of social relation. Woman would be the name of an objectification that recognizes itself as such, whereas the homosexual always colludes in his own deception, inviting the rape that constitutes him from behind. Arguing at one point the case of the active homosexual—that is, the beloved (the construction of activity through passivity is interesting: I am active by being loved)—Sartre observes how for Divine's lover Darling "the particularity of his lover escapes him. In fact he asks it to represent generality" (75). Divine is "a hand, any hand, all hands" (75). Sartre further observes—this time of the passive homosexual—that

this love is not addressed to the young hoodlum in his particularity. It is not at all concerned with the plans of the beloved and their success, that is, with his transcendence; it does not reflect him as a woman's love reflects the man she loves. It is addressed to a being who definitely has the appearance of a man and who is nevertheless an object, as is a woman, to a being who is utterly absorbed in criminal plans . . . Genet wants to be him whom he loves precisely insofar as the latter is already Genet. (85)

The same is not true of women, for whom social relations ground the possibility of reciprocity. Bersani, in fact, agrees with Sartre insofar as both deny reciprocity and relationality as components of homosexual desire once "socialized," but he projects into sublimity the social relations that such a desire might produce. For Sartre, the "transcendent" moment of homosexual desire would be a movement into the collective—it is quantitatively sublime—rather than beyond it.

Yes, the objectivity of my Being needs to be established by my becoming the object of another, but by identifying with this Other I take into myself the whole work of Being. Homosexuality—or prehomosexuality—would in fact function as a ruse, an attempt to usurp the role of the Other in the construction of identity. Specifically, for Sartre this is a desire—unlike a heterosexual feminine desire—that resists transcendence. Both the passive and the active homosexual—the lover and the beloved—seek not a specific object—or subject—but rather the general. Indeed, the mimetic relationship is interesting here: whereas women represent and reflect their lover, the "passive" homosexual *reenacts* the lover, subjecting the lover to precisely the same de-differentiation the lover himself seeks to impose. According to Sartre, what the homosexual deletes from the otherwise feminine position of desired object is the fiction of a reciprocity based on pleasure:

A woman receives pleasure insofar as she gives it, and whatever the violence, in other respects, of the sexual conflict between her and her lover, she has not leisure to betray him at the moment he satisfies her. But Genet, precisely because he rejects pleasure, has full latitude at the height of the other's pleasure, to practice mental restriction . . . He enters me until he becomes me, to the point of taking up, by the presence of his prick alone, all the place which I occupy, and then, at the extreme moment of leaving my personality." (128)

The very subjectivity of woman is what makes of her the perfect object for the man who seeks to reflect himself. The passive homosexual will always betray—and here we see how, as Bersani has argued, betrayal is encoded in homosexual desire—by refusing to enter into sexuality as a subject, by refusing to enjoy, refusing to cum. The woman is betrayed by her own pleasure, whereas the homosexual—in Sartre's presentation—inflicts rather than experiences pleasure. By making himself an object and refusing pleasure, the passive homosexual short-circuits the system whereby subjectivity will be conferred—through pleasure—by the object of his desire.

The passive homosexual seeks not a specific sexual partner but *the* abstract partner. In terms of the desire for the Blackshirts, it is the work of homogeneity rather than heterogeneity that such desire would perform, according to Sartre. The Other will never be acknowledged as anything other than its otherness. The Other is other precisely insofar as it is not other-than-itself; whereas I, by my very dependence on the Other, am always other-than-myself. However, this abstraction of the Other cannot be thought of as a mechanism for establishing the partner's self-transcendent subject-status for such an exchange instead characterizes "feminine" desire in Sartre's presentation. The partner does not function as the absolute Subject for the self-objectifying homosexual: the transcendence is not into the suprasensual but into the collective. The abstracted partner is not Man but men—that is, society, which takes us from behind. Genet's desire abstracts in a quantitative rather than qualitative manner: it is sensual rather than aesthetic in the limited sense. We need to understand this process in two complementary ways. First, as suggested in the passage above, in terms of a narcissistic self-closure: the homosexual takes the beloved into himself not in order to evacuate himself but rather to usurp the subjectivity of the Other. This, ultimately, would be the relationship of sexuality to murder: "For Genet, the answer is clear: love is a magical ceremonial whereby the lover steals the beloved's being in order to incorporate it into himself" (83). Genet must impossibly identify with that other that caught him stealing as a child, must take *himself* from behind in order that Being and Doing can coincide. The ideal would be a form of self-sodomy. But this leads us to a second, more concrete context—and, indeed, back to Sartre's collaboration essay. For the other with which Genet must identify will be a specific social instantiation: his antagonism toward society will derive from an immediate—that is to say, unmediated—relation to it. If transcendence passes through the collective, we must understand homosexual desire as a desire to give identity to that collective.

The split whereby Genet would like to be the one who observes himself stealing, and whereby he loves in order to steal the identity of the beloved, is at the same time a social split between the universality afforded by his groundless bureaucratic anonymity as a foundling and his existence as the little peasant child. The solipsistic split is immediately social, and results in an unmediated identification with society. The abstract lover that the homosexual seeks—the abstract that will not reconfigure as an identity—is *society*. Of course, the notion of an immediate relationship to society undercuts the very structure of mediation on which social links are predicated in any liberal understanding of the term. How to entertain an immediate relation to the principle of social mediation? How, in other words, to be both lover and beloved, preserving the split despite the conjunction? The answer would seem to lie in Genet's celebrated fascination with the aristocracy, feeding into the neofeudalism Sartre identified with collaboration. Genet "completes the sexual myth of the criminal by building a feudal system which he arranges with express purpose of reserving the lowest place in it for himself," Sartre claims:

Imagine a small military or quasi-military community which evolves on the fringes of real society. One enters it by virtue of an initiation, the three major ceremonies of which are crime, theft and anal intercourse. This parasitic minority, which is composed of a noble caste and its mob of vassals, is not permitted to engage in any work. It lives on the work of others, it is an association of consumers . . . And as they cannot be bound among themselves by a hierarchy of functions based on division of labor, they justify social distinctions by differences of nature or essence and divide the members of their society into two major categories: the tough and the soft. (115)

This relationship of tough and soft—a relationship abstracted from, but repeatedly instantiated in, sexual relations—recalls that direct relationship beyond all societal mediation of which the collaborator dreams.[12] Genet, in this account, identifies with the forces of the State against the forces of society. In other words, we should not see the stress on the aristocratic community as a simplistic *Gemeinschaft* placed in opposition to *Gesellschaft*, but as a mechanism for the revelation of the falsely communitarian values of society. What Sartre sees as passéism needs to be seen instead as a forward movement, as a protest against the bourgeoisie from the perspective of the *State*.

Sartre's characterization of this neofeudal community as a society of consumers is important, for it clearly distances the group from the self-reproductive task of the social order. Furthermore, Sartre links this consumption—or, at least, this abstention from production—as rooted in Genet's sexuality:

By virtue of his mere existence he disturbs the natural order and the social order. A human institution with its birth register and its bureaucracy has come between the species and himself. He is a fake child. No doubt he was born of a woman, but this origin has not been noted by the social memory. As far as everyone and, consequently, he himself are concerned, he appeared one fine day without having been carried in any known womb: He is a synthetic product. He is obscurely aware that he belongs legally to administrative bodies . . . We others who issue from the species have a mandate to continue the species. Genet, who was born without parents, is preparing to die without descendants. His sexuality will be sterility and abstract tension. (7)

Sartre links heterosexuality specifically to the species—not only to the biological need for self-reproduction but, implicitly, to the very notion of a species-being. What Genet, the homosexual, lacks—and what hinders communication in the everyday sense—is the sense of species-being, the Being of the species. His transcendence, therefore, will take him not into the transhistorical quasibiological realm of species but into the contingency of the social collective. More specifically, it is the bureaucracy of the *State* that differentiates Genet from his social milieu. In a very real sense—a sense more "real" than the realism of a collaborator or of Hegel, apologist of the State—Genet's self-consciously fake "transcendence" would be enacted through the State. This passage is crucial, therefore, in its suggestion of a necessary relationship between the homosexual and the State, between the "sterility" of homosexuality and the antifamilial origins of the displaced homosexual subject. As one exorbitant from the familial sphere of reproduction, the homosexual grounds himself in a community that is at the same time a negation of the very idea of communal immediacy. Such a possibility is figured through the State. Genet cathects that "administrative body" which bore him.[13]

To understand Sartre's presentation of homosexuality in terms other than relative, however, we need to move beyond the homosexual's antipathy to (heterosexual) reproduction and reexamine the very idea of consumption, in which Sartre grounds Genet's parasitic society.[14] We need to ask what is consumed, and how. At one point, demonstrating the complicity of the criminal with the social order, Sartre points out how "his thefts, far from challenging property, affirm it. This child who has enough to eat but whom society keeps at a distance wants by means of a solitary act, to integrate himself into the community. He is aiming at the impossible" (12). Sartre—who seemed not to have envisaged a radicality of nonrelational evil subsequently foregrounded by Bersani—in fact allows us here to see how the "solitary" might, in fact, constitute a port of entry to the social. Genet's real crime will be writing: the manifestation of evil. For in this feudal community, let us not forget, Genet has reserved for himself the most lowly place. He is the clerk—ambiguously both cleric and scribe, cleric, indeed, by virtue of his duties as a scribe—and his homosexuality serves, Sartre asserts, as a cassock:

A black aristocracy remains on the fringes of secular society. All the features of a feudal order are to be found in the knighthood of crime: parasitism, violence, potlatch, idleness and a taste for death, conspicuous destruction. All of them, even social conservatism, even religiosity, even anti-Semitism. Amidst these soldiers, Genet plays the role of a clerk. (203)

If, in the thieving child, the notion of consumption has already been uncoupled from that of self-preservation, the Black Mass of writerly communion will provide a very different means of understanding consumption—one that necessarily obliges Sartre to think the very instantiation of homosexuality as practice. Genet is an outsider to the principle of reproduction, but he is no less antipathetic to its complementary ideology of social consumption, as Sartre points out:

Outcast of a consuming society, the rites which he celebrates in secret reproduce the cardinal act of the society that excludes him: he sacrifices, he consumes. That is, he destroys. An object goes up in smoke, a piece of fruit melts in his mouth, his pleasure blossoms and fades, it is going to die. It is this process of dissolution that constitutes the entire ceremony. (13)

Consumption will be understood as destruction rather than as nourishment and reproduction. Tellingly, Sartre refers to this consumption as a "fictive communion," for the ceremonial of the communion best describes Genet's mode of consumption. This communion is fictive both in the sense of being merely mimetic and feigned, and also in the sense of being *creative*—it brings about the thing it pretends to be: communion as community. What does it "produce," this communion? Nothing but the fiction of community itself. Genet produces the community—in communion—by consuming it. He breaks the cycle of production and consumption: his consumption does not produce a self that might ultimately reproduce.

This melting in the mouth, this disintegration, smacks of a social scenario Sartre has already outlined: the disintegration of an agricultural producer community and the birth of a consumer society of bourgeois urbanites. If consumption is to be thought of as a communion—the fictive projection of a community—what is it that Genet consumes in this way? What is it he ingests that does not feed and regenerate him? And is there any relationship between this form of consumption that creates community and the aristocratic community of homosexuals Genet seeks to invoke? Indeed there is. For if this communion anchors the themes of community, writing, and communication, it is a Black Mass celebrated in the act of fellatio. Genet's desire is for "a rigidity that melts beneath contempt like barley sugar" (128):

We know now the secret weakness of the pimp's rigidity: it melts on the tongue. Thus, at the heart of his submission, Genet takes his revenge: the aim of his caresses is the softening of the male . . . In the last analysis, fellatio is castration. Coitus is the systematically pursued death of the beloved . . . The penis of the passive homosexual, still erect because he has refused pleasure, bears witness to his vigilance. (128–29)

Fellatio is a ceremony of communion; and the object of communion—the food for this communicant—is the phallus. The consumption that does not reproduce is the consumption of the seed, the very symbol of reproduction. This is the key passage in Sartre's analysis for thinking a linkage of homosexuality and fascism that subtends *Saint-Genet* even as it is disavowed. While Sartre's comparison of fellatio and castration is provocative, however, the equation is dangerously misleading and demonstrates the misunderstanding at the heart of Sartre's analysis. Castration is the detachment that makes possible a social and symbolic order by excluding a transcendent signifier from the system of exchange. Fellatio, on the contrary, resubjects that signifier to the economy of pleasure by forcing it to cum. The flaccidity of this phallus marks the detumescence of the symbolic order originating in castration. Fellatio *undoes* the work of castration. Read simply as a desire for the phallus—indeed, for the internalization of the phallus—fellatio would signify a desire for authoritarian order and, through ingestion, the transsubstantiation of the authoritarian into the totalitarian.[15] But as the action of one who withholds from ejaculation in order to subject the other to the rigors of pleasure, fellatio can only be understood as the humbling of the phallic order. What appears to be a fascination with power reveals itself instead to be a recycling of power against itself. The fascist—and the homosexual—does not desire the rigidity of a phallic order: the fellating of the phallus is intrinsically an act of aggression as well as desire. This paradox lies at the very heart of rightist anarchism: what is in fascism a desire for order (for the phallic) becomes in homosexuality a recognition of desire's impossible closure. "The tough" that Genet desires is, as Sartre points out, "he who defines laws for the other" (115), including the law of desire. To desire the transcendent principle of desire is to resubsume it, to recirculate it within an economy it can ground only by its exclusion. In other words, the closure of desire is also its undoing: the totalitarian impulse rejoins the anarchic. Perhaps, more than anything, this explains the ambiguously authoritarian and lawless nature of the fascist libido as elaborated by Theweleit.

This is not to say that homosexuality and fascism can, in these terms, be thought strictly as opposing strategies: the problem is that each operates within the other to some extent. As Bersani notes in his reading of the figure of Hitler in *Funeral Rites*, "we cannot comfortably say that operative political sympathies are entirely irrelevant to Genet's fantasmatic scenarios" (11–12). The phallus that one fellates, to put it another way, will not yet have been the signifier of fascism's detumescence. Fascism's totalitarian desire collapses not under the weight of something that opposes it but under the weight of the desiring mechanisms it sets in motion. "What excites Genet about a prick," Sartre will write, "is never the flesh of which it is composed but its power of penetration, its mineral hardness" (107). Desire is excited by rigidity—but produces flaccidity and emission. Once again, we need to think this sexual desire in terms of Sartre's overarching dichotomy of Being and Doing, for if the act of fellatio is intrinsically aggressive, its primary victim is the self. "Genet gobbles up his reflection with his eyes," (74) Sartre insists: thereby replacing primary narcissism with a vividly materialized image of sexuality. Whereas narcissism holds out the possibility of completion while operating all the while with the dyads created by its impossibility, Genet closes the circle. He sucks himself off—offs himself through sucking.

The political coding of all this is quite clear, even if Sartre never poses the political question in very direct terms. He will finally write:

Genet will later find an epic symbol for this omnipotence of the weakest: Hitler. Hitler declares in *Funeral Rites*—and it is Genet who speaks through his mouth: "I, puny and ridiculous little man, unloosed on the world a power extracted from the pure and clear beauty of athletes and hoodlums. For nothing but beauty could have elicited such a burst of love as that which every day, for seven years, caused the death of strong and fierce young creatures." Every day Genet, too, causes the death of fierce young men. And their death imparts to him "a power extracted from their beauty." (129)

The question we must pose in conclusion is whether Sartre's reading of Hitler is adequate to Genet's project. While Sartre's assertion would initiate an interesting rereading of *Funeral Rites*, Bersani has indicated the possibilities for such a reading and I do not propose to undertake one here. Instead, I wish to question Genet's putative desire for rigidity, and the discourse of beauty—the aesthetic—it sets in motion.

In short, I will equate the rigid phallus with the aesthetic, and the flaccid, fellated penis with what, in rather simplified terms, we have already called "the sensual." It seems that the question of aestheticization—as a model for reading fascist politics—depends on a certain reading of masculinity as experienced and reconstructed through homosexual desire. For all his sensitivity to Genet—and I would certainly no more claim Genet as a champion of gay consciousness than would Bersani—Sartre ultimately reads him (that is, reads homosexuality) as the work of, and toward, heterosexuality. To quote Bersani, "The symbolic is a product of the body, and it is a by-no-means-insignificant element of Genet's subversiveness that he performatively refutes the reactionary (Lacanian) doctrine that instructs us to think of language as castration, as cutting us off from the potentially revolutionary power of the body" (17). Fellatio seems to figure a sexual and linguistic mode that is not inaugurated by castration but that nevertheless bears a relation—*pace* Bersani—to the phallus it pleasures.

At stake, ultimately, are the terms we might use to understand the "aestheticization of politics" constitutive of fascism. Would aestheticization be "totalitarian" in the sense that it is self-enclosing and leaves no residue—or would it be "worldly"? Would it be desire for the rigid phallus or the venal and visceral subordination of the phallus to the appetites of desire (or what Bersani terms "frivolity")? Does fascism consist in the fascination with the phallus, or only in the desire to be penetrated by it? And does the desire to be penetrated acknowledge the impossibility of completion—the work of destruction it enacts on the phallus it desires? Or, in fact, is it between these two possibilities that the gulf between a totalitarian and a nontotalitarian aestheticization—between the fascist and the homosexual dandy—opens up? What, ultimately, differentiates the desire for the Blackshirt from the desire for the Black GI? The answer lies, I think, in the very notion of uniform: the desire for the Blackshirt recaptures the alterity of the other under the very uniformity of its otherness. But the embodiment of alterity in the American soldier marks that irreducible residue of the body that must resist both political and aesthetic—as well as Sartre's ethical—totalitarianism. When Bersani suggests that "it is perhaps Genet's homosexuality that allowed him to imagine a curative collapsing of social difference into a radical homoness in which, all relations with the other having been abolished, the subject might begin again, differentiating itself from itself and thereby reconstituting sociality" (16), he posits the exciting possibility of a regeneration of sociality from within the self-differentiating subject. At the same time, however, the "collapsing of social difference"—the erasure, in effect, of the difference of Blackshirts (homogeneous uniformity) and black bodies (heterogeneous sensuality)—is more his own than it is Genet's.

I do not wish to suggest some absolute divisibility; certainly, Genet's pronouncement that "Beauty is the perfection of organization" (98), seems, indeed, to manifest the impulse toward closure. What makes Genet so unsettling is precisely the interpenetration of what I have schematically presented as two modes of desire—the aesthetic/homogeneous and the sensual/heterogeneous. I am suggesting, however, the need to rethink the relationship of sexual to aesthetic sensuality—since the sexual predicates precisely that "interest" that the aesthetic precludes—an interest, that is, not only in the purposiveness of the object but in its very existence. Aestheticization—like castration—would be a desire that desires the nonexistence of the (ultimate) object, the removal of the phallus from circulation: the phallus must not palpably exist in order that it produce (order). Sensualization, meanwhile, would be Genet's fellatio, lusciously playing the penis around its mouth and coercing its expenditure toward no production: the penis must exist, in order that it produce nothing but cum. Homosexual desire—as enacted by Genet and traced by Sartre—would be completely antipathetic to fascist and *völkisch* notions of racial and national Being: it turns on an act of dissemination that would not be a Cumming into Being.

Miranda Pollard

Whose Sorrow? Whose Pity? Whose Pleasure? Framing Women in Occupied France

From the Resistance to 1968, from World War I to the Algerian War, women have been making an appearance in contemporary French histories.[1] A diverse range of approaches and methodologies seems about to rescue French women from the "condescension of history" and mainstream historians.[2] But what is really at stake in this "appearance"? For example, are we going to see and read the history of France during World War II *differently*? How and in what ways might women's presence change the dominant narrative conventions of Occupation history?

Answering these questions involves interrogating our pleasures and discomforts with existing histories in which women seem almost always absent. We must ask when and why we identify with certain representations of the past, and whether gender functions to uphold or to subvert our view of that past. How are women represented, for example, in wartime France?[3]

My chosen text for this discussion is Marcel Ophuls's film *The Sorrow and the Pity*, which has a unique cultural/iconographic status in French history. While there has been a host of wonderful films dealing with the Occupation, films by France's most accomplished directors (including Louis Malle's *Au Revoir les enfants* and *Lacombe Lucien*, François Truffaut's *Le Dernier métro*, Diane Kurys's *Entre nous*, and Claude Chabrol's *Une Affaire de femmes*), Marcel Ophuls's film stands out in terms of popular and oral history, visual text, and contemporary documentary cinema. Woody Allen's homage to the film (via its repeated appearances in *Annie Hall*) completes *The Sorrow*'s cultural canonization.[4]

While its influence and content have been subject to analysis ever since its controversial debut in 1971, I want to ask why and how *The Sorrow* still

141

fascinates us, in what ways we look to *The Sorrow* for "real" history, and in what ways masculinity and femininity operate in constructing that history. My interest in revisiting Marcel Ophuls's classic documentary is not to lament women's invisibility, nor to indict this text for its meager offering of one woman interviewed (counterposed to thirty-five men). Instead, I want to explore the film's "naturalizing" conventions, to investigate the "framing of women" in such histories. How do cinematic and historical "technologies of gender" really work in this film?[5] Whose sorrow and pity do we see and feel?[6]

Whether we are French or "outsiders," young or old, professional observers or survivors/*témoins*, the location and moment of our spectatorship surely affects more than our response to and ability to identify with the stories of "ordinary" French *people* living through those harrowing circumstances. It also affects our sense of the authenticity of this history, its faithfulness to lived experience. At the heart of this process, mediating these various identifications, is the "fact" of our gender, the ease with which we can locate ourselves in and throughout this text and how the film addresses "us." Ophuls does not seem to have a (sexed) spectator or subject in mind. And yet, as Stephen Heath remarks in another context:

in the last resort any discourse which fails to take account of the problem of sexual difference in its enunciation and address will be, within a patriarchal order, precisely indifferent, a reflection of male domination. It might be added, moreover, as a kind of working rule, that where a discourse appeals directly to an image, to an immediacy of seeing, as a point of its argument or demonstration, one can be sure that all differences are being elided, that the unity of some accepted vision is being reproduced.[7]

Is Ophuls presuming an undifferentiated spectator or presenting an undifferentiated history? Unlike many historical texts, *The Sorrow* contains multiple registers and multiple voices that enhance connection and identification as much as discomfort and alienation. This analysis explores how the apparent transparency of sexual (in)difference functions in this one (brilliant) documentary history and how gender constructs and (re)produces this highly influential historical chronicle.

Indeed, *The Sorrow and the Pity* is a brilliant film. It changed the way French people (literally) saw the Occupation, much as, at about the same time, Robert Paxton's book, *Vichy France: Old Guard and New Order* (1972), changed Vichy historiography forever. But *The Sorrow* is not just a documentary feat, not just another more or less factual, more or less complete record of the war and Occupation. It is itself an *historical text*, creating and sustaining social/sexual meaning. This film explicitly offers us a critical French history; it teaches us historical lessons about choice, justice, and compassion that are as politically necessary now as they were when the film first came out. *The Sor-*

row also reproduces and constructs a not-so-critical history of the relationship of French women and men to war, inscribing like the preceding chronicles, subliminally and explicitly, problematic messages about gender, class, race, sexuality, and political culture. Re-viewing this text, which is both classic and iconoclastic, may give us a particularly good sense of how fascism and gender are intimately connected through representation.[8]

I

> . . . c'étaient pas des ennemis personnels, si vous voulez, c'était pas du même côté. Moi, j'étais pour le Maréchal, les autres étaient de l'autre côté. Voilà, c'est tout. Moi, je pense.[9]

Pétainism can be thought of as a peculiarly "feminine" political phenomenon, both symbolically and materially. In 1940, the feeble eighty-four-year-old Marshal embodied France's defeat, the castration of a sovereign state; as Jean Guéhenno said, "Pétain no longer speaks with the voice of a man . . . but speaks like an old woman . . ."[10] But Pétain also embodied a "certain idea of France" that both presumed women's support and tried to appropriate "women" discursively in an antifeminist National Revolution.[11] Madame Solange, the hairdresser interviewed at the end of Marcel Ophuls's film *The Sorrow and the Pity*, who says she liked the Marshal, presents a compelling portrait of such Pétainism, and of citizenly fear, guilt, and ignorance. She gets up to lock the door to her salon, she twitches, she is filmed in half-light. Her pro-Pétainist attitudes are not stark and honest like those of the Resistance or collaborationist spokes*men* in this quasidocumentary film. Madame Solange is not even sure why she believed in the Marshal; she cannot justify herself; she did not consider—while undergoing torture at the hands of the Resistance— whether similar things happened under Vichy. Her situation is petty and personal, the result of jealousy, that most "feminine" of motivations. She accuses another woman of betraying her. She insists that she was not political. But what is "political" for Ophuls and for us, his audience? And what would be the price of identifying with this particular *témoin*, this woman?

By the time Madame Solange appears, at this late stage in the four-and-a-half-hour film, the viewer is well versed in the dangers of memory and denial. Inertia, inaction, ignorance—the purveyors of everyday fascism—are the real villains of *The Sorrow and the Pity*. Madame Solange represents the archetypical fascist "enabler."

The Sorrow demystifies the political phenomena of resistance and collaboration, blurring their boundaries; but even as it does so, curiously familiar subtexts about gender and rightist reaction seem to emerge. Women are intricately and subliminally cast as political actors, but it is usually as *women* or *woman*.

II

> ... if one has not been through ... the horror of an occupation by a
> foreign power, you have no right to pronounce upon what that
> country does which has been through all that.[12]

The Sorrow and the Pity was directed by Marcel Ophuls and produced by
Ophuls, André Harris, and Alain de Sedouy in cooperation with Swiss television. Turned down by French television (by whom it was originally commis-
sioned), it was first shown in a small cinema in Paris in 1971.[13] Supposedly the
chronicle of one city, Clermont-Ferrand, during the years 1939–44, it is com-
prised of two parts: *L'Effondrement* and *Le Choix*. It uses interviews con-
ducted by Ophuls and Harris, juxtaposed with contemporary newsreel, film,
and radio clips. Public figures, like Pierre Mendès-France, Jacques Duclos,
and Anthony Eden, ex-resistance and collaborationist activists, and local people in and around Clermont-Ferrand recall a variety of experiences from the
period of the war and Occupation.[14]

When it first appeared in France, the film attracted huge crowds and bitter
controversy. Although Ophuls denied that this was his intention, *The Sorrow*
was seen as a "destroyer of myths," particularly the myth at the heart of
Gaullism that all of France had supported the Resistance, had "resisted" the
German Occupation, had indeed unequivocally "resisted" Vichy, defeatism,
anti-Semitism, and Nazi domination. This film revealed ugly cracks in the
façade of heroic national unity and destroyed the reassuring polarities of resistance and collaboration by personalizing their histories. French critics at the
time called this film everything from "a film about a dishonored France," "a
history course in pictures," "a true cinematic masterpiece," and "a marvel of
honesty," to "a prejudiced film . . . of very relative impartiality."[15] Stanley
Hoffman, in his 1972 essay "In the Looking Glass: Sorrow and Pity?," remarked that "when the subject is nothing less than a nation's behavior in the
darkest hour of its history, it is not surprising that the reactions should be so
passionate."[16]

Ophuls wanted to bring politics home. The film was, according to him,
founded on this obsession with making politics part of everyday life, everyday
memory, of this determination to make a political story as exciting and moving
as a love story or an adventure film. He claimed—somewhat paradoxically
then—that *The Sorrow* was not primarily "a political film."[17] Postmodernist
and feminist critics can sympathize with this politicizing of everyday histories
and the denial of what constitutes an orthodox political film. Yet we must
surely remain skeptical about the seductions of adventure and romance narratives as a model for a new form of political text. Indeed, it is precisely at the

juncture where individualized "experience" meets a collective, recognizable "story" that we must be most wary. The film is very seductive in its use of realism, up-close interviews, and news footage, its creation of seemingly incontrovertible historical experience.[18] These *témoins* are speaking to us. The "honesty" of the interviews draws us in, allows identification, permits the ultimate historical voyeurism, even when we dislike or disbelieve the person interviewed. Unless, that is, we "resist" the gender conventions of the story and begin to investigate "our" part in the plot.

A feminist historian watching the film must be struck by the marginality of women to this—and other cinematic and historiographical—narratives of war and activism. Despite all its quirky and original features, the most conspicuous aspect of *The Sorrow* is its almost total omission of women. Of the thirty-six principal interviews, only one, right at the end of the film, is with a woman (Madame Solange). As in conventional histories, men are the protagonists, whichever angle we take: Tausend speaks for the German military occupiers, Mendès-France for the Third Republic's political elite, Anthony Eden for the British government, and Georges Lamirand for Vichy. But locally too, where we might expect women to be incorporated, men continue to represent individualized action. Men alone carry the plot, whether in the Resistance, like Colonel Gasper or the Graves brothers, or in the Waffen SS, like Christian de la Mazière. A circle encloses the three male interviewers, mostly unseen but always heard, and the men interviewed, who confidently interpret their historical experience. This circle is created cinematographically in the film technique, where the participants talk to each other *man to man*. But the circle represents, metaphorically, a political space that operates across and beyond women. It is not just that women did not have the vote or feature prominently in public life in 1939–45. In 1971, when the story is being told, there is both a reinscription of absence—female memory and female protagonists are not included—and a reconsolidation of masculinist historical narrative.

Yet *The Sorrow* is a "real" history, constructed according to familiar conventions of action, voice, plot—precisely fulfilling our expectations of heroism, virtue, romantic adventure—which men must represent. The most poignant moments of the film, even when tragic and/or ironic, confirm the link between masculinity and solemn historical reality: Mendès-France telling of his trial and sentencing to six years imprisonment for desertion; Claude Lévy speaking about anti-Semitism, about how France was the only country to collaborate and to enact racial laws even more harsh than the Nuremburg Laws; Emmanuel d'Astier de la Vigerie speaking about being afraid all the time in the Resistance, but loving life and never having considered suicide. These three men articulate and embody the dramatic, the tragic, the psychological, in a way that no woman's voice apparently could. And yet, even if such a clear set of gender conventions rules this film's historical discourse (no less than the current discourse of most professional historians of this period), is it simply the same old story of omission, ignorance, and neglect in the historical record?[19]

A reexamination of the text reveals how the issue is much more complicated than women's "underrepresentation." *The Sorrow*'s words and images build a story with which we can identify. This is not only the objective chronicle of France from 1939 through to 1944, which the merging of contemporary news footage and interviews emphasizes. Within this metanarrative are other stories, the juxtaposed and competing subjective stories of individuals, family, race, and sexuality, of politics. The film depends on both dimensions to construct a convincing historical portrait, giving us an orthodox master narrative and a commonsensical and normalizing framework from which to view this supposedly new "history." Yet both the objective and subjective dimensions, because they fall back on troubling masculinist authority, cause fractures or gaps of identification to emerge, and encourage a questioning of *The Sorrow*'s plot and characters, a critique of its multiple seductions.

III

> Moi j'ai fait fusiller une vieille, là, qui avait soixante ans, qui m'avait vendu à la Gestapo pour des sous. Pour des sous, Monsieur, et mon fils aussi, pour nous faire fusiller.[20]

Nothing in *The Sorrow* is superfluous or incidental, even when the storytelling seems most tangential to the political narrative. The film starts at a wedding (that of Herr Tausend's daughter). We hear bells, go into the church, meet the pastor, and for the subsequent interview with the unrepentant and jovial Wehrmacht enthusiast, we are guests at the wedding banquet. The film ends at the home of Monsieur Verdier, the pharmacist, the self-identified bourgeois, the one who thought the Defeat had been terrible, like losing a rugby match too fast and by too much. The family is assembled in the salon to witness to and provide an audience for Monsieur Verdier's tales.

Far from being trivial, these settings, at the wedding and in the salon, are both narrative pillars that render this history "familial" (both family-centered and familiar, intimate). They allow for resistance and collaboration literally to be brought home and retold to the children. Indeed, family is ever-present throughout the film to remind us of the little terrors and joys of the Occupation, the domestic perspective of "ordinary" history. Family is everywhere: in the newsreel images of a family eating rabbit for dinner; in the intimacy of the Graves brothers' farmhouse (in the village where they were born); in the story of Jean Zay's child being born while he was in prison; in the humor of de la

Vigerie telling about being the black sheep of his family until he was made a government minister; in the goodbye kiss from Madame Laval to her husband, the prime minister, as he heads off to work at Vichy; in Verdier's comment that he is a modern *père de famille nombreuse* whose preoccupation is to make money. Even the tourist guide at Sigmaringen, Pétain and Laval's last refuge, is filmed as he documents Hohenzollern family history and stops his tour in front of a portrait of Princess Stéphanie.

Family allows Ophuls to situate people and to provide the proper emotional backdrop to external, political events; family strengthens *The Sorrow*'s portrayal of ordinary social existence—so vital for the film's assault on myth and mystification.[21]

Part of the ordinariness and conventionality of this history is its representation of a different male and female sexuality, within and outside the family unit. This familiar and familial narrative is not just one-dimensional. It allows for a less "legitimate," if utterly recognizable, set of desires, too. Sex between German soldiers and French women is alluded to, in the section on Hitler's disparaging racialist attitudes to the French and in the interview with Germiniani, for example, about everyday life in Clermont. The issue of prostitution also does not unsettle the interviewees or the audience. Prostitution and brothels are mentioned casually and frequently in *The Sorrow*: by the Royal hotelier, by Tausend, by Louis Grave, and by de la Mazière. We realize that male sexuality and wartime in particular render prostitution an unremarkable fact of French life, an "open secret."

We are also treated to the normal and normalizing conventions of romantic, heterosexual love in wartime, with each heterosexual moment foregrounding crucial historical memories for the speaker. In London, the episode of the girls skylarking with French sailors in Hyde Park is recounted by Edward Spears, Churchill's delegate to the French, and marks out the tragedy of Mers-el-Kébir (when 1,600 French sailors were killed). The German soldier, Matheus Bleibenger, remembers his French girlfriend fondly, forcing us to consider how "love" traverses national and patriotic boundaries. The women of Clermont-Ferrand are filmed ecstatically kissing American GIs at the Liberation, giving us the quintessential image of victory.

Perhaps the most charming and memorable heterosexual "moment" in *The Sorrow* is Pierre Mendès-France's account of the man and woman courting outside the jail in Clermont, as he waited on a wall above them in the dark of a tree-lined avenue, anxious to make his escape: "There was a couple under the tree. You can guess the subject of their conversation; he had his mind made up; she was not decided. It seemed to go on for ages. She ended up by saying yes, but I felt she resisted the idea a long time. They went off. I jumped. For my part, I'm sure I was even happier than he was. I'd love to meet her again. I'd like to tell her how much I went through with her that particular night."[22]

Mendès-France was glad she had said yes eventually, but noted "how untimely *her lack of boldness* seemed." Fortunately, "love, luck, and escape finally won out."

Far from intruding or disrupting Ophuls's story, women here represent normality. Their presence is essential to the construction of "real life." These scenes and narrative links illustrate the very nature of existence—its heterosexual, romantic tenacity even in the face of adversity. Indeed, heterosexuality provides an "eternal" contrast to the inconstancy and historicity of the wartime narrative.

Women are not absent in the film. They are actually everywhere, naturalizing the plot, rendering the text credible. On camera, it is men who speak, almost exclusively. But between interviews, and especially in newsreel footage, we see women everywhere. Indeed women frequently carry the plot forward or amplify its message visually, in ways that men cannot. Women are seen, registered at multiple (un)conscious levels in powerful imagery: mothers and their children fleeing before the advancing Germans in the *exode*; young women crowding adoringly around Pétain; nurses waving enthusiastically to Hitler as his train passes; ladies fussing over their painted "stockings"; women workers expressing their admiration for Laval; film stars in their hats and furs, leaving the Gare de l'Est for a promotional tour in Germany; Clermont women celebrating the Liberation. Each scene resonates with (our) gendered expectations while, at the same time, it generates and heightens connections between the crucial events and phenomena at issue (Defeat, Collaboration, Nazism, Liberation) and femininity.

These events and phenomena are symbolized primarily through a certain reading of sexed citizens—of women—as victims, dupes, or opportunists. In addition to strong visual images, *The Sorrow* is also saturated with negative oral history, where certain women again signify political naivety or ignorance. For example, Mendès-France discusses the Parisian bourgeois women who wanted, during the period of the phoney war, to plant roses on the Maginot Line; Madame Tausend, smiling broadly at the camera when recollecting the triumph of *blitzkrieg* in 1940, admits being afraid for her Wehrmacht husband but enjoying the news of German successes; the champion cyclist Raphael Germiniani talks about how women going out with Germans were not well-thought-of (and were dealt with at the Liberation). In all these scenes, even where the anecdotes are humorously presented, women are ever present and ever ignorant of the historical or political significance of their actions. Thus, femininity and political danger are bound together.

The Sorrow mobilizes family, heterosexual romance, masculinity/femininity, and hegemonic social values to tell its story. The sexualized body appears within the film's frame and is conjured up beyond it, thoroughly marked by gender, by *difference*. This includes not only a captive femininity but also a potentially disruptive masculinity. Two discrete and powerful sexualized, masculine images stand out: one the propaganda clip of black Senegalese soldiers dancing, the other the English resister, Denis Rake, stroking his cat as he is interviewed. These two images of dissonant sexuality represent the "other" to the text's calling up of the "normal," the ordinary, the *French*.

Captured black African soldiers dancing signifies degeneracy. But is this only to the Nazi propagandists who staged this scene? Perhaps we—the audience—are also shaken by this scene. French men, we know, do not dance in defeat. This version of masculinity makes us uncomfortable; it does not fit. The contrast with the images immediately preceding and following this scene—the images of General Warlimont and Mendès-France, who are serious and "cultured"—is marked. These men give us "history" in their interviews; they understand the implications of their past and their identity. How do we read the juxtapositioning of (white) historical narrative (which incorporates and uses racist propaganda so effectively) and the utter otherness of people of color in this story? Is the black male subject not being re-presented as re-colonized and feminized in *The Sorrow*?

Similarly, the interview with Denis Rake, the English ex-radio operator, is positioned between interviews with Colonel Buckmaster, his SOE boss, and the Graves brothers in their wine cellar. We can see that Rake is not *like them*. In his self-confessed desire to prove his courage because he was homosexual, and in the very gesture of stroking his cat (which is focused upon in case we do not realize effeminacy is in play), Rake is set up: to tell us that the Resistance could encompass such alien and queer elements, but that its success and virtue actually depended on and derived from its very masculine-identified actions. Rake is an eccentric "extra," a literal and metaphorical (feminized) outsider to the main plot. The contrast of the Graves brothers, earthy peasant men with strong political convictions, and the chirpy girl, who had escaped from the Gestapo and who tells us in heavily accented English that she is happy to be in London working for General de Gaulle, is profound. The sweet subservience of young women is accentuated; the manly, if modest, character of the "real" Resistance hero is established without need for elaboration.

In these various ways gender is "at work" in the framing of the film. Men dominate *The Sorrow*, but femaleness and femininity are crucial to the narrative. Women belong, whether symbolically, on camera, or in visual "space-off." Indeed women's location in cinematic and metaphoric space-off is creatively used by Ophuls. In one extended scene, for example, the Graves brothers and Colonel Gaspar are being interviewed together in the Auvergne, sitting around the kitchen table of the Graves farmhouse. The wives pour the wine for the men, welcome two new arrivals, and occasionally interject acerbic comments—that some among the Resistance used the opportunity to steal and pillage, and that German and Nazi were synonymous ("ils étaient tous dans le même sac"). But these women's voices come from off-screen. The women stand or sit in the doorway, while the men sit at the table. This seems at once like a "real" cultural portrait, at least for southern rural France, and a "real" historical mirror. According to this account, the men were actors, the women served at home. Yet, listening and watching, the women re-present and embody the very passivity—*l'attentisme chez soi*—that the film silently indicts, the very being on the outside that this historical narrative builds itself against.

At this point in the film, in the section entitled "Le Choix," a break in our identification and seduction by the film is created. Were women not both uniquely threatened and active at home and in public throughout the years of the Occupation? Was this war experienced passively or peacefully by women? Were women really marginal in the face of arrests, deportations, extreme food shortages, the absence of two million POWs, and the German labor draft? There were obviously many ways in which homes—supposedly apolitical, private refuge, interior space—were invaded and politicized during the Occupation, so that this dichotomous framing of public/male versus private/female appears as a violent misrepresentation. Framing women "in the doorway," as though that is where women were *historically,* begins an unconscious but highly charged sexualized denouement in *The Sorrow.*[23]

IV

Est-ce que, pour un jeune, c'était quelque chose de crispant de voir une fille au bras d'un Allemand? Vous avez dû en voir?[24]

Toward the film's end, there are four consecutive episodes that constitute this sexualized conclusion. First, the complacent Verdier leads us back to the conversation in the peasant kitchen by saying that his view of the Occupation would have been very different if he had been personally affected like his friend Menut. "They didn't kill my wife or children," he says. "They took away and tortured Menut's wife." We then see a memorial plaque on a local street: "Marinette Menut, 1914–1944, heroine of Mount Mouchet, tortured and killed by the Germans."[25] Next, Menut himself recounts in detail how his wife was brutally tortured. He tells how her body could not be identified and how she was buried while still in a coma. When he goes on to say that he had heard that his wife's torturers raped her with a broom, his account is cut off by the agonized protests of the women in the doorway. We are never told what Marinette Menut actually did in the Resistance. What is presented to us is her complete victimization, the most horrible and sexualized destruction of her body. Her political and/or military work is erased.

The very next scene is in a Bavarian pub with the German soldier, Matheus Bleibenger, who does not understand why the passersby in Clermont-Ferrand spat on him as he lay injured and captive in the train station at Clermont in 1944. He protests that the French women who spat on him that day should have remembered their fathers or sons (who presumably were not being treated like this in Germany?).

The anecdote is not idly chosen, however; it provides a sexual link in the narrative. Bleibenger, who knew Clemont "like the back of his hand," praises his French girlfriend and says he would have escaped to the safety of her home if he could have. Years later, this smiling ex-Wehrmacht soldier, complacently drinking beer and clad in lederhosen, still articulates a proprietary knowledge of his wartime lover: "She was a very nice young girl and didn't hate the Germans at all."[26]

Again women are being framed: "nice young girls" may not be what they seem. As the camera zooms in on a woman whose head is being shaved, we realize that "horizontal collaboration," sexual betrayal, and female deviance are at stake. Here personal memory and public history agree, and we have Georges Brassens singing cheerily in the background about "the Beauty who slept with the Prussian King." This image—of a woman having her head shaved—is a privileged one in accounts of the Liberation, sometimes offset, as in *The Sorrow,* by a woman Resistance fighter brandishing her machine gun and the tricolor. Women with their heads shaved, their bodies beaten, spat upon and laid bare, uniquely signify the degradation, humiliation, and culpability of the vanquished and the power of the victors.

The narrative, moving from Occupation to Liberation, demands a shift from amorality to punishment, from abandon to retribution, from pleasure to danger; women's bodies stand in for all the (less visible) moral failings and more ambivalent collaborations of the Occupation.[27]

Women's hair links these two key sequences, connecting public and private space, gendered bodies, and sexual confession/retribution. From shaved heads in the town square, we move to a hairdressing salon, focusing ever inward on Madame Solange, who recounts her story of being falsely accused and arrested in August 1944. She was sentenced to fifteen years hard labor by the local Resistance court for denouncing a friend to the Gestapo. This is an unsettling interview. Curiously, it seems more disturbing than any of the other interviews, even contrasted with those who brazenly—in 1969—defended pro-Nazi and anti-Semitic activities during the war.

Christian de la Mazière, the French Waffen SS officer, the most notable "villain" of *The Sorrow,* is interviewed at Sigmaringen, in dark glasses, smoking. Shot among the chandeliers and shadows of the royal palace, he is relaxed, self-assured, filmed in a "comradely" style. He is allowed a lot of space to articulate his beliefs, to explain and justify his extremism. He knows why he fought for the Nazis. His admiration for the youthful bodies and discipline of German soldiers underscores his military background ("son of a soldier, a soldier myself") rather than destabilizing his gender identity, as the story of Denis Rake's male lover threatens to do. De la Mazière almost succeeds in winning our empathy for following his convictions as far as the Eastern front in 1944–45. De la Mazière is a self-confessed fascist; but at least he understood his actions and their significance.

Marius Klein, the shopkeeper who advertised himself in 1942 as being of an "ancient French family" because he did not want potential customers to think he was Jewish, is also interviewed as a negative political actor. But his "failing" is passive; he wanted to claim the privileges of belonging as a gentile, in a state that had become rabidly anti-Semitic.[28] Klein seems like a rather smug and disingenuous petit bourgeois. He denies his own prejudice, denies differentiating between those "who have done their duty to France." He is presented in an ironic, almost detached way. His responsibility is cast off, somewhat patronizingly, as an ideological delusion.

Much more sinister, and less easy to understand, is the part played by Madame Solange's story in the "master" narrative of the war and *The Sorrow* in particular. Is she a victim or a devious criminal? Madame Solange was arrested in the summer of 1944 by unknown resisters policing a local purge. She was held without formal charges, in the atmosphere of chaos and terror that was said to have characterized the Liberation of France. She recounts her own fear and puzzlement. She is accused of a denunciation that she disavows; she feigns innocence. She relates her torture and her trial. Her accuser was the wife of a friend, who ends up indicting herself. The tale is a sordid one of feminine spite, in which the politics of denunciation under Vichy are left unexamined, and the settling of personal and political accounts at the Liberation fades from view.

In some respects, Madame Solange's personal story is made historically irrelevant by the unsympathetic treatment accorded her by Ophuls, the unseen interviewer. It is not just that she is presented, in a fairly prolonged segment, as unnecessarily apprehensive (getting up to lock the door to prevent interruptions). We watch so much of her nervous twitching, as the camera focuses on her hands and face, that we imagine her guilt. Her words mark her gender— her unmistakable femininity—and her real "crime." Maybe she did denounce someone, maybe not. What is palpably self-incriminating is the position and identity she represents. She confesses in a brief, animated moment, that she liked Pétain, that she admired him ("perhaps his ideas"). Here is a fifty-year-old Catholic hairdresser who understands nothing of politics, nothing of history. She can only relate to the petty and the personal.

How does it happen that Madame Solange indicts herself and is indicted by us, the audience? She is not just a guilty person, an individual whose story finds its way, among others, into this chronicle of a city in wartime. Madame Solange, this sole female witness, in some ways stands in for *women, the category of historical Other.* She confirms the marginal relationship of all women to the really significant plot, to the proper business of history. Twitchy, inarticulate, *emotional,* Madame Solange underlines the historical gullibility and the potential danger that women represent to mainstream political culture. De la Mazière, analyzing his youthful fascist enthusiasms, can assert "Only fools never change their opinions." Three decades later, Madame Solange has not changed her opinions. She backed Pétain, "fascism," antidemocratic ideas (and the loser). She still can't explain why.

V

Vous avez la franchise de dire que vous étiez pour Pétain . . .

J'étais pour le Maréchal. Je ne faisais pas de politique, mais j'étais pour le Maréchal.

. . . je trouvais cet homme très bien, d'ailleurs.

Vous le trouvez encore?

Oui . . . oui.[29]

These four scenes toward the end of *The Sorrow* move the viewer along a sexualized and gendered narrative trajectory where femininity is increasingly used to underscore "the chronicle." The first represents woman as heroine/victim: the tortured Resistance fighter, Madame Menut; the second, Bleibenger's Clermontoise girlfriend, the pro-German "nice young girl"; focused on collective rather than individual female guilt, the third scene also illustrates "horizontal collaboration," women selling out to the enemy. The final scene of the four, the tortured but not virtuous or heroic Pétainist, Madame Solange, concludes the sexual/political plot. Each scene proves the narrative necessity of women but also their captive status within the narrative, how their identities rely on well-established tropes of feminine representation.

Each of these women's stories has been told in relation to her man, be it the grieving French husband, the Bavarian soldier, the German lovers, or the "Father" of defeated France, Pétain. Within this historical drama, only Madame Solange is given an on-scene presence, a voice. The others have to remain silent, inarticulate, and/or unseen objects of our gaze.

VI

I don't care what's down below
Let it rain
Let it snow
I'll be up on a rainbow
Sweeping the clouds away

(sung by Maurice Chevalier)[30]

This cheerful refrain and the image of a triumphant General de Gaulle end *The Sorrow and the Pity*. It still remains to ask, Whose sorrow? Whose pity? Whose pleasure? Is *The Sorrow* irredeemably masculinist? How do we position ourselves in and against this remarkable film, this version of history that has fully earned its iconographic and iconoclastic status from Paris to New York. Neither as a feminist historian nor Francophile teacher am I prepared to forego the pleasures of this film. Rather, my sense is that we must be critical and reflective about the pleasures of *The Sorrow and the Pity*, precisely because it is an extraordinarily accomplished historical, and a profoundly, seductively, en-*gendered* text.

A reflective critique of this history must operate on at least two levels. The first and most obvious approach is to consider how the visual and narrative absence of women in a formal and participatory way skews the framing of this French wartime history. The second level is to analyze how women and gender get implicitly incorporated in such a history, to see how "normalizing" strategies mediate and delimit a feminine and/or female presence.

Undoubtedly, had he so wished, Ophuls could have interviewed women *témoins*. Female voices would have enhanced the film's portrayal of the ambiguities and hardships of the war and Occupation. Having women present, on camera, instead of in "space-off," or having a women's version of this story might not change the plot. Depending on the women interviewed, one could imagine a reconsolidation of the story, as told.

But perhaps there might be a proliferation of voices and a destabilizing of the metanarrative, a quite different account. Women speaking of the war, the *exode,* the deprivations of the Occupation, their daily fears and uncertainties; women recounting how they saw their lives and their identities faced with the social and political turmoil, the arrests and deportations, the material deprivations of those dark days of war—this might alter the terms of the historical chronicle being told. In Clermont-Ferrand and nationally, many women, reflecting the class and political diversity of French opinion, could have been found to witness to the unique hardships of the Occupation.

It clearly would have been disruptive cinematically to ask the peasant women in the doorway what they saw and experienced, while their hero-husbands were busy in the Resistance, or in POW camps, or in Pétain's Legion. It would certainly have been refreshing to have a woman interviewer to undermine the male authorial voice that structures the entire film.

But the "problem" of gender in this film is not the by-product of Ophuls's (or any individual's) faulty consciousness. Rather the film works so well because of its appeal to familiar (hegemonic) narratives. The gendered history of *The Sorrow,* and the heterosexual contract that upholds it, would not be undone by the "affirmative" additions of some more women here or there in the text. Though apparently neutral and documentary, this film has a plot that is remarkably conventional, a plot that reproduces and parallels the very history it is designed to disrupt. Occupation, collaboration, and resistance, French political and social life during war, far from being redefined or demystified, are in fact reified and reworked as masculinist phenomena. Women are secondary historical actors, passive, malleable, sexually embodied in ways that men are not—not because Ophuls creates them in a "sexist" manner but because this is the dominant discourse available, and one that we will recognize and legitimate. In short, women are trapped within discourses of eternal womanhood, not invisibilized but contained, dehumanized. This in a film that is extraordinary precisely for the detail, the character, the empathy and charm, the *humanity* of its approach. The paradigms of masculinity and femininity, like the contours of racial and sexual difference, are safely embedded and contained within the text, protected by our own desires for "real" history. We want to see and identify with these French "people," to read into their testimony and their lives our own social and political desires, desires that, whether we (as historians and feminists) recognize it or not, are NOT floating free of the gendered scripts of "History." It is these desires, as much as this one brilliant film, that need revision.

Leah D. Hewitt

Vichy's Female Icons:
Chabrol's *Story of Women*

> The judicial world is only the reflection of the real world, sometimes its deforming mirror. Certain trials, by themselves, summarize better an era than many history books.
>
> Francis Szpiner, *Une Affaire de femmes*

Following the course of the "Vichy Syndrome," memories of World War II continue to work their way through French consciousness in recent films and literature, as well as in the news media. France's confrontation with a guilty past has widened the debates on collaboration, not just with the Germans, but also with the Vichy regime. Clearly, when President Mitterrand told a television audience of millions in 1994 that he maintained close ties until 1985 with a René Bousquet, ex-head of Vichy police, the event undoubtedly made history rather than just recounting it.

Because of film's accessibility and popularity, it is perhaps the most forceful of art forms in articulating a public sense of the historical and political stakes of the war. In addition to its capacity to reflect and shape popular views of past events, film also allows for and promotes the airing of current concerns through the lens of memory's (re)creations. The concurrent (although not necessarily overlapping) reappraisals in the seventies of World War II on the one hand, and of women's sociopolitical positions in France on the other, have fostered in the eighties and nineties a new commitment to both the portrayal and analysis of French women's involvement in the war. Because women's roles during the Occupation of France have often been overlooked or neglected in both fictional renderings and historical accounts, there is a sense for both critics and creators alike that it is time to review the intersections of women's lives with the history of the Occupation.

What is also becoming apparent in this review is the repeated depiction of women as powerful figures of the unresolved ambivalence in the opposition resistance/collaboration. In films such as Louis Malle's *Lacombe Lucien*, François Truffaut's *The Last Metro*, Claude Chabrol's *Story of Women* (in French, *Une Affaire de femmes*) and Claude Miller's *L'Accompagnatrice* ("The Accompanist"), as well as in (fictional) memoirs such as Marguerite Duras's *War*, female characters are focal points for the working through of France's uneasy relationship to a past in which "collaborators" and "resisters" inhabit the same space and sometimes the same body, thereby problematizing tidy political distinctions. Even in such cases as *Lacombe Lucien*, where the emphasis is clearly on a young Frenchman who becomes a member of the fascist militia working for the German police, the women characters in the film provide troubling variants of France's duplicity: for example, the young Jewish woman who becomes involved with the fascist Lucien is named France, as if ironically to underscore questions involving national identity, anti-Semitism, and betrayal. In *The Last Metro*, the lead female character turns away a Jew wishing to work in her theater because she wishes to protect her Jewish husband. Again, women's acts of heroism and betrayal dwell in the same ambivalent moment. Because the separation of public and private spheres has continued to be an issue and a problem for women more than for men, female characters seem to embody all the more forcefully the ways in which France's inhabitants remember and live the contradictions between their private desires and actions on the one hand and the public sphere of ethical responsibility and State law on the other.

In what follows, I concentrate on one of the more recent examples of filmic ambivalence concerning women in the war: Claude Chabrol's 1987 film *Story of Women*. This work is particularly crucial to the study of women's representations because it offers a double focus: it not only allows us to question the ways Vichy's versions of fascism enter into women's lives in the historical period, it also enables us to explore the ways this filmic representation/performance of history shapes the contemporary public's attitudes toward women's issues when they are filtered through the recreation of France's Vichy. What can this spectacle tell us of the past represented and of ourselves as its spectators?

· · ·

Near the end of *Story of Women*, we watch Chabrol's protagonist, Marie Latour, as she is led to the guillotine in 1943 for having performed abortions, that is, in Vichy's pro-fascist, pro-natalist terms, for having committed "crimes against the State." Chabrol, taking his inspiration from Francis Szpiner's 1986 account of the life and execution of the abortionist Marie-Louise Giraud,[1] has chosen to dramatize an actual historical event from the Occupation that no doubt feeds into ongoing debates in Europe and the United States on the issue of abortion.[2] The film eventually makes it quite clear that Marie Latour's deeds have been judged by a deceitful, murderous "French State" incapable of hiding the inequities and contradictions in its policies toward women. We come to realize, as do Marie and her defense lawyers, that Marie is a scapegoat accused of creating the ills of Occupied France, depriving it of its children, while the government unhesitatingly sends French workers to forced labor camps in Germany (the Service de Travail Obligatoire) and ships out communists, resisters, and Jews of all ages to death camps, when it does not have them killed on French soil. Chabrol creates a stark contrast: on the one hand, abortion is sanctimoniously defined as a State issue of morality—this occurs at the end of the film during Marie's trial; on the other hand, the earlier sections of the film emphasize the individual plight of women, mostly uneducated, poor, working class, who have become pregnant—by their husbands, lovers, German soldiers—and who cannot afford financially and/or personally to bring the pregnancy to term. Although uneducated herself, Marie astutely remarks to a cellmate at the end that rich women don't have to go through the same difficulties and suffering, because they can buy their way out of the problem. Thus the law's victims are those who are the least economically privileged.[3] Clearly, such economic disparities, when it comes to the affordability of abortion, remain contemporary in both France and the United States.

As spectators of the film, however, we are made to feel at least some complicity with the judges and their reprehensible, outrageous position: up until her arrest, we have been witnesses to Marie Latour's less than perfect conduct during the war, and are implicitly called upon to judge her moral shortcomings—shortcomings that play into Vichy propaganda condemning individualism, materialism, and immorality, *especially* in women.[4] Ultimately one comes to wonder if Marie isn't condemned for these faults as much as for being an abortionist. In Chabrol's film, it is Marie's own husband who turns her in to the authorities, and his reasons have more to do with the fact that he is being shamelessly cuckolded than with Marie's abortion activities. Chabrol makes his viewers recognize the workings of collaboration by placing us in the compromising position of judges. The spectators, sitting in neat rows of armchairs facing the screen, constitute the contemporary jury that is to pass sentence on Marie's actions.

There are two sides of this issue that I would like to emphasize: first, I am concerned with the final image left for us to ponder, that is, the victimized woman's destruction as it plays into national politics, with woman becoming national symbol, albeit an ambivalent one. How do a government *and* a filmmaker use women's issues to raise questions of collaboration and patriotism during the war? In a sense, we are being asked to judge France via Marie as national symbol. Although Chabrol is not known as a feminist filmmaker, his construction of an effective, mythic version of the Szpiner account enacts through the individual woman's life story the sociopolitical ambiguities and harsh difficulties of survival in France in 1942–43, at a time when much of the population began shifting alliances from Pétain to the resistance. In a second section, I explore the ways the final scenes require a rereading of the film as a whole, a rereading that reveals to us how complicity takes place, as we are called upon to pass *our* judgment on Marie Latour, not just as abortionist but as woman.

Woman as National Symbol

For a French public, what is conspicuous in the image of this woman about to be executed are her associations with Joan of Arc and Marie-Antoinette and the paradoxes that arise from the expressly visual ties to Joan the Patron Saint of France (the nation's savior-victim), Marie-Antoinette (the traitor to the Republic), and Vichy's National Revolution. The guillotine symbolically conflates opposing "revolutions," that of 1789 and of Vichy's antidemocratic, antirepublican cause, making us contemplate Marie Latour's ties to France's tradition of turning its female victims into national symbols (principally Joan, but to a lesser degree, Marie-Antoinette as well). The indirect references to Joan of Arc also bring together in one figure patriotic appeals of the Left and the Right: on the Right, we find the frequent propaganda links to Joan during the Occupation, which helped to legitimate Marshal Pétain's role as savior of the French people. (In another recent film, Jean Marboeuf's 1993 *Pétain*, the comparison between Pétain and Joan of Arc is explicit.)[5] On the Left, the peasant girl from Domrémy is associated with that other liberator, General de Gaulle, who hailed from the province of Lorraine as did Joan, and who ardently cultivated the comparison between himself and Joan, making the cross of Lorraine the very symbol of French independence and resistance against the Germans and the Vichy government.[6]

The links to Joan of Arc and Marie-Antoinette in Chabrol's film are numerous even if they go unspoken.[7] The first markers that associate them lie in Marie's preparation for her beheading: the nuns, who are her jailers, have her hair cut off before the fateful morning, almost as if to prefigure the actual beheading. Marie's hair is left in a crude, blunt cut, with her neck exposed. On the day of her death, she wears a dark dress made of coarse material and dark socks that hang around her ankles. Her worn, simple shoes complete a look that makes her seem almost childlike although she is forty years old. Finally, the small stature of Chabrol's Marie, played by Isabelle Huppert, makes the character seem all the more vulnerable at the end. In the procession led by the priest and attended by policemen, lawyers and Vichy officials (all symbols of the powers bringing about her death), Marie is more or less dragged toward the guillotine with her hands bound behind her back. In this final instant, her appearance strikingly resembles portraits of Joan of Arc and Marie-Antoinette. It is not, of course, the warrior Joan of Arc clad in armor that we recall, and it is not to the actual history of Joan's death that we are led. (Joan's head was reportedly shaved before her burning.) The cropping of Marie's hair and her subsequent beheading are obviously reminiscent of Marie-Antoinette's end. Marie Latour in the final scenes does in fact bear a resemblance to David's famous pen sketch of the queen en route to her death. But Chabrol's protagonist *also* reminds us of the representations of Joan of Arc as poor peasant girl and martyred victim. In the film, the haircut and drab peasant clothing are all the more conspicuous because, as was the case for Marie-Antoinette, we have witnessed Marie's increasing attention to her appearance—hairstyle, makeup, clothing— up to the point when she is arrested. Like the haircut, the stripping of Marie's outward beauty and sensuality presages the beheading and takes on the function of a feminine castration. Concurrently, both Marie and Marie-Antoinette are also turned into quasi-monsters in order to merit fully their punishment: Marie is accused of depriving the country of its children; Marie-Antoinette was accused of sexually abusing her son.

Marina Warner's work on Joan of Arc provides several examples of artistic images of Joan that intersect with her political significance and that are pertinent to our discussion of Chabrol's Marie Latour.[8] Of particular interest are two visual portrayals that show Joan's recuperation by Vichy and by the Gaullists. The 1943 Vichy propaganda poster, "Assassins Always Return to the Scenes of Their Crime," evokes Joan burning at the stake in Rouen and clearly suggests that the English (rather than the Germans) are once again the enemies of France. Joan looms larger than life in the background against a red sky full of black smoke as the Allied bombings, portrayed in the foreground, cause Rouen to go up in flames. Joan herself, like Marie, is dressed simply: she wears robes reminiscent of a choir girl's and has her hands manacled. Her eyes are closed as if she were in prayer, and her haircut is reminiscent of Marie Latour's.[9] Like Chabrol's protagonist, this Joan also has a childlike quality. It should be noted, however, that everything about Vichy's Joan is carefully staged, the perfect icon, whereas Marie's blank look and ill-kept appearance are devoid of the calm assurance visible in Joan's demeanor. Marie leaves us instead with an unsettled and unsettling image, seemingly combining martyr and betrayer, Joan *and* Marie-Antoinette.

The picture of the Gaullist Joan is even more stylized: enclosed in a frame within the picture, Joan is an elongate figure, dressed in a flowing white robe (and in an almost sensual pose, revealing bare feet and a bare shoulder), tied to the stake, with her smiling head raised to the burning sky, while what is perhaps a spiritual mother (a nun or the Virgin Mary?) looms protectively over

I think the weather was beautiful on July 30, 1943...

Courtesy of MK2 Productions and New Yorker Films.

her. At the very bottom of the print we see knights with drawn swords, and to each side of the scene is the Cross of Lorraine, as if the Gaullist symbol were meant to enshrine Joan. In contrast to this Gaullist Joan, it is interesting to note that Marie, like the Vichy Joan, is not represented as a sexual being when she is executed: in Chabrol's film, Vichy makes sure that Marie is stripped of the exuberant sensuality she has unabashedly displayed up to the end; Vichy's Joan wears robes that camouflage her to the point that she could just as easily be a boy as a girl. In this context, Joan's famous androgyny is merely an absence of sexuality rather than an ambivalence. The same goes for Marie, whose sexuality, as we shall see later, is ambivalently represented in the earlier parts of the film and then denied totally at the end. The sensual portrayal of the Gaullist Joan, on the other hand, reminds us of the frequent references by de Gaulle to a feminine France that he felt destined to save.

Like these predecessors, Marie Latour becomes a symbol to be manipulated, in her case, by the Vichy government, as well as by the contemporary filmmaker.[10] The similarities with Joan's story are in fact striking. Both Joan and Marie undergo trumped-up trials in which the State and the Church align themselves against an uneducated woman who is actually betrayed by her own people: the initiative against Joan is led by Frenchmen (Pierre Cauchon under the auspices of Jean de Bourgogne) who sympathize with the English cause rather than with Charles VII; Chabrol's Marie is denounced anonymously by her husband, and then prosecuted by representatives of the French government of Vichy.[11] It is no doubt one of the fascinating and horrifying ironies of these

Courtesy of MK2 Productions and New Yorker Films.

histories that it is certain traitorous Frenchmen who help to crush the person who then becomes the very symbol of their patriotism. The presence of the nuns as prison guards and of the priest who officiates at her death underscores in Marie's case the complicity between Church and State. Collaboration with foreign powers and complex national politics also inflects the two cases. In both, the steamrolling procedures by which the accused are tried are too complex or hermetic for either Marie or Joan to be able to understand completely just what they are supposed to have done. In the heresy trial of Joan by the Inquisition (composed primarily of French Inquisitors), Joan is never informed of what her crimes might have been. Warner explains:

The Inquisition did not bring formal charges against a suspect; but its duty was the diagnosis and eradication of heresy. The plaintiffs could never be defended against specific accusations, because the actions that had brought them under suspicion were never set forth clearly by the accusers, but appeared only under the veils of their questions. Joan's trial has the nightmarish ambiguity, formlessness, confusing menace of *The Trial* or *The Castle*: she has no means of knowing where the interrogation is driving, what the concealed charge is.[12] (117)

Marie's difficulty in grasping what is happening to her is a similar nightmare. She has erroneously assumed that Vichy's State Tribunal only tries communists, and is thus confused about her own trial when she learns that it is a State matter. Under normal circumstances, the abortions she admits to having performed would have led at most to a prison term, but certainly not to a death sentence for what was considered a minor crime under the Third Republic.

Marie's understanding is at the level of standard judiciary practices: she does not realize that the government is making of her a diabolic symbol that it will then consider its obligation to crush. She is told to sign a document by a Justice Ministry official without understanding just what she is signing. And when a cellmate asks what she is being tried for, her response is both comical and tragic, revealing the extent to which the process has overwhelmed her: she tells her cellmate that she didn't really understand (or trust) her lawyer's description of her case, that he told her she had assassinated the president of the Republic. By this, she refers to the accusations against her for crimes against the State. Although Chabrol's spectator may not realize it, the metaphor also reflects the actual phrasing of Vichy's law of February 15, 1942, stating that abortionists are assassins of their country.[13] Clearly, the accusations against Marie are much more severe than she has ever dreamed of. Her tragicomical remark is all the more ironic because it shows that Marie has not fully realized what it means for France no longer to be a Republic during the Occupation. That there is only a "French State" with a "Chief" is in fact crucial to the way her case is being treated.[14] Her explanation unwittingly reveals the important change, precisely the one that will allow for a bogus trial. When her lawyer explains to Marie that the State prosecution plans to make an example of her, she naively repeats: "an example of what?" We are made to realize that the outcome of her case depends less on evidence and jurisprudence than on the Vichy government's vengeful sadism and vacuous discourse on morality. In the film, the melodramatic 1808 painting by Pierre Prudhon, "Justice and Divine Vengeance Pursuing Crime," hangs above the presiding magistrate.[15] The camera silently zooms in on this icon as an ironic, mythic reminder of the overblown rhetoric used to condemn Marie, a rhetoric that, like the painting, unites the powers of law and religion to carry out the pursuit of this woman.[16] In the discourse of Chabrol's judge, Marie's crime as abortionist is rendered a capital offense because it involves accepting money for her actions (the abortions, and renting rooms to prostitutes). The fact that Marie performs the first abortion just to help out a friend in need and then later is able to give her two children and husband a degree of security and material comfort is irrelevant to the self-righteous magistrate. As we noted earlier, Vichy's moralizing discourse affirms Marie's culpability over her resourcefulness: it is particularly vehement against materialism even though Vichy's police officials and thugs were known to abscond with the belongings of Jews and others they were tracking down.[17]

Another similarity between Joan and Marie that underscores the ambivalent quality of the icon conjoining woman and national symbol lies in their abjurations. Joan's abjuration, Warner tells us, has often been overlooked when her story is retold (140–41). It is perhaps not featured because Joan later says she was tricked into signing her recantation. But it is also probable that the episode is underplayed because it does not fit well into the tidy (pure) image that a patron saint must provide. In Marie's case, the equivalent of an abjuration would be her acceptance of guilt in the terms that Vichy's ideology advocated. Whereas Joan's death is triumphant, Marie's only confirms her victimization.

Marie's disavowal of her own actions unfolds in two steps and remains much more ambivalent than Joan's. After a certain vacillation on her part about the nature of her deeds, the forces of State and Church eventually triumph over her. Following her trial, she is placed in a freezing cell by herself and, sitting alone with tears in her eyes, she begins to recite a "Hail Mary." But her vehement words betray the contrite figure she *appears* to be: "Hail Mary, full of shit. The fruit of your womb is rotten." Marie repudiates her namesake, the Virgin Mary, and then angrily rips off a religious medallion, in (implicit) recognition of the Church's role in condemning her. Were the film to stop here, spectators might be able to appropriate Marie either as a symbol of feminist strength (on the Left) resisting all too powerful forces, or as a symbol of blasphemy (on the Right) deserving of God's wrath. Chabrol would have reproduced a more standard symbol within the field of nationalist iconography. The penultimate scene undercuts such unequivocal interpretations of Marie, however. After going to confession, Marie articulates a certain repentance for her actions in a most revealing way: "Marshal Pétain was right," she says to the young intern lawyer sent to see to her needs before the execution. Paradoxically, it is the victim who now espouses the condemnation as she seeks forgiveness, whereas Vichy's representative sees through the falseness of the "family values" that Pétain was advocating: the legal intern (sent by Marie's lawyer, who is too much of a coward to face her himself) almost tells Marie not to believe in the validity of the judgment, but checks his remark, no doubt realizing that it will do Marie no good to know she has been tricked by the Pétainist ideology. The unsettling visual image of Marie we noted earlier is perfectly consonant with this painful image of the woman's defeat and the State's treachery.

The end of *Story of Women* leaves us with no doubt about the caricatured, hypocritical nature of the switch from the Revolution of 1789's secular trinity, "Liberty, Equality, Fraternity" to the "New Order's" hollow equivalent, "Work, Family, Homeland." In a park where "good" mothers stroll with their babies in carriages, Marie's lawyer expresses his disgust with his own and the general French complicity with Vichy, but it is described in terms of male mutilation and castration: "They're cutting off our balls. They're carving up our flesh." Ultimately, however, as the blade drops, it is *Marie's head* that will fall. There is a repeated impression that the woman's head must be cut off in order to avoid a masculine castration. Superimposed on the final image of the guillotine is a biblical-style injunction that belies Vichy's treachery: "Take pity on the children of those who are condemned." The individual case of Marie ultimately supposes many more victims than just Marie: stigmatized, unwanted children born from "illicit encounters" or those (like Marie's) who lose their mother; women who have no choice to decide their own fate (to become mothers or not); mothers, some of whom will have their heads shaven at the end of the war as the sign of their truck with the Occupant; women having been accused of aborting or helping others to abort . . . etc. But all this is lost under the layers of propaganda, with the State machine harming women and children in the name of family and country. As Chabrol's symbol, Marie Latour embodies to the end the paradoxical double icon of victimization and betrayal under Vichy's pro-fascist policies.

• • •

Given my description thus far, someone who had never seen *Story of Women* would undoubtedly wonder how on earth the spectator could possibly feel any complicity at all with sadistic justice officials who speak of amputating the gangrened limbs of society when referring to Marie, or even with cowardly lawyers who do their jobs with a bad conscience. I am not trying to suggest, in fact, that spectators identify with these characters. Our early negative evaluations of Marie are, of course, incommensurate with the subsequent treatment she receives. It is rather an issue of perspective: I am concerned with who is looking at Marie's life. What position does the spectator occupy when watching the depiction of Marie before and during her trial? What kind of visual rhetoric has created the negative viewpoint, and what allows the spectator to shift to a sympathetic one?

Throughout most of the film, the audience does not really have a clear idea of who is telling this story, of whose eye the camera might embody. It is not until the final scenes that we have the sense of a definable perspective thanks to a voice-over in the seconds before the execution. The last voice we hear, the one that gives a retrospective meaning to the film we have just witnessed, is in fact the voice of Marie's little boy, Pierrot—now a grown man—who describes having learned about the execution as we watch his mother approaching the scaffold: "The weather must have been very fine on that morning, July 30, 1943. The neighborhood children told me about it. Your mother was guillotined. It's hard to believe, even when you're seven years old. It's like a big black hole inside you. She was sometimes so cheerful and she loved to sing so much." Although it is an adult who utters these words, we acknowledge in them the child mourning his mother's death, a child who (in the last scene in which he appears) beats his head against the wall as a reaction to that death. If we approach the first parts of the film through the little boy's perspective on his mother and on the past we have just seen, this rereading makes clearer the mark of a male viewpoint that feeds into Vichy's patriarchal discourse condemning Marie at the end. It will confirm the complicity between the two parts of the film (before and after Marie's arrest).[18]

Rereading Motherhood

There are several early episodes in the film where the gaze of the young son, Pierrot, colors the way we evaluate Marie, particularly as a "bad" or unfit mother.[19] Before Marie ever thinks of helping out her neighbor who wishes to end an unwanted pregnancy, she is viewed with a certain suspicion by the spectator. In the opening scene of 1942, Marie, whose husband has been a prisoner of war for some time, scrounges for food along the bleak, if beautiful, cliffs outside Cherbourg with her son, Pierrot, and baby daughter, Mouche. Although the spectator may not notice it the first time around, Pierrot's voice is the first (as well as the last) one we hear in the film, as if to confirm the importance of his point of view as frame for the story. Before we see any of the characters, the audience hears Pierrot crying, and then the camera focuses briefly on his face. Then we see Marie chide Pierrot and lightly swat his cheek when he begins to cry that the nettles are stinging him as they collect food.[20] Eventually we will understand that impatience and frustration, in the context of a poverty-stricken life, ignite this impulsive act, but there is no visual justification to soften our negative impression at the very beginning. It is a sort of defining act that will be confirmed in the next scene, when Pierrot gazes at his mother's tender care of Mouche, while Marie says to neighbors that having Mouche was her one success. The camera emphasizes Pierrot's silent, watchful presence in this scene, and his feelings of being neglected are rendered explicit when he later asks his mother: "And me, when I was born, were you happy then too?" Marie explains to him that boys are automatically considered a success. The spectator infers that she is commenting on the gender hierarchies of society (i.e., it is traditionally "better" to produce a boy than a girl), but Pierrot's sense of unfair exclusion stays with the spectator nevertheless.

These first episodes (and subsequent negative ones) are balanced by many others where Marie shows love and caring for both her children, but because of the ordering of events (with the negative sequences establishing a framework), Marie appears very early on to be biased against her son (in favor of her daughter) and ultimately is portrayed as self-centered. When we later see Marie dancing with her friend Rachel in the local café (rather than with the men there),[21] or when she shows that she is not in love with her husband who returns from a prisoner-of-war camp, or when she befriends the prostitute Lulu (after Rachel is deported because she is Jewish), Marie's frequent preference for the company of women seems relatively well established and it is not entirely in a sympathetic light that her friendships are viewed. What also seems clear, however, is that if we are aware of the way Pierrot's perspective on his mother's life shapes our attitudes (in the rereading of the film), the negativity is easily explained as a function of the subject (Pierrot) as much as of the object

(Marie). It is certainly not unusual for a child to remember selectively key moments of hurt or neglect by the most important person in his life, Mother. Pierrot's love for his mother is insatiable, and her attention to girls and women leaves him an outsider gazing in, even when that attention is not a denial of Marie's maternal love for Pierrot. His father, upon returning to the family, is portrayed similarly as an unwanted intruder in Marie's life.

It should be noted here that in the subsequent trial, Chabrol's Marie is not accused of maternal negligence. Szpiner's account, on the other hand, stresses the thousands of anonymous accusations and denunciations that Vichy and the Germans received during the Occupation and states that many of Marie-Louise Giraud's female neighbors actually did accuse her (in either anonymous or signed letters) of being a bad mother. Chabrol thus greatly downplays women's roles in these kinds of pernicious actions, since the only anonymous letter (of denunciation) that is sent in the film is from Marie's husband. In terms of the actual Giraud trial, Szpiner tells us that Marie-Louise Giraud successfully defended herself against the accusations of maternal neglect. Chabrol, instead of making Marie's care of her children an explicit topic of accusation in the trial, has the silent camera eye present the case to the spectators, leaving us to ask uneasily: which of us (viewers) might have written accusatory letters concerning Marie's childrearing the way Marie-Louise's neighbors did during the Occupation?

Pierrot's role as visual filter for our understanding of Marie is actually thematized in the film: he is actively portrayed as a voyeur spying on his mother. He is curious in his own right about his mother's actions: Pierrot senses something is going on in secret that involves taboo issues concerning sex and women's bodies, even if he doesn't understand exactly what he's seeing. But Pierrot's father, Paul, also uses the boy as his private informant to try to find out with whom Marie spends her time and how she acquires more and more money to support the family. The camera repeatedly fixes on Pierrot as he watches his mother, either with her knowledge or surreptitiously through the keyhole, especially when she performs abortions in her kitchen.

Pierrot and his father both unwittingly embody a certain logic of the Vichy collaborator. In a café scene where the father orders plenty of wine for Pierrot (no doubt to loosen his tongue about his mother's activities), the family conversation is interrupted when the boy rushes to pick up and return a coin to a German soldier who has dropped it. Pierrot even knows enough German to respond to the soldier's thanks in German. The boy has unquestionably learned his civics lesson well: the scene symbolically enacts Vichy propaganda fostering Franco-German cooperation. The complicity with the German cause enacted by this little boy (whose family listens faithfully to Pétain's radio speeches) seems all the more natural or at least understandable given the context: this is a scene in which the father asks his unsuspecting son to betray his mother's secrets. Again, the ordering of events is significant: after Pierrot has rendered service to the German, his father, Paul, then remarks that he doesn't really care after all about how Marie gets her money, as long as they get a better apartment. It may be that when Paul realizes, through Pierrot's responses, that Marie spends most of her time with women rather than men, he stops worrying about the personal threat to his "manhood." Pierrot's public action (assisting the German soldier) is consonant with his father's willingness to look the other way when his wife's potentially objectionable actions benefit him. Paul's private betrayal of Marie to the Vichy police merely uses Vichy's public rhetoric concerning the sanctity of the family to exact a personal revenge on a wife who has ignored his feelings and bristled at his advances. And although the spectator feels a certain sympathy for him in the middle parts of the film (when, jobless, he cares for the children or is neglected by Marie), his anonymous accusation makes him fully a partner in the hypocrisy and deception of the State discourse and actions in Marie's case.

The symbolism of Pierrot's voyeuristic treachery is most poignantly brought to our attention in a wish he makes when blowing out a candle at a family celebration. He tells his family matter-of-factly that he has made a wish to become an executioner. As we reread the film, this startling, horrifying remark from a seven-year-old suggests complicity in his mother's future execution (perhaps feelings of guilt on the adult Pierrot's part), and also links him to the handsome Vichy thug, Lucien, who first captures Marie's fancy by winning a town competition set up by the German authorities.[22] This contest consists of trying to lop off the head of a goose with a sword while the contestant's head is covered by a huge mask (reminiscent of the cowl worn by an executioner) in the shape of the head of Mother Goose. The winner and eventual lover of Marie, presents to her his prize, the headless goose, a gift symbolically presaging Marie's own beheading, but also materially valuable at a time when severe food shortages and deprivation are part of daily existence.[23] The official contest is an execution of sorts, and one that plays into the local politics of collaboration between Vichy and Germans as they control the French population by trying to placate them with a rare food stuff that, says the German official, is not from the black market. (It is thus a legitimate, legal slaughter.) Marie's lover, husband, and son thus enter into the network of Vichy's legalities, its collaborations and executions, symbolic and real. Marie's own role remains ambivalent, in that she is both a passive adherent of the Vichy regime and a victim of it.

The Politics of Gender and Collaboration

Given that Marie's activities and political affinities exceed the comprehension of her young son, this last section explores, in addition to or beyond the "bad mother" image, Marie's relationship to Vichy before her arrest. We have already seen that one of the key perspectives on Marie can be defined as male and collaborationist. Although this viewpoint is an important frame for the negative judgment of Marie, the spectator need not identify solely with it. Because the gaze is rendered so visible to the spectator *within* the film, we are more apt to take it as just one possible attitude toward Marie. Let us consider how politics and gender interact where Marie and the other female characters are concerned.

The women in *Story of Women* are involved in cooperative efforts for survival, both emotional and physical. Marie's friendships and associations with other women suggest a loose, informal solidarity across certain boundaries.[24] Marie does not judge the women who come to her for abortions: what does it matter that their pregnancies are the result of relations with a husband who then leaves for the forced labor camps, with a German soldier, or a French lover, if in each case there is no way to provide for the child (made all the more difficult when the encounter is outside marriage)? Loneliness, poverty, and a stifling daily life are things Marie understands well. The women are forced to rely exclusively on one another, because, ultimately, Vichy's "New Order"— and to a lesser extent our own society—consider such problems to be women's business ("une affaire de femmes") even if officials mouth a rhetoric of caring, concern, and protection of women and children.[25]

Marie is also (unconsciously) attracted to women relegated to the margins of French society during the Occupation. Her friendship with Rachel is on an individual level that does not take into account the kinds of markings that racist public policies and sociopolitical divisions emphasize: before her friend's disappearance, Marie doesn't have a clue that Rachel is Jewish and doesn't have a clear idea of what the implications of this fact might be. "Rachel has never been Jewish," says Marie (when she learns Rachel has been taken away), as if one could choose and cast off origins like clothing or political beliefs. Being Jewish is like being a communist: Marie is aware that both are hunted down by the government, but never stops to ask why. All that is evident to her is the immense grief she feels at the loss of her friend. The spectator (especially in the film's rereading) wonders whether Rachel isn't turned in by one of the men in the café who watch the two women dance.[26]

Marie's friendship with the prostitute Lulu flows smoothly from a pleasure they derive in each other's looks and company to a commercial association that mutually benefits them: Marie rents out bedrooms to Lulu.[27] (The smooth shift from neighborly assistance in an abortion to financial gain by performing abortions suggests the same pattern.) Lulu's politics are particularly revelatory in the context of the Occupation: she tells Marie that, contrary to popular thinking, the Germans are no more brutal toward prostitutes than the French. Although the patriotic spectator might be offended by Lulu's steadfast treatment of German soldiers as individuals rather than as a national

group of invaders, in her own small way Lulu is a resister to the German Occupation, because, as she tells Marie, as a matter of principle she fleeces them
whenever she gets a chance. (This contrasts with Pierrot's returning the coin to
the German soldier.) Lulu's gesture is reminiscent of the small acts of defiance
that the French began to make after the 1940 defeat.[28]

As for Marie's conscious ties to national politics before her arrest, we may
note that her patriotism is full of the paradoxes and contradictions of the times:
like substantial numbers of French in 1942–43, she remains faithful to Pétain,
but also declares herself for the Resistance, while continuing to take advantage
of her ties to her collaborating lover, Lucien. She acts according to personal
dictates of pragmatism (survival), self-gratification (a certain greediness), but
also of caring and friendship. Her strong ties to her own working class, especially to poor women for whom an unwanted pregnancy intensified the deep
personal distress and financial hardships that the war had already imposed,
make of Marie a resister of sorts. Critics and historians have come more and
more to realize the importance of survival as a major form of resistance during
the war. Marie's help to the women who seek her out benefits both herself and
them as they attempt to persevere in difficult times. Chabrol seems to make a
symbolic connection between Marie and the Resistance when a resister who
has just been shot by the authorities dies looking intently into Marie's face.
Marie is haunted by the man's gaze: "it's as if he knew me," she says, symbolically suggesting the recognition between kindred souls who die for their actions under Vichy.

What is perhaps most remarkable about the solidarity among women in
Chabrol's film is that even Vichy's staunchest, most vivid female representative does not betray Marie to the authorities after her sister-in-law has died following an abortion (that may or may not have caused her death). When this
woman shows up with two of her dead sister-in-law's six children, her disapproval of Marie is unwavering. Her Catholic beliefs match Vichy's image of
women as childbearers ready to sacrifice themselves for the family. She explains that she is going to raise the children herself because the children's father has committed suicide following his wife's death. The surviving sister-in-
law's choice of self-abnegation and self-righteousness contrasts with an earlier
scene in which the mother of the six children had begged for an abortion after
a thoroughly moving description of painful pregnancies, of raising unwanted
children in an impoverished household with no control over her own body's
reproductive system. Both sisters-in-law are victims of social pressures that
Church doctrine and State policy promote. It is to Chabrol's credit that his
film presents both sides of the abortion issue—for and against—through
women characters who live the problem in a concrete historical framework
that shows Vichy's inflated pronouncements to be hollow and beside the
point. Although the woman who takes on the task of raising her sister-in law's

children moralizes about abortion in a discourse consonant with Vichy's pro-family policy, *she nevertheless pays Marie for her sister-in-law's abortion and does not tell the police about the incident.*[29] The Catholic woman's overriding concern for the well-being of her orphaned nieces and nephews foreshadows the final words written across the screen: "Take pity on the children of those who are condemned." This is one of the crucial issues that Vichy consistently neglects in its "family" policies. Both Marie and the sister-in-law attend to the necessities of survival (of women, of children). Their forbearance contrasts sharply with the dead husband's suicide: his death reveals weakness and an inability to face up to a difficult life of child care and economic hardship.

· · ·

Chabrol has made of Marie Latour an icon around which swirl the complex interactions among gender, class, and politics during the Occupation. In the process of mythmaking, Chabrol alters Szpiner's account in significant ways. The film strategically concentrates on an imperfect individual victim to suggest the connections among Vichy politics, the difficulties of women's lives during the period, and the general issue of French collaboration during the war. Francis Szpiner's account, on the other hand, underscores more the generalized discrimination against women, particularly poor women (without neglecting the moments when women denounce women). Although we are certainly aware in the film of other women's predicaments, Chabrol concentrates on Marie as *the* victim of Vichy, the symbol of state treachery. Szpiner emphasizes the fact that all the women involved in Marie-Louise Giraud's abortion case—from her clients to her assistants—were tried with her and punished, and that her husband, who was involved in the abortions (having disposed of a fetus by burying it), went scot-free.[30] In Chabrol's version, Marie alone is on trial and her husband is more obviously associated with Vichy's bogus justice than with his wife's actions, since he is the author of the unsigned accusation against Marie. (According to Szpiner, Marie-Louise Giraud's accuser was never named.) Chabrol thus more clearly identifies the private male resentments and biases toward women with Vichy's hypocritical public policies. It would seem that in his wish for a sympathetic, although ambiguous portrayal of the abortionist, Chabrol sacrifices the extremes that often become the clichés of womanhood (women's "natural" perfidy and victimization), while simultaneously polarizing the gender divisions. Chabrol's transformation of Marie-Louise Giraud into the national symbol of Marie Latour involves, no doubt, a certain amount of Hollywood-style idealizing to make us more sympathetic to Marie Latour's story than a large public might have been to Marie-Louise Giraud's: Isabelle Huppert is beautiful whereas Giraud was homely and had a criminal record before the abortions began. Marie is thus morally more palatable and aesthetically more seductive to the film viewer than Giraud would have been. The female neighbors and maid of Giraud denounced her at will, whereas Marie Latour's female entourage shows solidarity for the most part. The only women who are sympathetic to her undoing are the representatives of the Church and State (the jailer-nuns, for example) and certain inmates. These anonymous characters are more associated with sociopolitical groups than recognized as individuals. Latour is also at least symbolically associated with the Resistance, whereas Giraud was not. Finally, Chabrol gives Marie Latour a Jewish friend whereas this was never an issue in Giraud's story. At least one critic complained that Marie's not knowing that Rachel was Jewish was unlikely. Chabrol is criticized with failing to make the public anti-Semitism of the period more visible.[31] And yet, given that the friendship is itself a fictive embellishment and that Marie's friendships consistently depend less on recognized ethnic origins and political awareness than on other, personal affinities, the friendship with Rachel is not so incongruous. It certainly seems credible that Marie would not think of associating her best friend with the hateful, anti-Semitic propaganda and laws initiated by Vichy, particularly if that friend were trying to conceal her origins to keep out of harm's way.[32] Chabrol's addition of the Jewish friend does, on the other hand, appear to reflect our contemporary obsession with the Holocaust and France's responsibility in the deportations.

· · ·

If Chabrol's embellishments on events act to counterbalance the patriarchal viewpoint promoted by Vichy to which Marie is subject in the film, Marie's transformation into pure heroine (or saintly victim) is far from complete. Our ability to evaluate Marie's actions and character is precisely what is at stake in Chabrol's version of the story: is she merely an opportunistic, calculating, callous, and shallow woman, as viewed through the lens of an excluded male gaze, or is she a courageous, gutsy, resourceful woman who falls prey to Vichy?[33] Clearly, neither description fully does her justice. By retaining a certain opacity to her character—we glimpse her through the filmic peephole just as Pierrot spies on her through the kitchen keyhole—Chabrol leaves it up to us to think through the value of her actions, tending to nudge us alternately toward and away from Marie: yes, she helps out her neighbor for free, but later, she revels too much in the material success of her enterprises. If we grant that Chabrol's Marie is indeed self-centered, tough, manipulative,[34] the director nevertheless makes us wonder to what extent this is negative *because* she is a woman. Do a man's "enterprising, resourceful" talents become "calculating and callous" when enacted by a woman? Chabrol's gender polarization in the story (whether intentional or not), intensifies the question. As one film reviewer put it: "The case for a 'selfish' woman is still a tough one to make, demanding that filmmakers overcome the knee-jerk assumption—held by women as well as men—that women justify their actions by what is good for others."[35] Both the Vichy magistrate and the Vichy mother wholly subscribe to such an assumption. In the first part of the film, Chabrol attenuates the case against Marie's self-interest by first emphasizing her poverty and desperation (the early scenes are bleak, dark, depressing), and then by showing her sharing her new monetary gains with her children and husband. But bit by bit, Chabrol seamlessly leads us through the network of gazes toward disapproval of Marie, making *us* take on the negative view. These gazes, whether male (the boy's, the father's, the magistrate's) or female (Lulu's, the Vichy mother's, the neighbors'), all condemn the "selfish" woman. Because Chabrol does not make us privy to Marie's unspoken thoughts, motivations, and intentions, we have no privileged position through which to understand her point of view. Whereas Szpiner's account constantly rushes to Marie-Louise Giraud's defense, Chabrol places the responsibility for evaluating Marie Latour squarely on our shoulders. It is up to the viewer to determine the nature and value of her actions. And while many could probably agree that Marie is a pragmatic, immoral woman who increases her own and her family's wealth and comfort beyond the point of "good taste" or social acceptability, we must ask to what extent this negative attitude toward her remains a function of gender expectations: the material gains in her own life do not wipe out the very real assistance she provides to the numerous desperate women who come to her for abortions.

· · ·

Were it not for Chabrol's embellishments on Giraud's story, how many more spectators would be tempted to don the Vichy judge's hat and pronounce her guilty for the "sin" of self-interest, as well as immorality? At issue, too, is the danger of sliding from these moral judgments concerning Marie's character flaws to fatal juridical pronouncements: it is as if the filmmaker temporarily lured us into watching Marie through a progression of collaborationists' eyes: her son's, her husband's, the judge's. Chabrol's feat is to have made visible this collaborationist gaze of Vichy (in its private and public dimensions) through our own eyes while also filling us with the outrage of that gaze's injustice. *Story of Women* invites the conflation of moral and juridical judgments in order then to make us all the more aware of the danger of slipping too easily from one to the other. To appreciate Marie's self-interest as a sign of survival (*and* pleasure) one need not make of her a saint or a demon. She is at once the unique symbol of women's difficult survival during the war, the victim of Vichy's duplicitous treatment of women, especially in reproductive issues, and the unsettling national symbol of a French public whose daily survival choices and self-interest often made it at least passively complicit with Pétain and Vichy. For those who yearn for a position of purity, Marie cannot fail to elicit strong reactions: Chabrol calls upon us to rethink our assumptions about this woman who becomes the icon of France's ambivalence toward its own past, representing all at once complicity, survival, victimization, heroism, and opportunism. Her multifaceted portrait defies a simple appropriation by the Left or the Right and makes us more keenly aware of the difficult negotiations the French are still making with their nation's collaborationist past. Unlike France's patron saint, Chabrol's protagonist is more a symbol for reflection than for celebration.[36]

Melanie Hawthorne and
Richard J. Golsan

Righting Gendered Writing:
A Bibliographic Essay

In 1992, with great fanfare, Editions Gallimard published its massive three-volume *Histoire des droites en France*. A history of the reaction in France from the Revolution to the present, the series offered an apparently exhaustive study of right-wing ideologies, political parties and movements, cultural and religious attitudes, myths and symbols, and sociological data. The three volumes together constituted more than twenty-five hundred pages, and the respective titles of the three books—*Politique, Cultures*, and *Sensibilités*—suggested that no stone had remained unturned in an effort to understand the Right in all its ideological, political, and cultural manifestations in modern France.

And yet a perusal of the table of contents and many of the articles comprising the three volumes of the *Histoire des droites en France* confirms that scant attention at best is paid to the topic of gender. Little analysis is devoted, for example, to right-wing attitudes toward and representations of women, or to the role played by women in the long and complicated history of reactionary politics in postrevolutionary France. With the exception of a lengthy chapter devoted to "Jeanne d'Arc et la mémoire des droites" in the second volume, entitled *Cultures*, not a single chapter focuses exclusively on women, although their roles, or more accurately, the roles assigned them within the family and on the broader social and cultural scene, are mentioned in passing. But even here, discussions are occasionally woefully inadequate. In an otherwise excellent essay on right-wing attitudes toward universal suffrage, Odile Rudelle makes only the briefest reference to Charles de Gaulle's April 1944 ordinance including women in the democratic process. Rudelle notes simply: "at last women had the right to vote" (3:298). The increase in the size of the electorate from ten million to twenty-five million voters seems to deserve no further attention or analysis.

If the *Histoire des droites en France* downplays and perhaps even marginalizes gender issues in its analysis of the Right in France, what of other studies dealing with the issue in broad as well as more specific terms? There is certainly no lack of scholarly as well as public attention given to the Right and above all the extreme Right in contemporary France, especially given the resurgence of the latter as evidenced in the Front National's electoral successes and the nation's obsessive preoccupation with the Vichy years. Books on the extreme Right and Vichy continue to pour out, but they, too, generally ignore gender issues or treat them only as a very secondary concern. For example, following Gallimard's publication of its *Histoire des droites en France*, the Editions du Seuil followed in the next year (1993) with two books on the extreme Right in modern France, Michel Winock's *Histoire de l'extrême droite en France* and Pierre Birnbaum's *La France au Français: Histoire des haines nationalistes*, both in the prestigious *XX Siècle* series. While dealing with topics as diverse as Edouard Drumont's *La France juive*, Vichy's biological racist Georges Montandon, the Dreyfus Affair, Boulangism, the National Front, and so on, no essay or chapter in either book deals explicitly or exclusively with women, gender attitudes, or the like. Similar observations hold true for major recent works on the Vichy regime. In *Vichy et les Français*, a massive collection of essays dealing with virtually every aspect of Vichy's domestic political, cultural, and social agenda, only two out of some fifty-five essays deal with women. In Philippe Burrin's highly praised 1995 history of the Vichy years, *La France à l'heure allemande*, a volume of over five hundred pages, not a single chapter is devoted to women and their role and representation in Pétain's National Revolution.

Many other examples of what might best be described as scholarly negligence could be cited,[1] but the additional evidence would only confirm what is already clear: in discussions of the Right in all its redactions in modern France, the issue of gender has been largely relegated to the margins. The role of women in right-wing ideologies, their involvements in right-wing politics and cultural practices, and their representations in right-wing iconography have been treated in a minor key by historians and political scientists as well as literary and film critics.[2] The same can be said, of course, of gays and lesbians.

Work combining right-wing ideology and gender has been carried out in contexts other than France, however, and the results have been impressive. Because of Germany's dominant historical role, much of the work relating gender to right-wing thought has been done in this field. The pioneering essays collected in *When Biology Became Destiny* (1984), for example, examine a number of ways in which Nazi policy sometimes embraced contradictions, coopted feminism, and appealed to women. Policies rewarding motherhood and giving women access to birth control could exist alongside forced sterilization in the Nazi eugenics program. Far from being a contradiction, these two stances represented the two kinds of women admitted by the fascist state: the idealized and the abjected. Reproductive issues are also the object of study in *Maternity and Gender Policies* edited by Gisela Bock and Pat Thane (1991), in Cornelie Usborne's *The Politics of the Body in Weimar Germany* (1992), and Atina Grossman's *Reforming Sex* (1995). Claudia Koonz expands on Jill Stephenson's pioneering surveys such as *Women in Nazi Society* (1975) and *The Nazi Organisation of Women* (1981) in her important 1987 study, *Mothers in the Fatherland*, aimed at the general reader. More recently (1993), in her collection of interviews *Frauen*, Alison Owings has challenged the long-held assumption that because women did not officially serve on the frontlines of battle, their experiences of World War II were not worth recording. Women's experiences on the home front not only have their role to play in the dissemination and perpetuation of right-wing ideology, but some of Owings's findings also illustrate how resistant ideology can be when the truth clashes with dogma. Nancy Reagin's *A German Women's Movement* examines the role of women over several decades in one provincial center (Hanover) in order to understand in greater detail why women found national socialism appealing.[3] Needless to say, when we generalize from her findings, it becomes clear that the attraction of right-wing ideology is far from being confined to the remote past of one distant town in one country's provinces.

In addition to historical studies, cultural studies have yielded insights into the role of gender in the Weimar and Nazi periods. Linda Mizejewski's study *Divine Decadence* focuses on Sally Bowles as recreated by Christopher Isherwood and made famous in the film *Cabaret*, while Maria Tatar's *Lustmord* examines the theme of sexual murder in Weimar film and literature, showing the formation of patterns of misogyny that Klaus Theweleit has identified as characteristic of fascist thinking in the years that marked the Nazi rise to power.

Germany is not the only national context in which the role of gender in right-wing thought has been addressed. Victoria de Grazia has studied (to use the title of her book) "how fascism ruled women," arguing that Italian fascism "nationalized" women as though they were just another natural resource. She begins her work by showing how the neglect of women's issues on the part of preceding liberal governments made it easy for fascism to "seduce" and co-opt women by seeming to pay attention to their demands for civic rights, a reminder that the Left neglects women at its peril. Karen Pinkus's study of advertisement in Italy in the 1930s, *Bodily Regimes*, examines various representations of the fascist body, in particular the way fascist advertising covers the body in protective "armor," causing the body (and its gender) to disappear, and splitting the male subject into a feminized interior and male exterior. Work addressing the Italian context continues to appear, and recent publications include Perry Willson's *The Clockwork Factory* (1993) and Robin Pickering-Iazzi's *Mothers of Invention* (1996). Cinzia Sartini Blum's study of Marinetti, *The Other Modernism*, looks at the connection between gender, right-wing ideology, and literature.

There have also been studies of women's participation in right-wing movements in the United States. In *Women of the Klan*, Kathleen Blee studies women's participation in the Ku Klux Klan in the 1920s, focusing especially on the connection between racism and gender, while more recently, Glen Jeansonne's *Women of the Far Right* shows how certain women used the rhetoric of women's pacifism to promote a reactionary, isolationist, and anticommunist agenda during World War II.

The role of gender in recent French history has not escaped attention altogether, but it has tended to focus on the Left, rather than on the Right. The role of women in the Resistance, for example, has received increasingly extensive treatment. The history of the Resistance during the German Occupation was begun even before the war was over, but it was not until the 1975 conference organized at the Sorbonne by the Union des Femmes Françaises that women's contributions to the Resistance effort began to be addressed explicitly. Many women came forward at the conference and spoke of their experiences, and the conference proceedings were published in 1977, leading to a flood of first-hand accounts as well as historical surveys. Since then, the topic of women in the Resistance has continued to mobilize attention and to be a prominent topic in World War II French history.[4] Numerous autobiographies of women who participated in and organized resistance work have been published, and works such as Claire Chevrillon's *Code Name Christiane Clouet* (1995) continue to appear. These primary materials are particularly popular because of their human interest and accessibility, especially for Americans "fascinated by fascism." In addition, the recent fiftieth anniversary celebration of the D-Day landings has stimulated the interest of a new generation and revived the interest of a public glad to seize on a narrative of the unambiguous victory of good over evil. As a result, such primary sources are often readily available in translation (unlike some of the more scholarly studies). One such recent work of autobiography, Lucie Aubrac's *Outwitting the Gestapo*, was picked up as a selection by several national book clubs when it was published in the United States in 1993.

There are also works devoted entirely to women's roles in the Resistance, such as Margaret Rossiter's *Women in the Resistance*, as well as studies in which the focus has been expanded to include not only women in the Resistance but women's experiences of the war in general, such as Celia Bertin's *Femmes sous l'Occupation.*[5] Yet paradoxically this focus on women as active participants in the Resistance movement has in some ways diverted attention from larger questions of gender and its relation to ideology. Thus, in one of the most recent and important works, *Sisters in the Resistance* (1995), Margaret Collins Weitz attempts to offer analytical rather than merely anecdotal insight into women's roles. But while Weitz acknowledges that "The role of gender in assessments of collaboration merits attention" (268), an exhaustive treatment of right-wing women is beyond the scope of her book and she devotes only one chapter to all the phenomena of "collaboration."

In addition to documenting the roles women have historically played, the question of gender can be examined at a more theoretical level and in ways that interrogate masculinity as well as femininity, sexuality as well as sex roles. Such are the implications of studies such as Theweleit's two-volume undertaking, *Male Fantasies*. While there have been important contributions to this area in French studies, most notably Alice Kaplan's *Reproductions of Banality* and Mary Louise Roberts's *Civilization Without Sexes*, the topic is far from exhausted.

In addition to understanding masculinity as a manifestation of gender ideology that is every bit as important as femininity, German studies have gone a step further in bringing out another aspect of the sex/gender system by examining the intersections of sexual expression and fascism. This aspect was already implicit in the work of historians focusing on reproductive policies (such as abortion and forced sterilization), but a new wave of autobiography and biography has opened up a new area of study: reactionary politics and sexual expression, fascism and homosexuality.

Until recently, the issue of Nazi homophobia was seldom discussed in studies of Nazism, the Third Reich, World War II, or camp survivor literature. Richard Plant, one of the foremost authorities on the subject and author of *The Pink Triangle*, notes the complete absence of the topic in such classic works as Shirer's *Rise and Fall of the Third Reich*, despite widespread knowledge of Himmler's obsession with the extermination of homosexuals. Plant concludes, "There is simply no excuse for the widespread silence on what was clearly an important aspect of Nazi ideology and action" (18).

Excuses or not, little attention was paid to the topic of the persecution of gays under the Third Reich until the 1970s, when the first full-length autobiographical account of a gay concentration camp survivor was published, thereby paving the way for others (just as the 1975 conference had done for women in the French Resistance). Heinz Heger's *Männer mit dem rosa Winkel* was published in Germany in 1972 (in translation, it was published in the United States as *The Men with the Pink Triangle* in 1980).

Heger's book broke a long silence. Still today, few people—men or women—have told their story. Although an estimated ten to fifteen thousand men wore the pink triangle, the Nazi code for (male) homosexuals, Klaus Müller, a consultant for the Holocaust Memorial Museum in Washington, D.C., and author of the Introduction to the 1994 edition of the translation of

Heger's book, notes that "not more than fifteen gay Holocaust survivors have spoken of their experiences, and many of them have asked for anonymity" (13). In part this is because, unlike other Holocaust survivors, homosexuals were not considered to have been wrongly imprisoned. Men such as Karl Gorath who sought the same compensation as other victims of the Nazis after World War II were denied reparations. (The courts argued that prejudice against gays existed before the Nazis came to power, and therefore their treatment was not the result of specifically Nazi persecution.) Indeed, the Nazis' antihomosexuality legislation remained in effect until 1969 (after being upheld by a supreme court decision in 1957), and men such as Gorath, after having survived the concentration camps, continued to serve prison sentences.[6]

Heger's book was followed by Richard Plant's *The Pink Triangle* (1986), which attempts a comprehensive history, and more recently by *The Hidden Holocaust* (1995), in which Günter Grau makes available numerous important source documents, complementing the effort begun in *The Weimar Republic Sourcebook* (1994).

But Nazi antihomosexuality laws (enacted in 1935 and known as "Paragraph 175") applied only to men, thus the history of sexual expression and its repression in the Third Reich looks significantly different for men and for women. Nazi policy, with its insistence on racial eugenics, saw male and female homosexuality differently. Nazi policy on sexuality was as contradictory as on other issues: just as abortion was considered a crime against the state for Aryan women but encouraged for non-Aryans, (male) homosexuality was only a problem insofar as it was perceived to interfere with the reproductive duties of the Aryan man and therefore to threaten the survival of the race. Thus Aryan men came in for greater scrutiny and punishment than non-Aryans. A woman's sexual orientation was immaterial: it did not interefere with reproduction, so it was thought, and was therefore irrelevant. Consequently, female homosexuality was not strictly illegal, and lesbians were not treated the same way as gay men by Nazi policy. According to Klaus Müller, there are "only a few documented cases of lesbians being incarcerated in the concentration camps solely because of their sexual orientation" (Introduction, 11).

If the history of gay men is largely untold, the history of lesbians is virtually unknown, though it has begun to emerge thanks largely to the work of Claudia Schoppmann. In addition to her untranslated work, the recent publication of her book *Days of Masquerade* (1996) makes available through interviews the day-to-day life of lesbians during the Third Reich. Schoppmann's overview is given depth by another recent publication, *Aimée and Jaguar* (1995), the story of Elisabeth (Lilly) Wust as told to journalist Erica Fischer. A Nazi officer's wife and mother of four, Lilly (Aimée) met Felice Schragenheim (Jaguar), an "underground" Jew, in Berlin in 1942. They fell in love, but Felice was arrested on August 21, 1944, and deported first to Theresienstadt and subsequently to Bergen-Belsen, where she died in 1945. It is clear, however, that Felice was arrested because she was Jewish, not because of her sexuality. Since her testimony has been lost to history, the book tells very little about the gay subculture in prewar Berlin (in which Felice seems to have taken an active role), nor can it tell about her observations of life as a lesbian in the camps, except through hints in her surviving letters. The work of Schoppmann and others shows that to the extent that "Aryan" women were willing to conform to Nazi ideology that viewed women as a source of reproductive labor, they could avoid punishement, but that lesbians suffered the same destruction of their culture as gay men.

While official Nazi policy punished homosexuality for Aryan men, however, others have noted the homosociality and homoeroticism fostered by official Nazi culture. As Richard Plant notes, the accusation of "degenerate" sexuality was also used against the Nazis by their enemies who attempted to suggest that it was they who were "simply homosexual perverts" (Plant, 16). Until the purge of the notoriously homosexual Roehm, Hitler's second-in-command and leader of the SA, on the "night of the long knives" (June 28, 1934), the Nazi organization could be seen as condoning male homosexuality. Even after this purge, the Nazi movement was considered by some to promote male homosociality and a form of male bonding that overlapped with homosexuality through its promotion of physical fitness and hypermasculinity. Organizations such as the Hitler Youth and the Wandervögel offered a sexually ambiguous model for male youth. The translation and republication of works documenting these experiences testify to the renewed interest in this aspect of Nazi culture. Daniel Guérin's *The Brown Plague* (published in translation in 1994), for example, makes available his first-hand experiences with such groups in the years of Hitler's rise to power.

Guérin went on to become a gay activist in France, but it was another generation of activists who would address the question of homosexuality during the war years in France. Heger's book again paved the way here, prompting Pierre Seel to speak out for the first time about his own experiences, recorded in *Moi, Pierre Seel* (1994; translation 1995), and usefully annotated by Jean Le Bitoux. In addition to documenting the deportation of gay men (as an Alsatian, Seel was considered "German" by the Nazis and therefore his sexuality was a matter of state concern), Seel's memoirs reveal that French police kept illegal files on homosexuals that, when seized by the Nazis, enabled them to identify their targets. Seel shows the role of the French government (and not just the reactionary Vichy government) in failing to protect its citizens from the Germans and in making the Germans' job easier. In addition, the government had violated the civil rights of its citizens by keeping secret files at a time when homosexuality was not a crime. To date, the experience of French lesbians has been treated only in works of fiction by novelists such as Hélène de Montferrand.

There remain, then, many avenues to explore in order to gain a deeper understanding of the role of gender in right-wing politics in France. Other national cultures have followed certain paths in bringing out the ways gender inflected their respective right-wing culture(s). Time will tell if France will prove to be similar or different to these models.

Notes

Introduction

1. This question was originally formulated as "Can Fascism Be Assigned *a* Sexual Identity?" by David Carroll in *French Literary Fascism: Nationalism, Anti-Semitism, and the Ideology of Culture* (Princeton: Princeton University Press, 1995), 147.
2. Ibid., 148.
3. Zeev Sternhell, Mario Sznajder, and Maia Asheri, *The Birth of Fascist Ideology* (Princeton: Princeton University Press, 1994), 4.
4. Roger Griffin, *The Nature of Fascism* (London: Routledge, 1993), xi.
5. In his *A History of Fascism, 1919–1945* (Madison: University of Wisconsin Press, 1995), Stanley Payne attempts to bridge the gap in stating: "Fascist ideas have often been said to stem from opposition of the Enlightenment or the 'ideas of 1789,' when in fact they were a direct by-product of aspects of the Enlightenment, derived specifically from the modern, secular, Promethean concepts of the Eighteenth century. The essential divergence of fascist ideas from certain aspects of modern culture lay more precisely in the fascist rejection of rationalism, materialism, and egalitarianism—replaced by philosophical vitalism and idealism and the metaphysics of the will, all of which are also intrinsically modern" (8).
6. Pierre Milza and Serge Berstein, *Dictionnaire historique des fascismes et du nazisme* (Brussels: Editions Complexe, 1992), 7.
7. Robert Soucy, *French Fascism: The Second Wave, 1933–1939* (New Haven: Yale University Press, 1995), 24.
8. Robert Musil, "Ruminations of a Slow-witted Mind," *Critical Inquiry* 17.1 (Autumn 1990): 52. Many scholars now would of course disagree with Musil's claims, since the intellectual terrain for Nazism was prepared by, among others, Ernst Jünger, Carl Schmitt, and, arguably, Martin Heidegger, as well as others.
9. Along these lines, see especially Jeffrey Schnapp, "Epic Demonstrations: Fascist Modernity and the 1932 Exhibition of the Fascist Revolution," in *Fascism, Aesthetics, and Culture*, ed. Richard J. Golsan (Hanover, N.H.: University Press of New England, 1992), 1–37.
10. Sternhell et al., 3.
11. We refer here especially to the work of the American Robert Soucy and the Israeli Zeev Sternhell. In Sternhell's case, his charge in *Ni Droite ni gauche: L'idéologie fasciste en France* (Paris: Seuil, 1983) that the political ideas of Bertrand de Jouvenel were essentially fascist landed him in court in 1983. Sternhell was found guilty of defamation. For a discussion of the trial and its implications, see Robert Wohl, "French Fascism, Both Right and Left: Reflections on the Sternhell Controversy," *Journal of Modern History* 63 (March 1991): 91–98.
12. In his classic study of the Vichy regime, *Vichy France: Old Guard and New Order, 1940–1944* (New York: Columbia University Press, 1982), Robert Paxton argues

that the regime was not fascist, since it did not constitute "a mass anti-liberal, anti-communist movement, radical in its willingness to employ force and in its contempt for upper-class values of the time, sharply distinct not only from its enemies on the left but also from its rivals on the right . . ." (229). Paxton continues: "The Vichy National Revolution clearly occupied a place on such a spectrum nearer the conservative than the fascist end. Pétain felt himself closer to Franco and Salazar than to Hitler" (230). As their essays indicate, a number of the contributors to the present volume disagree with this assessment.

13. For a discussion of the term "true France" as it is used here, see Herman Lebovics, *True France: The Wars over Cultural Identity, 1900–1945* (Ithaca: Cornell University Press, 1992).

14. Bernard-Henri Lévy, *L'Idéologie française* (Paris: Grasset, 1981).

15. In July 1995, President Jacques Chirac formally acknowledged French culpability in and complicity with the Nazi Final Solution. Chirac's gesture initially cooled passions stirred by recent events such as the trial of Paul Touvier and revelations concerning François Mitterrand's Vichy past and postwar friendship with the former head of Vichy police, René Bousquet. But the "Vichy Syndrome," as Henry Rousso has so aptly labeled it, could erupt again at any time. For example, the recent court hearings in Bordeaux over whether or not to try the former Gaullist Minister Maurice Papon for crimes against humanity for actions committed during the Occupation made front-page news throughout France. If Papon is actually tried, the event will almost certainly stir as much controversy as the trial of Paul Touvier.

16. See Jacques Julliard, *Ce Fascisme qui vient . . .* (Paris: Seuil, 1994).

17. For a translation of the petition and a discussion of the issues at stake, see the special issue "The French New Right: New Right—New Left—New Paradigm," *Telos* 98–99 (Fall 1993–Winter 1994).

18. Along these lines, see Carroll's assessment of Adorno's and Sartre's texts on the subject in *French Literary Fascism*, 147–52.

19. Sartre implies that collaborationism was sexually as well as politically "suspect" because of the prevalence of homosexual collaborationists among the Parisian intelligentsia, especially Robert Brasillach. Sartre's linkage of homosexuality and collaborationism has been taken up subsequently by historians as well as novelists dealing with the period, most notably the British historian Richard Cobb in *French and Germans, Germans and French* and the novelists Patrick Modiano in *Les Boulevards de ceinture* and Michel del Castillo in *Le Démon de l'oubli*.

20. For a brief discussion of the impact of the application of feminist perspectives and gender issues to the study of fascism and especially Nazism, see Tim Mason, "Whatever Happened to Fascism?" included as an appendix in *Reevaluating the Third Reich*, ed. Thomas Childers and Jane Caplan (New York: Holmes and Meier, 1993), 256–57.

21. For a discussion of what has appeared on the subject of women and Vichy, and French fascism more generally, see the bibliographical essay at the end of this volume.

22. Carroll, 155.

23. Judith Butler, *Gender Trouble: Feminism and the Subversion of Identity* (New York: Routledge, 1990), 6.

24. Ibid., 1.
25. Ibid., viii.
26. One could argue that the so-called "White Nurse" that Theweleit describes in volume 1 of *Male Fantasies* constitutes an authentic "fascist woman," but there are difficulties with this perspective. First, the White Nurse is hardly a woman in any real sexual sense, since she manifests no sex drive but instead fills the role of an idealized mother who comforts the dying and on occasion needs protection from her "warrior son." Moreover, she rarely if ever has a sexual partner, since her husband is either dead or removed from her for other reasons. Nevertheless, in having a spouse she is no longer available to others, even if they come to desire her. But the biggest obstacle to casting the White Nurse in the role of authentic fascist woman is that she is primarily the figment of the imagination of the fascist warrior: she is a literary construct that Theweleit detects and analyzes in diaries and journals of the Freikorps members he studies. See *Male Fantasies*, 1: 90–100.
27. *Male Fantasies*, 2: 323. Elsewhere Theweleit suggests that men desire other men because women are by definition excluded from what he defines as "the pleasure-intensities of public activity" and are therefore inherently less appealing. Men are more "experienced," they nurture "dreams of a life of heroes, of strength and *esprit*, of rising to power and glory," and the richness of these dreams and ambitions contributes to their desirability. For many men, Theweleit continues, women are simply incapable of realizing such high aspirations. See *Male Fantasies*, 2: 332–33.
28. Ibid, 319–20.
29. Carroll, 154.
30. In their "Foreword" to the second volume of *Male Fantasies*, Anson Rabinbach and Jessica Benjamin also stress the extent to which Theweleit's approach derives from the perspective of the post-1968 German Left. In their view, this imposes certain limits on his theories. For a discussion of this perspective, see *Male Fantasies,* vol. 2, *Male Bodies: Psychoanalyzing the White Terror* (Minneapolis: University of Minnesota Press, 1989), x.
31. Theweleit's more theoretical approach to links between fascism, gender, and sexuality was accompanied in the late 1980s and early 1990s by the publication of influential and comprehensive historical studies of women in Nazi Germany and fascist Italy. These include Claudia Koonz's *Mothers in the Fatherland* (New York: St. Martin's Press, 1987) and Victoria de Grazia's *How Fascism Ruled Women: Italy, 1922–1945* (Berkeley and Los Angeles: University of California Press, 1992). Like Theweleit's study, these works have also contributed to a shift in the debate over fascism to include more centrally issues of gender and sexuality.
32. Payne, 7.
33. It should be noted, however, that, as Robert Soucy has pointed out recently, a number of fascist movements in the thirties, including the Croix de Feu, advocated the political enfranchisement of women by giving them the vote. Their reason for advocating this policy, however, had nothing to do with the liberation of women in social terms. The Croix de Feu leadership simply assumed that women in their roles as housewives and mothers would vote conservatively for the Catholic Right. See Soucy, 163.

34. Michèle Bordeaux, "Femmes hors d'Etat Français, 1940–1945," in *Femmes et fascismes*, ed. Rita Thalmann (Paris: Tierce, 1986), 138.
35. Ibid.
36. Rabinbach and Benjamin, xviii.
37. Quoted in Pierre Péan, *Une Jeunesse française: François Mitterrand, 1934–1937* (Paris: Fayard, 1994), 198.
38. See William R. Tucker, *The Fascist Ego: A Political Biography of Robert Brasillach* (Berkeley and Los Angeles: University of California Press, 1975), 258–60.
39. Philippe Burrin, "La France et le fascisme," *Le Débat* 32 (1984): 65.
40. De Grazia, 2.
41. Miranda Pollard, "La Politique du travail féminin," in *Vichy et les Français*, ed. Jean-Pierre Azéma and François Bédarida (Paris: Fayard, 1992), 245.
42. This being said, it should nonetheless be noted that misogyny and antifeminism did not, generally speaking, play a central and explicit role in left-wing ideologies as they did in fascist ideology.

Female Anti-Semitism during the Dreyfus Affair

1. For a discussion of these questions as they relate to fascism, see David Carroll, *French Literary Fascism: Nationalism, Anti-Semitism, and the Ideology of Culture* (Princeton: Princeton University Press, 1995), 147–70.
2. Sibylle-Gabrielle Marie-Antoinette de Riquetti de Mirabeau, comtesse de Martel de Janville, 1849–1932. On Gyp, see Willa Z. Silverman, *The Notorious Life of Gyp: Right-Wing Anarchist in Fin-de-Siècle France* (New York: Oxford University Press, 1995).
3. Stephen Wilson, *Ideology and Experience: Antisemitism in France at the Time of the Dreyfus Affair* (Rutherford, N.J.: Fairleigh Dickinson University Press, 1982), 596.
4. See Julie Sabiani, "Féminisme et Dreyfusisme," in *Les Ecrivains et l'Affaire Dreyfus*, ed. Géraldi Leroy (Mayenne: Presses Universitaires de France, 1983), 199–206.
5. Other notable female *antidreyfusardes* include Marie Maugeret, Marie Duclos, Marie-Anne de Bouet, and the duchesse d'Uzès.
6. For a transcript of Gyp's deposition, see "La Haute Cour," *L'Eclair*, 17 Dec. 1899.
7. Léon Blum, *Souvenirs sur l'Affaire* (Paris: Gallimard, 1982), 68. All translations are the author's unless otherwise indicated.
8. Charles Maurras, "Les Images puissantes: Un ménage dernier cri," *La Gazette de France*, 9 Aug. 1903: 1–2.
9. Philippe Barrès, "Gyp, ou la féerie," *Les Nouvelles littéraires*, 9 July 1932: 2.
10. Zeev Sternhell, *La Droite révolutionnaire, 1885–1914: Les origines françaises du fascisme* (Paris: Seuil, 1978). Several historians, and Sternhell most insistently, view this radical Right, especially in its French variety, as a precursor of a fascist Right that would emerge after World War I. See, for example, Zeev Sternhell, *Ni Droite, ni gauche: L'idéologie fasciste en France* (Paris: Seuil, 1983), Introduction, pp. 15–43, and George Mosse, *Toward the Final Solution: A History of European*

Racism (New York: Harper Colophon, 1980), ch. 10, pp. 150–68. Other historians, however, caution against assimilating the pre- and postwar periods and note that the type of virulent anti-Semitism espoused by Gyp, for example, was not always an essential element of fascism. See Pierre Birnbaum, *Un Mythe politique: La 'république juive' de Léon Blum à Mendès France* (Paris: Fayard, 1988), Introduction, pp. 7–39.

11. Michel Winock, *Edouard Drumont et Cie: Antisémitisme et fascisme en France* (Paris: Seuil, 1982), 38.

12. Gyp, letter to Henri Rochefort, [1894], Naf 16802, #120–23, Bibliothèque Nationale, Paris (henceforth BN).

13. Gyp, *Souvenirs d'une petite fille*, vol. 2 (Paris: Calmann-Lévy, 1928), 25; vol. 1 (Paris: Calmann-Lévy, 1927), 48. Ellipses in original.

14. This regret is a recurrent theme in Gyp's writings. In her *Souvenirs*, for instance, she recreated a dialogue between Colonel de Gonneville (her grandfather) and Marshal Canrobert, in which the colonel expresses his dismay about the girl's gender: "I understood that, on the way, Grandfather and he had spoken about the fact that I was not a boy! . . . I'm often reproached for not being a boy! . . . And no one, of course, regrets it as much as me! . . ." *Souvenirs*, vol. 1, 113. Ellipses in original.

15. François Bournand, *Les Juifs et nos contemporains: L'antisémitisme et la question juive* (Paris: Pierret, [1898]), 134.

16. Quoted in Bournand, 136.

17. Quoted in Bounand, 135.

18. Léon Blum identifies the successes of a handful of bourgeois Jews—"the indiscreet intrusion of nouveau riche Jews or the penetration, deemed too rapid, of Jewish intellectuals"—as one of the primary causes of fin-de-siècle anti-Semitism. Blum, 68.

19. Rachilde, rev. of *Israël*, by Gyp, *Le Mercure de France* 16 (Apr.–June 1898): 231.

20. Gyp, letter to Georges Calmann, 3 Aug. 1909, Calmann-Lévy Archives (henceforth CL), Paris.

21. Gyp, letter to [?] Calmann-Lévy, 28 July 1909, CL.

22. Gyp, *Souvenirs*, vol. 1, 213. Ellipses in original.

23. On the emergence of the "New Woman" at the fin de siècle and the resulting antifemale backlash and "cult of masculinity," see Michelle Perrot, "The New Eve and the Old Adam: Changes in French Women's Condition at the Turn of the Century," in *Behind the Lines: Gender and the Two World Wars*, ed. Margaret R. Higonnet, Jane Jenson, Sonya Michel, and Margaret Collins Weitz (New Haven: Yale University Press, 1987), 51–60; and Debora Silverman, *Art Nouveau in Fin-de-Siecle France: Politics, Psychology and Style* (Berkeley and Los Angeles: University of California Press, 1989).

24. Gyp, letter to Ludovic Halévy, 10 Mar. 1895, MS 4485, #414, Institut de France, Paris.

25. Gyp, letter to Paul Déroulède, [Aug. 1900?], 401AP9, #7548, Archives Nationales, Paris.

26. Wilson, 597. The double rejection of woman and the Jew as physically and morally inferior beings—a leitmotif of the fin de siècle—was most clearly developed during that period in the influential works of Otto Weininger, the Viennese theorist

who wrote in *Sex and Character* (1903): "Whoever has thought about woman and the Jews at the same time will have been able to observe without surprise to what extent the Jew is imbued with this femininity which is nothing other than the negation of all masculine qualities." Weininger's obsessive anti-Semitism and misogyny, remarks Christine Buci-Glucksman, were symptomatic of "his own self-hatred as a converted Jew, his own anguish about a feminized sexuality." Christine Buci-Glucksman, "Culture de la crise et mythes du féminin: Weininger et les figures de l'Autre," in Rita Thalmann, ed., *Femmes et fascismes* (Paris: Tierce, 1986), 21. On Weininger, see Jacques Le Rider, *Le Cas Otto Weininger: Racines de l'antiféminisme et de l'antisémitisme* (Paris: Presses Universitaires de France, 1982). To some analysts, the same repudiation of the feminine and the concomitant glorification of a "masculinist" discourse of violence, destruction, and self-denial, typifies fascism. This is the thesis, for example, of Klaus Theweleit's *Male Fantasies*, 2 vols., trans. Stephen Conway (vol. 1) and Erica Carter and Chris Turner (vol. 2) (Minneapolis: University of Minnesota Press, 1987 and 1989). On the connection between antifeminism and fascism in the French case, see, for example, Richard Golsan, "Henry de Montherlant: Itinerary of an Ambivalent Fascist," in *Fascism, Aesthetics, and Culture,* ed. Richard Golsan (Hanover, N.H.: University Press of New England, 1992), 143–63.

27. Quoted and translated in Wilson, 154. Wilson notes that an unusually high proportion (10 percent) of the contributors to this fund were women.

28. Jean-Paul Sartre, *Réflexions sur la question juive* (Paris: Gallimard, 1954), 23.

29. Gyp, *Le Friquet* (Paris: Flammarion, 1901), 131.

30. Gyp/Bob, "Histoire de la Troisième République," *Le Rire,* 14 Nov. 1896.

31. See Wilson, 154–55, and, on the castration complex as the root of anti-Semitism (in Freud's view), 164. Wilson notes that this "attribution of special and frightening sexual power to the Jew" (155) was prevalent among such subscribers to the Monument Henry as the one who described herself as a "working girl seduced by her Jewish employer," (154) and, more recently, in the so-called "rumor of Orléans" of the late 1960s, which held that Jews were abducting young girls from the dressing rooms of boutiques into the white slave trade. See also, on the Jew as murderer and predator, Sander Gilman, *The Jew's Body* (New York: Routledge, 1991), 104–27 and passim.

32. Sartre, 54.

33. Wilson discusses sexual anti-Semitism as an "externalization and projection of a sexuality that is for some reason repressed; and the sexual mode in each case expresses sentiments that are profoundly ambiguous, and, for that reason, extremely powerful" (585). See also Birnbaum, *Un Mythe politique,* 196–236.

34. Edmond and Jules de Goncourt, *Journal: Mémoires de la vie littéraire,* vol. 3 (1887–1896), ed. Robert Ricatte (Paris: Laffont, 1989), 930 and 1204.

35. Gyp, letter to Maurice Barrès, June 1923, Fonds Barrès, BN.

36. George Mosse, *Nationalism and Sexuality: Respectability and Abnormal Sexuality in Modern Europe* (New York: Howard Fertig, 1985), 10.

37. See Erik Erickson's discussion of abstinence, nationalism, and anti-Semitism in the case of Hitler in *Childhood and Society* (New York: Norton, 1963), 342. See also Mosse, *Nationalism and Sexuality,* Introduction and discussions of Krafft-Ebing and Weininger.

38. Daniel Halévy, "Apologie pour notre passé," *Cahiers de la quinzaine*, Cahier 10, Series 11, Oct. 1907–Jan. 1910.

39. A pamphlet describing the outrageousness of this obese, hard-drinking delegate to the Estates General was entitled "Unheard-of Indecency of Vicomte de Mirabeau and Abbé Maury toward the Nation."

40. Eugénie Buffet, *Ma Vie—mes amours—mes aventures* (Paris: Figuière, 1930), 48.

41. René Dubreuil, "Le Procès Déroulède-Habert," *Le Siècle*, 1 June 1899.

42. Laurent Tailhade, "Lettre casquée—Sermo Galeatus—à Gyp—Comtesse de Mirabeau-Martel—Gyp," *L'Action*, 10 Dec. 1903.

43. Abel Hermant, "La Vie littéraire," *Le Temps*, 24 Sept. 1918.

44. Marc Angenot, *Ce que l'on dit des Juifs en 1889: Antisémitisme et discours social* (Saint-Denis: Presses Universitaires de Vincennes, 1989), 132.

45. I am referring, for example, to Sydney Vigneaux's *Le Baron Jehovah* (1886), Edmond Haraucourt's *Shylock* (1889), Félicien Champsaur's *La Gomme* (1889), Paul Adam's *L'Essence du soleil: Roman social sur l'or des juifs* (1890); George Ohnet's *Nemrod et Cie* (1892), Paul Bourget's *Cosmopolis* (1893), Eugène Melchior de Vogüé's *Les Morts qui parlent* (1899), etc.

46. Quoted in Michel Missoffe, *Gyp et ses amis* (Paris: Flammarion, 1932), 64.

47. *Les Gens chics* (Paris: Charpentier et Fasquelle 1895), *Ohé! les dirigeants!* (Paris: Chailley, 1896), *Le Baron Sinaï* (Paris: Fasquelle, 1897), *En Balade* (Paris: Montgrédien, 1897), *Journal d'un grinchu* (Paris: Flammarion, 1898), *Les Cayenne de Rio* (Paris: Flammarion, 1899), *Les Izolâtres* (Paris: Juven, 1899), *Les Femmes du colonel* (Paris: Flammarion, 1899).

48. On the Jewish character and anti-Semitism in French literature through the period of the Dreyfus Affair, see Robert Byrnes, *Antisemitism in Modern France*, vol. 1 (New Brunswick, N.J.: Rutgers University Press, 1950), 104–10; Moses Debré, *The Image of the Jew in French Literature from 1800 to 1908*, trans. Gertrude Hirschler (New York: Ktav, 1970); Charles C. Lehrmann, *The Jewish Element in French Literature* (Rutherford, N.J.: Fairleigh Dickinson University Press, 1971); Béatrice Philippe, *Etre juif dans la société française* (Paris: Montalba, 1979) 206–17; Léon Poliakov, *Histoire de l'antisémitisme*, vol. 4 (Paris: Calmann-Lévy, 1977), 45–83; Earle Stanley Randall, *The Jewish Character in the French Novel* (Menasha, Wis.: Banta, 1941).

49. Rachilde, rev. of *Israël*, by Gyp.

50. Albert Keim, rev. of *Israël*, by Gyp, *La Cité d'art* 3 (Mar. 1898): 106.

51. Georges Sénéchal, rev. of *Israël*, by Gyp, *La Nouvelle Revue* 111. (3) (Mar.–Apr. 1898): 753–54.

52. Susan Rubin Suleiman, *Authoritarian Fictions: The Ideological Novel as a Literary Genre* (New York: Columbia University Press, 1983).

53. Fredric Jameson, *Fables of Aggression: Wyndham Lewis, The Modernist as Fascist* (Berkeley and Los Angeles: University of California Press, 1979), 27. On the use of metonymy and other forms of popular polemical rhetoric during the Dreyfus Affair, see Richard Griffiths, *The Use of Abuse: The Polemics of the Dreyfus Affair and Its Aftermath* (New York: Berg, 1991).

54. Gyp, *Souvenirs*, vol. 2, 309.

55. Albert Sonnenfeld, "The Poetics of Antisemitism," *Romanic Review* 76.1 (Jan. 1985): 77.

56. See Alice Yaeger Kaplan, *Reproductions of Banality: Fascism, Literature, and French Intellectual Life* (Minneapolis: University of Minnesota Press, 1986), 31–32.

57. Sonnenfeld, 79. Drumont dwells at some length on the Jews' perversion of language. For a discussion, see Gilman, 10–37; Sonnenfeld, 80; and Wilson, 607, 614 and passim.

58. Gyp, *Les Gens chics*, 74.

59. Ibid., 50.

60. Ibid., 25.

61. For more on Gyp as an anti-Semitic caricaturist, see Jacques Lethève, *La Caricature sous la IIIe République* (Paris: Armand Colin, 1986), 86–90; and Phillip Dennis Cate, "The Paris Cry: Graphic Arts and the Dreyfus Affair," in *The Dreyfus Affair: Art, Truth and Justice*, ed. Norman Kleeblatt (Berkeley and Los Angeles: University of California Press, 1987), 62–95.

62. Suleiman, 180–81.

63. Drumont harps on the theme of aristocratic decadence in *La France juive*, often drawing curious parallels between Jews and aristocrats, as in "the aristocrat's brain is, ordinarily, very feebly organized." Edouard Drumont, *La France juive*, vol. 2 (Paris: C. Marpon and E. Flammarion, 1886), 77.

64. Susan Suleiman, "Malraux's Women: A Re-Vision," in *Witnessing André Malraux: Visions and Re-visions,* ed. Brian Thompson and Carl Viggiani (Middletown, Conn.: Wesleyan University Press, 1984), 140–58.

65. Sheri Benstock notes that Stein, like Gyp, "saw herself playing roles traditionally assigned to men, adopting a male persona against the feminine weakness to which her womanhood apparently consigned her." *Women of the Left Bank: Paris 1900–1940* (Austin: University of Texas Press, 1986), 19.

(En)Gendering Fascism

1. David Carroll, *French Literary Fascism: Nationalism, Anti-Semitism, and the Ideology of Culture* (Princeton: Princeton University Press, 1995), 169.

2. See, for example, *Leni Riefenstahl: A Memoir* (New York: St. Martin's Press, 1993).

3. Claudia Koonz, *Mothers in the Fatherland: Women, the Family and Nazi Politics* (New York: St. Martin's Press, 1987).

4. See Philip V. Cannistraro and Brian R. Sullivan's *Il Duce's Other Woman* (New York: William Morrow, 1993).

5. Stanley Payne, *A History of Fascism, 1914–1945* (Madison: University of Wisconsin Press, 1995), 13.

6. Klaus Theweleit, *Male Fantasies*, vol. 1, *Women, Floods, Bodies, History* (Minneapolis: University of Minnesota Press, 1987), and Vol. 2, *Male Bodies: Psychoanalyzing the White Terror* (Minneapolis: University of Minnesota Press, 1989).

7. Theweleit's speculations are echoed in the work of theorists such as Roger Griffin, who, in his recent attempt to define fascism, suggests that it included a "radical misogyny or flight from the feminine, manifesting itself in a pathological fear of

being engulfed by anything in external reality associated with softness, with dissolution, or the uncontrollable." *The Nature of Facism* (London: Routledge, 1993), 198.

8. See the section entitled "Very Early History: The Woman from the Water" (1:288–94). Clarifying that he is not referring to a cultural or ideological perception, Theweleit writes: "In her impresive work *The Descent of Woman*, Elaine Morgan establishes a link between women and water that is anything but mytholgical" (1:288).

9. Minneapolis: The University of Minnesota Press, 1986. References to this work will be given in the text.

10. Judith Butler, *Gender Trouble: Feminism and the Subversion of Identity* (New York: Routledge, 1990), 16–17.

11. Nancy Chodorow, *The Reproduction of Mothering: Psychoanalysis and the Sociology of Gender* (Berkeley and Los Angeles: University of Califoria Press, 1978).

12. Referred to in connection with Theweleit's theory by Ehrenreich in the introduction to volume 1. See also Kaplan, *Reproductions of Banility*, 4–6 and 12.

13. See Alan Sinfield, *The Wilde Century: Effeminacy, Oscar Wilde and the Queer Movement* (New York: Columbia University Press, 1995).

14. I am not using the being/becoming opposition here in the same philosophical sense that Simone de Beauvoir uses it in her famous formulation of the difference between natural and socially constructed facts ("one is not born a woman"). Rather, I am making a distinction about what occurs in the process of social construction itself.

15. Sigmund Freud, "Fetishism," in *The Standard Edition of Complete Psychological Works of Sigmund Freud*, ed. James Strachey (London: Hogarth Press, 1953–74), vol. 21, 147–57.

16. For challenges to Freud and discussions of female fetishism, see Emily Apter, *Feminizing the Fetish: Psychoanalysis and Narrative Obsession in Turn-of-the-Century France* (Ithaca: Cornell University Press, 1991); Elizabeth Grosz, "Lesbian Fetishism?" in *Space, Time, and Perversion* (New York: Routledge, 1995), 141–54; Teresa de Lauretis, *The Practice of Love: Lesbian Sexuality and Perverse Desire* (Bloomington: Indiana University Press, 1994); Anne McClintock, "Psychoanalysis, Race and Female Fetishism," in *Imperial Leather: Race, Gender and Sexuality in the Colonial Contest* (New York: Routledge, 1995), 181–203; and Naomi Schor, *Bad Object Choices* (Durham: Duke University Press, 1995).

17. I am not suggesting that these characteristics are essentially male or grounded in biology, but that they are culturally defined as male. For example, "independence" might be a universal human characteristic, but in a certain historical moment it might be so strongly associated with the cultural definition of masculinity as to "masculinize" whatever context it appeared in. The fact that women displayed this characteristic didn't challenge the perception that it was a male trait or cause the trait to be redefined; rather, women who displayed independence were thought to have been masculinized.

18. See, for example, Bernard-Henry Lévy, *L'Idéologie française* (Paris: Grasset, 1981); Stanley Payne, *A History of Fascism, 1914–1945* (Madison: University of Wisconsin Press, 1995); Zeev Sternhell, *Ni Droite ni gauche: L'idéologie fasciste en France* (Paris: Seuil, 1983).

19. See also Daniel Goldhagen, *Hitler's Willing Executioners: Ordinary Germans and the Holocaust* (New York: Knopf, 1996), 45.

20. Benedict Anderson, *Imagined Communities: Reflections on the Origin and Spread of Nationalism*, revised ed. (London: Verso, 1991).

21. As Anne McClintock states: "All nationalisms are gendered, all are invented and all are dangerous (*Imperial Leather*, 352).

22. See Paul Lagarde, *La Nationalité française* (Paris: Dalloz, 1975), 169–76. In Britain, a similar asymmetry prevailed. The Naturalization Act of 1870 stated that "A woman shall be deemed to be a subject of the state of which her husband is for the time being a subject." Subsequent legislation added confusion without addressing the underlying inequality, which was only eliminated in the British Nationality Act of 1981, according to which no spouse of a British subject—man or woman—automatically acquires British citizenship. See Ann Dummett and Andrew Nicol, *Subjects, Citizens, Aliens and Others: Nationality and Immigration Law* (London: Weidenfeld and Nicolson, 1990).

23. *The Birth of Fascist Ideology*, 3.

24. See Willa Silverman's article in this volume on Gyp, whose life and career paralleled in so many ways that of her friend Rachilde.

25. *Pourquoi je ne suis pas féministe* (Paris: Editions de France, 1928).

26. See Robert Soucy, *Fascism in France: The Case of Maurice Barrès* (Berkeley and Los Angeles: University of California Press, 1972); Zeev Sternhell, *Maurice Barrès et le nationalisme français* (Paris: A. Colin, 1972); and David Carroll, *French Literary Fascism: Nationalism, Anti-Semitism, and the Ideology of Culture* (Princeton: Princeton University Press, 1995).

27. Rachilde recounts their meeting in *Portraits d'hommes* (Paris: Mornay, 1929).

28. The preface was first published in the 1889 Brossier edition and has been reprinted in the 1977 Flammarion edition.

29. See Marguerite Bonnet, ed., *L'Affaire Barrès* (Paris: Corti, 1987).

30. The letter is in The Harry Ransom Humanities Research Center, the University of Texas at Austin.

31. *Les Hors-Nature* initially appeared serially in the *Mercure de France* under the title *Les Factices* from December 1896 to March 1897, before being published as a book by Mercure de France in 1897. The short story "Les Vendanges de Sodome" was originally published in the *Mercure de France* in March 1893 and was subsequently reprinted as part of the collection *Le Démon de l'absurde* (1894). Marinetti praised the entire collection, but also singled out this story for mention.

32. For interpretations of the gender politics of *Mafarka*, see Alice Kaplan, *Reproductions of Banality*; Karen Pinkus, *Bodily Regimes: Italian Advertising under Fascism* (Minneapolis: University of Minnesota Press, 1995); Cinzia Sartini Blum, *The Other Modernism: F. T. Marinetti's Futurist Fiction of Power* (Berkeley and Los Angeles: University of California Press, 1996).

33. The rediscovery of this document was made by Zeev Sternhell and published in *La Droite révolutionnaire, 1885–1914: Les origines françaises du fascisme* (Paris: Seuil, 1978). The event is highlighted in Alice Kaplan's "Fascism: Etymologies and Political Usage," the introductory section of *Reproductions of Banality* (xxvii–xxix).

34. All quotations from "Les Vendanges de Sodome" refer to *Le Démon de l'absurde* (Paris: Mercure de France, 1894). A translation by Brian Stableford entitled "The Grape-Gatherers of Sodom" appeared in *The Dedalus Book of Decadence*, ed. Brian Stableford (Sawtry, U.K.: Dedalus, 1990) and is reprinted in Paul Hallam, ed., *The Book of Sodom* (London: Verso, 1993), 261–66.

35. Claude Lévi-Strauss, *The Elementary Structures of Kinship* (Boston: Beacon, 1969). References to this edition will be given in the text.

36. Jean de Palacio in his introduction to Rachilde's *Les Hors-Nature* (Paris: Séguier, 1994), 11. All future references to the introduction and novel will be given in the text.

37. Umberto Eco, "Ur-Fascism" in *The New York Review of Books* (22 June 1995), 14.

38. Among them, as I am indebted to Margaret Waller for pointing out, is that this original title is, uncannily, virtually an anagram of "les fascistes."

39. The problem of "l'hommosexualité" described by Luce Irigaray in, for example, *Speculum of the Other Woman* (Ithaca: Cornell University Press, 1985). Although others have shown how the homosexual couple can be read as reconstituting heterosexuality, for example in the discourse of the sexologists. See Christopher Craft, *Another Kind of Love: Male Homosexual Desire in English Discourse, 1850–1920* (Berkeley and Los Angeles: University of California Press, 1994).

40. See, for example, Kaplan, 16.

41. The image is found, for example, in Sartre's essay "Qu'est-ce qu'un collaborateur?" in which he characterizes the relations between Germany and France as "sexual union in which France plays the role of the woman." See the analysis in David Carroll's *French Literary Fascism*, especially pp. 147–52. See also Andrew Hewitt, this volume.

42. For a critique of Lévi-Strauss, see Gayle Rubin's article "The Traffic in Women: Notes on the 'Political Economy' of Sex," in *Toward an Anthropology of Women*, ed. Rayna R. Reiter (New York: Monthly Review Press, 1975), 157–210. See also Judith Butler's recent interview of Gayle Rubin in *differences* 6.2+3 (Summer–Fall 1994): 62–99.

43. Gayle Rubin, "The Traffic in Women."

44. *Modernism/Modernity* 1.3 (1994): 55–87.

45. Claudia Koonz, *Mothers in the Fatherland*, 25.

46. John Halperin, *Eminent Georgians: The Lives of King George V, Elizabeth Bowen, St. John Philby, and Nancy Astor* (New York: St. Martin's Press, 1995), 212.

47. See Glen Jeansonne, *Women of the Far Right: The Mothers' Movement and World War II* (Chicago: University of Chicago Press, 1996).

48. On the topic of the paradox of avant-garde women's fascist sympathies, see also Shari Benstock's "Paris Lesbianism and the Politics of Reaction, 1900–1940," in *Hidden From History: Reclaiming the Gay and Lesbian Past*, ed. Martin Bauml Duberman, Martha Vicinus, and George Chauncey, Jr. (New York: New American Library, 1989), 332–46; and Wanda Van Dusen's "Portrait of a National Fetish: Gertrude Stein's 'Introduction to the Speeches of Maréchal Pétain' (1942)," in *Modernism/Modernity* 3.3 (1996): 69–92.

49. See, for example, the interview with Beverly LaHaye in Susan Faludi's *Backlash: The Undeclared War Against American Women* (New York: Crown, 1991), in

which Faludi subtly contrasts the feminine markers in LaHaye's office (the use of pink, for example) with the underlying political ambitiousness of her political agenda (253–56). I am grateful to Pamela Matthews for bringing this example to my attention.

50. Virginia Woolf, *Three Guineas* (London: The Hogarth Press, 1947), 8. All future references will be given in the text.

51. For more on the antifascist message of *Three Guineas*, see Marie-Luise Gättens's *Women Writers and Fascism: Reconstructing History* (Gainesville: University Press of Florida, 1995). For more on Woolf's resistance to fascism, see Patricia Klindienst Joplin's "The Authority of Illusion: Feminism and Fascism in Virginia Woolf's *Between the Acts*," in *South Central Review* 6.2 (1989): 88–104.

52. "Sources" is the name of a series of poems appearing at the beginning of *Your Native Land, Your Life: Poems* (New York: Norton, 1986).

53. *Claiming an Identity They Taught Me to Despise* is the title of a volume of poetry by Michelle Cliff (Watertown, Mass.: Persephone Press, 1980) for which Rich supplied a "blurb."

54. New York: Norton, 1991.

55. All quotations in this paragraph are from Adrienne Rich, *The Dark Fields of the Republic* (New York: Norton, 1995).

56. Victoria de Grazia, *How Fascism Ruled Women: Italy, 1922–1945* (Berkeley and Los Angeles: University of California Press, 1992).

The Bouboule Novels

1. Although this misogyny seems to express itself with particular intensity in the fiction of the Right, writers of all political stripes seem hard on women. The women characters of the liberal Roger Martin du Gard are criticized for their efforts to play a role in war in the final volumes of *Les Thibault*, and women do not fare well in Louis Guilloux's homefront epic, *Le Sang noir*. Only Louis Aragon attempts to make women into heroes, as in *Les Cloches de Bâle*, and even here his portraits are fraught with ambivalence.

2. Mary Louise Roberts, *Civilization Without Sexes: Reconstructing Gender in Postwar France, 1917–1927* (Chicago: University of Chicago Press, 1994), p. 7.

3. Ibid., 5–6.

4. *Fiction in the Historical Present: French Writers and the Thirties* (Hanover, N.H.: University Press of New England, 1986).

5. In a letter written on October 12, 1994, a representative of Flammarion informed me: "Nous avons effectivement publié nombre d'ouvrages de cet auteur mais, malheureusement, les archives que nous pourrions posséder sont inutilisables pour le moment." Trilby's works are listed in the *Catalogue Général des Livres Imprimés* (Paris: Bibliothèque Nationale, 1965–1967), 353–68.

6. See, for example, René Rémond, *La Droite en France de 1815 à nos jours* (Paris: Aubier Editions Montaigne, 1954); Pierre Milza, *Fascisme français: Passé et présent* (Paris: Flammarion, 1987) and *Les Fascismes* (Paris: Seuil, 1991); Zeev Sternhell, *Ni Droite ni gauche: L'idéologie fasciste en France* (Paris: Seuil, 1983).

7. Robert Soucy, "French Fascism and the Croix de Feu: A Dissenting Interpretation," *Journal of Contemporary History* 26 (1991): 163. See also his *French Fascism: The First Wave, 1924–1933* (New Haven: Yale University Press, 1986), and *French Fascism: The Second Wave, 1933–1939* (New Haven: Yale University Press, 1995).

8. William L. Irvine, "Fascism in France and the Strange Case of the Croix de Feu," *Journal of Modern History* 63 (June 1991): 272.

9. Robert Soucy discusses the ways in which La Rocque's discourse on fascism and the parliamentary system fluctuated according to the political circumstances in which the movement found itself. Soucy finds La Rocque most loudly denying his fascism at moments when it was most politically expedient to do so. Similarly, in Trilby's text the word fascist appears only as an accusation made by those hostile to the Croix de Feu, who connect the term with antiparliamentarianism. In a politically ambiguous anecdote recounted in *Bouboule chez les Croix de Feu*, two shepherds who hear charges of fascism leveled against the Croix de Feu nevertheless decide to join it; whether their approval of the movement includes its possible fascist leaning is left unclear.

10. Victoria de Grazia, *How Fascism Ruled Women: Italy, 1922–1945* (Berkeley and Los Angeles: University of California Press, 1992), 73.

11. Roberts, 72.

12. Ibid., 2.

13. Although Ginette plays an activist role in this movement, Trilby does not imply that women play a central role in the Camelots du Roi: she points out that Ginette is allowed to participate only through the membership in the movement of her male cousin.

14. *Bouboule, dame de la IIIe République* (Paris: Flammarion, 1931), 23.

15. Roberts, 10.

16. *Bouboule, dame de la IIIe République*, 12.

17. De Grazia, especially pp. 41–59.

18. *Le Flambeau*, April 1, 1934: 4.

19. For example, *Bouboule chez les Croix de Feu* (Paris: Flammarion, 1936), 9, 136.

20. In *Bouboule chez les Croix de Feu*, Bouboule muses, "Oui, mais ces hommes obéiront-ils comme on doit obéir? Il ne faut jamais discuter les ordres d'un chef, même quand on ne les comprend pas, il faut savoir attendre avec confiance l'heure que le chef choisira. Les Français ont perdu l'habitude de la discipline" (133).

21. Ibid., 250.

22. *Bouboule en Italie* (Paris: Flammarion, 1933), 40–41.

23. Ibid., 220.

24. Claudia Koonz, *Mothers in the Fatherland: Women, the Family and Nazi Politics* (New York: St. Martin's Press, 1987).

25. Françoise Thébaud notes that even French feminists of the interwar period failed to protest the reigning social model of woman as housewife and mother, and the identification of femininity with motherhood seemed to characterize the thought of socialists and communists, as well as that of the conservative right. "Maternité et famille entre les deux guerres: Idéologies et politique familiale," in *Femmes et fascismes*, ed. Rita Thalmann (Paris: Tierce, 1986).

26. Nancy Huston, "The Matrix of War: Mothers and Heroes," in *The Female Body in*

Western Culture, ed. Susan Rubin Suleiman (Cambridge: Harvard University Press, 1985), 119–36.

27. Margaret H. Darrow, "White Angels on the Battlefield: The Myth of Feminine War Experience in World War I France," unpublished paper.

28. In *Bouboule chez les Croix de Feu,* Bouboule observes: "La seule chose que j'ai critiquée le quatorze juillet c'était la présence, dans le défilé, d'infirmières, elles s'efforçaient de marcher au même pas que leurs camarades hommes, elles étaient rouges, congestionnées, et vraiment ne semblaient pas à leur place. Elles ont fait la guerre, elles ont été, elles aussi, souvent très exposées, mais qu'importe, les femmes ne doivent pas suivre des marches militaires, elles y sont toujours un peu ridicules" (169). Bouboule does explore the possibilities of nursing in *Bouboule dans la tourmente,* when she and her daughter care for the wounded during the February riots. Although Claire later undergoes nurses' training in the Croix Rouge, Bouboule rejects the nursing role as offering insufficient opportunity for real participation.

29. De Grazia, 117.

30. Ibid., 98.

31. *Le Flambeau*, September 1, 1933: 4.

32. *Bouboule chez les Croix de Feu*, 282.

33. Ibid., 201.

34. "Le Congrès social de la section féminine," *Le Flambeau*, November 2, 1935: 2.

35. The attention given to women in the pages of *Le Flambeau* seems to decline radically after the dissolution of the Croix de Feu by the Popular Front government in July of 1936 and its reemergence as the Parti Social Français. This change may well reflect women's lack of electoral power. Replacing news of the local associations and the *section féminine* is an increased attention to sports and aviation, especially as represented by the heroic pilot Mermoz. The columns on recipes and household hints continue sporadically in 1936 before disappearing altogether, and even the ads are more clearly directed toward men.

36. "Section féminine du Regroupement National autour de Croix de Feu," *Le Flambeau*, April 1, 1934: 4.

37. The Croix de Feu was not known for its anti-Semitism, and several prominent Jews were among the movement's supporters. However, as the threat from the Popular Front grew, a discourse aimed at the threat posed by "immigrants" introduced a thinly veiled anti-Semitic element; a similar development occurs in the Bouboule series.

38. *Bouboule chez les Croix de Feu*, 269.

39. Ibid., 111.

40. Ibid., 263.

41. An article accompanying the notice of Nadine de La Rocque's death appeared on page 3 of *Le Flambeau* on September 1, 1934, under the title "Nadine de La Rocque." The brief editor's note attributes authorship to a woman member of the movement who has insisted on anonymity. A second article, simply entitled "Nadine," appears on August 3, 1935, accompanied by a snapshot of Nadine sitting on the arm of her father's chair. This article is signed with the name "Ottavi."

42. From its inception the Croix de Feu had celebrated the *fête* of Joan of Arc in May

and articles in *Le Flambeau* frequently expressed the esteem with which she was regarded by the movement.

43. Huston, 128.

44. Ibid., 130.

Seducing Corinne

1. Colin Mercer sees consent as a necessary paradigm in the success of popular culture in "Complicit Pleasures," *Popular Culture and Social Relations* ed. Tony Benett, Colin Mercer, and Janet Woolacott (Philadelphia: Open University, 1986), 3. See also Noam Chomsky's recent videorecording in *Manufacturing Consent: Noam Chomsky and the Media* (Montreal, Quebec, Canada: Necessary Illusions, 1992).

2. The relationship of France in general and of the Vichy government in particular with fascism has been discussed by the following landmark works: Robert Paxton, *Vichy France 1940–1944: The Old Guard and the New Order* (New York: Knopf, 1972); Bernard-Henri Lévy, *L'Idéologie française* (Paris: Grasset, 1981); Zeev Sternhell, *Ni Droite ni gauche* (Paris: Seuil, 1983); Ariane Chebel d'Appollonia, *L'Extrême droite en France de Maurras à Le Pen* (Brussels: Editions Complexe, 1988); and Michel Winock, *Histoire de l'extrême droite en France* (Paris: Seuil, 1993).

3. Michèle Cointret-Labrousse, *Vichy et le fascisme* (Brussels: Editions Complexe, 1987).

4. Andrew Shennan, *Rethinking France: Plans for the Renewal 1940–1946* (Oxford: Oxford University Press, 1989), 5.

5. Pascal Ory questions this influence in *Les Collaborateurs* (Paris: Seuil, 1976).

6. Mercer, 51.

7. All quotations from Corinne Luchaire, *Ma Drôle de vie* (Paris: Sun, 1948) (cited in text as *DV*) are my translations.

8. Otto Abetz, *Pétain et les Allemands* (Paris: Gaucher, 1948), 32.

9. David Welsh, *Nazi Propaganda: The Power and the Limitations,* (Totowa, N.J.: Barnes and Noble, 1983), 3.

10. See Pierre Bourdieu's work on the role of language in the social sciences: "[The social sciences] must examine the part played by words in the construction of social reality . . . ," in *Language and Symbolic Power* (Cambridge: Harvard University Press, 1991), 105, 127–36.

11. Renate Bridenthal, Claudia Koonz, and Susan Stuard, *Becoming Visible* (Boston: Houghton Mifflin, 1987), 4.

12. Cine Dauphin, et al.,"Women's Culture and Women's Power: Issues in French Women's History," *Writing Women's History,* ed. Karen Offen, Ruth Roach Pierson, and Jane Rendall (Bloomington: Indiana University Press, 1991), 128.

13. Dauphin, 500.

14. Nancy Tuana, *The Less Noble Sex* (Bloomington: Indiana University Press, 1993), 3.

15. Claudia Koonz, *Mothers in the Fatherland: Women, Family and Nazi Politics* (New York: St. Martin Press, 1987). See also Gisela T. Kaplan and Carole E. Adams, "Early Women Supporters of National Socialism," in *The Attraction of Fascism,* ed. John Milfull (New York: Berg, 1990), 186–204.

16. What Raymond Aron qualifies as German "Korrection," in *Histoire de Vichy* (Paris: Fayard, 1954), 185.
17. Elizabeth Badinter, *XY: De l'identité masculine* (Paris: Odile Jacob, 1992), 14–15, 107.
18. For an internal view of the loss of self-identity of "men at war" and the attraction of war see Glenn Gray's article "Enduring Appeals of Battle," *Rethinking Masculinity: Philosophical Explorations in Light of Feminism,* ed. Larry May and Robert Striwerda (Lanham, Md.: Littelfields Adams Paperbacks, 1992).

"L'Envers de la Guerre"

1. Violette Leduc, *La Bâtarde,* trans. Derek Coltman (London: Virago Press, 1985), 339. The original French edition of *La Bâtarde* was published by Gallimard in 1964. Subsequent references to the Coltman translation appear within the text. I would like to thank the members of my Reno reading group, Kathleen Boardman, Stacy Burton, Martha Hildreth, and Gaye Simmons, for the careful and insightful attention they brought to this article in draft form.
2. Susan Gubar, "'This Is My Rifle, This Is My Gun': World War II and the Blitz on Women," *Behind the Lines: Gender and the Two World Wars,* ed. Margaret Randolph Higonnet, Jane Jenson, Sonya Michel, and Margaret Collins Weitz (New Haven: Yale University Press, 1987), 227–59.
3. Joan W Scott, "Rewriting History," in Ibid., 27.
4. Sarah Fishman, *We Will Wait: Wives of French Prisoners of War, 1940–1945* (New Haven: Yale University Press, 1992). Like Fishman, Pollard is a feminist historian of Vichy France. Pollard's call for the study of "less respectable" narratives, those which allow us to imagine more marginal women's tales, appears in her review of Fishman's valuable book, "Forgotten Women," *The Women's Review of Books* 10.2 (November 1992): 21–22.
5. This expression appears on page 304 of the original French text (Paris: Gallimard, 1964). It is inexplicably missing from the Coltman translation and I have thus used my own translation here. In the passage in question, Leduc follows a German soldier as he walks through the streets of Paris hand-in-hand with a young French girl: "Le boulevard des Capucines me montraient l'envers de la guerre. Un guerrier promenait une jeune fille" (304). This is Leduc's first sighting of "an enemy in the street," and, significantly, this encounter introduces the Occupation to her reader as a conventional wartime drama with sexual connotations, conquests, and consequences for French women in which Leduc, a marginal figure, neither young nor beautiful, often adopts the role of voyeur.
6. Denise Riley, "Some Peculiarities of Social Policy concerning Women in Wartime and Postwar Britain," *Behind the Lines,* 260.
7. Quoted in Michèle Bordeaux, "Femmes hors d'Etat français, 1940–1944," *Femmes et fascismes,* ed. Rita Thalmann (Paris: Tierce, 1986), 138: "La Révolution nationale est une réaction très virilement humaine à une république féminisée, une république de femmes ou d'invertis."

8. For further analysis of these terms as manipulated within Vichy discourse, see Michèle Bordeaux, 138–39.

9. Denise Riley, *"Am I That Name?": Feminism and the Category of "Women" in History* (Minneapolis: University of Minnesota Press, 1988), 2.

10. I borrow this phrase from Jacqueline Piatier's review of *La Bâtarde* in *Le Monde*, 10 Oct. 1964: 13.

11. Leduc's first work, *L'Asphyxie*, chronicles her unhappy childhood and her troubled relationship with her mother (Paris: Gallimard, 1946).

12. Beauvoir began writing her autobiography in 1957. *Mémoires d'une jeune fille rangée* dates from 1958, *La Force de l'âge* from 1960. She concluded *La Force des choses*, the third volume of her autobiography, in March 1963. This volume was followed by an account of her mother's death, *Une Mort très douce* (1964). The final volume of Beauvoir's autobiography, *Tout compte fait*, appeared in 1972. Beauvoir encouraged Leduc to write an autobiography after witnessing the relative lack of popular success of Leduc's earlier works. According to Isabelle de Courtivron, Leduc spent four years writing *La Bâtarde*, from 1958 to 1962. *Violette Leduc* (Boston: Twayne, 1985), 29.

13. J. Piatier, *Le Monde*, 30 May 1972: 28, as quoted by Pièr Girard in *Œdipe masqué* (Paris: des femmes, 1986), 18: "J'ai raconté ma vie comme elle est arrivée, mes livres, mes erreurs, mes désespoirs, en somme ma vie d'écrivain raté" (my translation).

14. For further discussion of the question of autobiography and self-representation in Leduc's work, see Michèle Respaut, "Femme/ange, femme/monstre: *L'Affamée* de Violette Leduc," *Stanford French Review* 73 (Winter 1983): 365–74; Isabelle de Courtivron's ground-breaking critical overview, *Violette Leduc*, and her subsequent exploration of Leduc's relationship in life and writing with Simone de Beauvoir, "From Bastard to Pilgrim: Rites and Writing for Madame," *Yale French Studies* 72 (1986): 133–48; Pièr Girard's *Œdipe masqué*, a psychoanalytic reading of *L'Affamée* (Paris: des femmes, 1986); Martha Noel Evans's important chapter on Leduc in her book on twentieth-century French women writers, "Violette Leduc: The Bastard," *Masks of Tradition* (Ithaca: Cornell University Press, 1987); Shirley Neuman's "'An appearance walking in a forest the sexes burn': Autobiography and the Construction of the Feminine Body," *Signature* 2 (Winter 1989): 1–26; Eileen Boyd Sivert, "Permeable Boundaries and the Mother-Function in *L'Asphyxie*," *Tulsa Studies in Women's Literature* 11.2 (Fall 1992): 289–307. More recently, *Nord'*, a journal devoted to the literature of Northern France, published a special issue on Leduc's life and writing: *Nord'* 23 (June 1994).

15. De Courtivron, *Violette Leduc*, 32.

16. In my work in progress, *Between the Lines: Women, Witnessing, and the Occupation of France*, a study of literary testimony to the war years by Colette, Violette Leduc, Simone de Beauvoir, Marguerite Duras, Charlotte Delbo, and Elsa Triolet.

17. The term "anti-memoir" is only appropriate to the extent that Leduc clearly does not say "the right things" about the Nazis, about her Jewish neighbors, or about the war in general. Her refusal to do so should not be interpreted as a bald-faced rejection of the genre of autobiography or memoir, but as a provocation to literary convention and to social and readerly expectations.

18. For information concerning Maurice Sachs, I am drawing on Leduc's portrayal of him in *La Bâtarde*; Henri Raczymow's biography, *Maurice Sachs* (Paris: Gallimard, 1988); and Isabelle de Courtivron, *Violette Leduc*, 2–4.

19. De Courtivron, *Violette Leduc*, 3.

20. Isabelle de Courtivron, "From Bastard to Pilgrim," 136.

21. Violette Leduc, *La Folie en tête*, 231 (as translated and quoted by de Courtivron, "From Bastard to Pilgrim," 136).

22. De Courtivron, "From Bastard to Pilgrim," 138.

23. The final section of Duras's *La Douleur* focuses on a recurring Durassian figure, Aurélia Steiner, a young Jewish girl who, in this version, observes the world from her hiding-place window (Paris: *P.O.L.*, 1985). Earlier in the work, however, within the diary "La Douleur," the girl remains unnamed.

24. In the original French, this reads quite differently: "La nuit je rêvais que la guerre était finie, que les valeurs rentraient . . ." (349). Leduc's fear of a return of social and moral "values" that condemn her lesbianism and criminality is, of course, less offensive than her anti-Semitism and her related conflation of Jews, among the "people of ability" to whom she has previously referred, with wealth (339).

25. Although the magazine is not named in *La Bâtarde*, it is identified in a later work as *Pour Elle* (*La Folie en tête*, 107). Dominique Veillon notes, in *La Mode sous l'Occupation*, that *Pour Elle* was a weekly women's magazine founded in August 1940 (with the approval of the German authorities) that lasted until March 1942 (Paris: Payot, 1990), 48.

26. Judith Butler, *Gender Trouble: Feminism and the Subversion of Identity* (New York: Routledge, 1990), 145.

27. Guylaine Guidez, *Femmes dans la guerre* (Paris: Perrin, 1989), 219.

28. My use of the phrase "coming to writing" relies on Nancy K. Miller's elaboration of the scenarios through which a woman "authorizes" herself, not only as a writer, but as a female/feminist subjectivity negotiating within the social. Whereas Leduc's previous journalistic writing had started her on the road to her vocation, I place her "coming to writing" at this later moment in which she begins writing for (her own) good. See Miller's *Subject to Change* (New York: Columbia University Press, 1988), 16, 158 n.3.

29. The circumstances of this "coming to writing" somewhat resemble those of Colette, who, famously, began to write her schoolgirl memoirs at the behest of her husband, Willy. Lest we be misled by Leduc's indirection, it should be noted that, once begun, her career as a writer was undertaken seriously over the next thirty years until her death in 1972, and certainly not simply to please Maurice Sachs (or later, Simone de Beauvoir). Leduc continued writing in spite of the lack of success of her books: *L'Asphyxie* (1946), *L'Affamée* (1948), *Ravages* (1955), *La Vieille fille et le mort* (1958), *Trésors à prendre* (1960). Beauvoir insists that Leduc was an extremely disciplined writer, in spite of her lack of acceptance and her recurrent bouts of mental illness. It was not until the publication of *La Bâtarde* in 1964, written under the sign of total failure, that Leduc was to gain true critical and popular success. None of her subsequent books came remotely close to matching the bestseller status of this first volume of her autobiography: *Thérèse et Isabelle* (1965), *La Femme au petit renard* (1966), *La Folie en tête* (1970, vol. 2), *Le Taxi*

(1971), *La Chasse à l'amour* (1973, vol. 3; posthumous publication edited by Beauvoir).

30. See Raczymow for the details surrounding Sachs's decision to go to Germany and the circumstances of his death there.

31. This was not the first time that Sachs had proposed motherhood to Leduc He had, in fact, asked if she would like to have a baby with him earlier in the war, after the collapse of her marriage to Gabriel. Leduc was flattered, sickened, and tempted by his ambiguous proposition: "Did he want to make me a mother in order to save me? It's not impossible" (353–54). This offer was also rejected.

32. Chabrol's film is loosely based on the life of Marie-Louise Giraud, a black-market abortionist convicted of treason by Vichy and guillotined on 29 July 1943. Giraud was the last woman to be executed within the French penal system. For an important analysis of Chabrol's film, see Rosemarie Scullion, "Family Fictions and Reproductive Realities in Occupied France: Claude Chabrol's *Une Affaire de femmes*," *L'Esprit Créateur* 33.1 (Spring 1993): 85–103. Concerning Vichy and abortion laws, see Miranda Pollard, "*Femme, Famille, France*: Vichy and the Politics of Gender," Ph.D. diss., Trinity College, Dublin, 263–89. Before writing *La Bâtarde*, Leduc had described the life-threatening illness caused by the abortion in her novel *Ravages* (1955).

33. Leduc had published fashion articles during the war in *Paris-Soir.*

34. Violette Leduc, *Mad in Pursuit,* trans. Derek Coltman (New York: Farrar, Straus and Giroux, 1971), 14–15.

35. The Gallimard re-edition dates from 1988 It is currently available in the "Blanche" and "Folio" editions, thereby rendering it a more likely candidate for classroom use.

The Historical Nullification of Paul Morand's Gendered Eugenics

1. Diane Rubenstein, *What's Left? The Ecole Normale Supérieure and the Right* (Madison: University of Wisconsin Press, 1990), 140–63.

2. Robert Brasillach, "Paul Morand ou ce qui se porte," *Oeuvres complètes de Robert Brasillach*, vol. 7 (Paris: Plon, 1935; Club de l'Honnête Homme, 1964). Diane Rubenstein offers excellent insights into the Normalien, elitist rhetoric that Brasillach deployed in his treatment of Morand (97–98).

3. Paul de Man, *Wartime Journalism, 1939–1943 by Paul de Man*, ed. Werner Hamacher, Neil Hertz, and Thomas Keenan (Lincoln: University of Nebraska Press, 1988), 151. Unless otherwise indicated all translations in this article are my own.

4. Paul Virilio and Sylvère Lotringer, *Pure War*, trans Mark Polizotti (New York: Semiotext(e), 1983), 40.

5. Paul de Man, "Literary History and Literary Modernity," *Blindness and Insight: Essays in the Rhetoric of Contemporary Criticism* (Minneapolis: University of Minnesota Press, 1983), 147.

6. Edgardo Cozarinsky's documentary, "La Guerre d'un seul homme," contains numerous examples of these clips.

7. Jean-Paul Sartre, *Qu'est-ce que la littérature?* (Paris: Gallimard, 1948), 237.

8. Ibid, 111–12.

9. David Carroll, *French Literary Fascism: Nationalism, Anti-Semitism, and the Ideology of Culture* (Princeton: Princeton University Press, 1995), 151.

10. Sande Cohen, *Historical Culture: On the Recoding of an Academic Discipline* (Berkeley and Los Angeles: University of California Press, 1986), 297.

11. Sartre, 236.

12. "The precise mechanism of the bicycle contests the languorous dreams of the harem one lends to the passage of this veiled creature; but at the same time whatever remains of the voluptuous, magic depths between these painted eyebrows, this narrow brow, in its turn, contests mechanization"(37). This sight was arresting enough to have been recycled by Sartre for his reading of Morand. It originally comes up in the context of a passage on the writer Valéry Larbaud. See *Les Carnets de la drôle de guerre (novembre 1939–mars 1940)* (Paris: Gallimard, 1983), 179.

13. Paul Morand, "Réflexions sur la natalité," *Excursions immobiles* (Paris: Flammarion, 1944), 62–63.

14. Robert A. Nye, *Masculinity and Male Codes of Honor in Modern France* (New York: Oxford University Press, 1993), 83, 97.

15. Paul Morand, *Nouvelles*, vol. 1, ed. Michel Collomb (Paris: Gallimard, Bibliothèque de la Pléiade, 1992), 1:420. All page references from this volume and volume 2 (also editied by Collomb and published in 1992) of Morand's *Nouvelles* will appear hereafter in parentheses in the body of this article.

16. Nye, 187.

17. Ibid, 188–89.

18. Ibid, 190.

19. Ibid, 187. "Indeed, the contrast between 'Semites' and 'Aryans' that Drumont drew in his *La France juive* in 1886 did more than anything else to initiate the epidemic of 'Jewish' duels of the following twenty-five years." Nye, 205–206.

20. In Ginette Guitard-Auviste, *Paul Morand (1888–1976): Légendes et vérités* (Paris: Hachette, 1981), 387. The year 1958 is coincidentally the year Morand stood for election to the Académie Française.

21. Carroll Smith-Rosenberg, *Disorderly Conduct: Visions of Gender in Victorian America* (New York: Oxford University Press, 1985), 282–83. This study also covers European influences and traces the development in perceptions of gender over the twentieth century. Smith-Rosenberg provides an excellent summary (275–80) of the theories of Havelock Ellis's work on sexual deviance, theories that Morand was familiar with: "Ellis was above all a eugenicist. The stereotypic definitions of masculinity and femininity (the complementarity of the genders), he argued, were rooted in genetic difference . . . Feminism, lesbianism, equality for women, all emerge in Ellis's writings as problematic phenomena. All were unnatural, related in disturbing and unclear ways to increased female criminality, insanity, and 'hereditary neurosis'" (278–79).

22. Paul Morand, "Poncifs," *Excursions immobiles*, 141.

23. Ibid, 142.

24. "Un Nouvel Exotisme," *Excursions immobiles*, 120.

25. Cohen, 290.

26. Ibid, 290.
27. Favorably biased accounts of Morand's activities during this period appear in Gui-
    tard-Auviste's biography and in an autobiography by Jean Jardin's son, Pascal,
    Vichy Boyhood: An Inside View of the Pétain Regime, trans. Jean Stewart (London:
    Faber and Faber, 1975). Michel Collomb's "Chronologie" of Morand's life in the
    first volume of the Nouvelles presents a somewhat more neutral version of these
    years.
28. See Henry Rousso, *The Vichy Syndrome: History and Memory in France since
    1944*, trans. Arthur Goldhammer (Cambridge: Harvard University Press, 1991).
29. Charles Bernheimer, "1880: Prostitution in the Novel," in *A New History of French
    Literature*, ed. Denis Hollier (Cambridge: Harvard University Press, 1989), 783.
30. Nye, 106. Dominique Rémy, *Les Lois de Vichy* (Paris: Romillat, 1992), 92–97.
31. For example, "Delphine," "Les Amis nouveaux," "Eloge de la marquise Beausem-
    blant," and *Lewis et Irène*.
32. Rousso, 65–66.
33. Ibid, 67.
34. Ibid, 66.
35. This small detail appears in Michel Collomb's "Chronologie."

Sleeping with the Enemy

1. I have dealt with the literary and theoretical aspects of this conflation—though
   without reference to Genet—in *Political Inversions: Homosexuality Fascism, and
   the Modernist Imaginary* (Stanford: Stanford University Press, 1996).
2. Theodor W. Adorno, *Minima Moralia: Reflections from Damaged Life*, trans. E. F.
   N. Jephcott (London: New Left Books, 1974), 46.
3. Larry David Nachman, "Genet: Dandy of the Lower Depths," *Salmagundi* 58–59
   (Fall 1982–Winter 1983), 369.
4. I have in mind particularly Benjamin's "Pariser Brief <1>," *Gesammelte Schriften*,
   vol. 3, ed. Hella Tiedemann Bartels (Frankfurt: Suhrkamp, 1972), 482–95.
5. Jean-Paul Sartre, *Saint-Genet: Actor and Martyr*, trans. Bernard Frechtman (New
   York: Pantheon, 1963), 119. Hereafter *SG*.
6. Interview with Bertrand Poirot-Delpech in *L'Ennemi déclaré: Textes et entretiens*,
   ed. Albert Dichy, in *Oeuvres complètes*, vol. 6 (Paris: Gallimard, 1991), 233–34.
   Cited in Edmund White, *Genet: A Biography* (New York: Vintage, 1994), 161–62.
7. We should note, however, that the convergence of sexual desire and protofascist
   ideology is not always based on an absence of political sensibility. For example,
   Genet's anti-Semitism—referred to by Sartre—is directly sexually inflected: he
   could never sleep with a Jew. Sartre's attempts to explain this particular sexual
   taste seem unconvincing in the framework of his broader argument. Jews are victims—like Genet—not the "real men" he wants. But Sartre also points out that
   Genet's "real men" are not really "real men" either, but their ciphers. Moreover, the
   insistence on alterity in sexual desire always reverts to a narcissistic identification
   in Sartre's analysis—an identification that another "victim" could facilitate.
8. Jean-Paul Sartre, "Qu'est-ce qu'un collaborateur?" *Situations III: Lendemains de*

guerre (Paris: Gallimard, 1949), 58 (orig. in *La République francaise*, 1945). My translations.

9. Leo Bersani, "The Gay Outlaw," *Diacritics* 24.2–3 (Summer-Fall 1994): 5–18.

10. Moreover, such writing is communicable in the manner of a disease: it homosexualizes Sartre as a reader. It is contagious. Commenting on the slippage in and out of the first person in Genet (a technique particularly noticeable in *Funeral Rites*, and most particularly with respect to Genet's impersonation of Hitler), Sartre observes:

> If I have the slightest inclination for men, even if it is repressed to my very depths, I am caught, constrained, in the shame of avowing my tastes to myself, the Other. If I really have no partiality for boys, then I become, in myself, the Other. Another uses me to desire what I cannot desire; my freedom lends itself, I am possessed by a homosexual zar, and, what is more, voluntarily possessed. (500)

Either one accepts the identification and accepts homosexuality—or one does not, one remains other: which is, of course, precisely to be homosexual. Sartre—as a reader—is caught in this communication. This writing sodomizes, enacting a desire, or rendering you passive as the recipient and instrument of that desire.

11. We should perhaps note here the importance of the title *Saint-Genet: Actor and Martyr*, for what is at stake is a question of mimesis, and the reduction of Being to representation. Protofascism would not be—as Sartre implies in the passage just cited—the state of mimetic falsification or doubling of a true Being, but the desire to act (out) Being at all as an existential possibility. In other words, the problem is not that acting is secondary or derivative. In her presentation of Céline, Kristeva presents a figure who—in the terms of the subtitle of her chapter 6—is "neither actor nor martyr." Might we posit a homo- and a heterosexual route to the ideology of collaboration, one that distinguishes—by way of a pun—between Genet's writing and Céline's "active" collaboration? "Céline," Kristeva writes, "has us believe that he is true, that he is the only authentic one" (134). Céline "has us believe"—he is a better actor, perhaps, but an actor still. Genet never has us believe. Céline's heterosexual—"active"—collaboration would derive from a belief in the object of mimesis—the objective self. Genet's, instead, is a fascination with the performativity of mimesis. If Céline is an evildoer, Genet reserves Evil for his writing. See Julia Kristeva, *Powers of Horror: An Essay on Abjection*, trans. Leon S. Roudiez (New York: Columbia University Press, 1982).

12. In his *Male Fantasies,* 2 vols., trans. Stephen Conway (vol. 1), Erica Carter and Chris Turner (vol. 2) (Minneapolis: University of Minnesota Press, 1987–89), Klaus Theweleit comments on why we cannot think of this as homosexuality: "In the end," he writes of Nazi transgressors, "they faced a second double-bind, a second dilemma to parallel the double-bind that simultaneously prohibited and commanded incest between men: thou shalt love men, but thou shalt not be homosexual. A second commandment: thou shalt do what is forbidden, yet still be punished, if those in power so desire." In other words, "the legalization of homosexuality was seen as likely to eliminate one of the key areas of *transgression* into which the fascist had to be initiated and accepted" (2:339). Genet, of course, was never interested in homosexual liberation as a political phenomenon precisely because he too depended on the transgression apparently encoded in his sexuality.

13. I have rather consciously avoided the terminology of psychoanalysis in this piece, if only because Sartre's own reworking of Freud would render the valence of certain terms ambiguous in this context. Indeed, Sartre's insistence that Genet "was born without parents" suggests interesting ways in which a certain homosexual fantasy might necessarily move beyond the orbit of the familiar Oedipal framework. Nevertheless, since I am arguing that the trajectory of Genet's desire runs toward the physical embodiment of abstract social relations, we must acknowledge the bodily functions of the State that "bears" or at least "fosters" the writer. Of particular interest would be the potential collapse of male and female polarities in Genet's cathexis of the State—a "masculine" order that nevertheless acquires a maternal function in this context.

14. Obviously, the dyad of production and consumption and the gloss I will place on them in what follows suggest links to Bataille's analysis of both fascism and sexuality. However, I find Sartre's presentation more suggestive in its elaboration of a sexual economy than Bataille's anthropological presentation of homo- and heterogeneity as quasi-ontological states. See Georges Bataille, "The Psychological Structure of Fascism," trans. Carl Lovitt, in *Visions of Excess: Selected Writings 1927–39*, ed. Allan Stoekl (Minneapolis: University of Minnesota Press, 1985).

15. Having cited Adorno as a prime example of the conflation of fascism and homosexuality from a psychoanalytic perspective, I should point out that this desire for the phallus would not, in fact, correspond to his analysis, which turns, instead, on the *collapse* of political agency in a post-Oedipal society. See, for example, "Freudian Theory and the Pattern of Fascist Propaganda," *The Essential Frankfurt School Reader*, ed. Andrew Arato and Eike Gebhardt (New York: Continuum, 1982), 118–37.

Whose Sorrow? Whose Pity? Whose Pleasure?

1. This paper was originally given at the 1990 Berkshire Conference on the History of Women held at Rutgers University. I am grateful to various people for their comments on drafts of this article or for conversations about the film: Julie Abraham, Roderick Kedward, Tricia Lootens, Greg Mann, Sharon Moore, and Joan Scott. I am especially grateful to Siân Reynolds for sending me a copy of her article "The Sorrow and the Pity Revisited: or, Be Careful, One Train Can Hide Another," *French Cultural Studies* (June 1990), following the Berkshire Conference.

2. Histories specifically dealing with various aspects of women or gender in contemporary French society are also proliferating. See, for example, Claire Duchen, *Women's Rights and Women's Lives in France, 1944–1968* (London: Routledge, 1994); Sarah Fishman, *We Will Wait: Wives of French Prisoners of War, 1940–1945* (New Haven: Yale University Press, 1991); Margaret Higonnet, *Behind the Lines: Gender and the Two World Wars* (New Haven: Yale University Press, 1987); Francine Muel-Dreyfus, *Vichy et l'éternel féminin* (Paris: Seuil, 1996); Mary Louise Roberts, *Civilization Without Sexes* (Chicago: University of Chicago Press, 1994); Joan Scott, *Only Paradoxes to Offer* (Cambridge, Mass.: Harvard University Press, 1996); *Femmes et fascismes,* ed. Rita

Thalman (Paris: Tierce, 1986); Dominique Veillon, *La Mode sous l'Occupation* (Paris: Payot, 1990).

3. See Miranda Pollard, *Woman and the National Revolution: Mobilizing Gender in Vichy France, 1940–1944* (Chicago: University of Chicago Press, forthcoming).

4. *Annie Hall,* dir. Woody Allen, 1977.

5. *The Sorrow* does not simply "reflect" some inherent or inevitable sexism. This film constitutes an important historical and gendered discourse. More broadly, as Teresa de Lauretis argues: "The construction of gender goes on today through the various technologies of gender (e.g. cinema) and institutional discourses (e.g. theory) with power to control the field of social meaning and thus produce, promote, and 'implant' representations of gender. But the terms of a different construction of gender also exist, in the margins of hegemonic discourses. Posed from outside the heterosexual social contract, and inscribed in micropolitical practices, these terms can' also have a part in the construction of gender, and their effects are rather at the 'local' level of resistances, in subjectivity and self-representation." Teresa de Lauretis, *Technologies of Gender* (Bloomington: Indiana University Press, 1987). On film theory and sexuality, see also Screen, *The Sexual Subject: A Screen Reader in Sexuality* (London: Routledge, 1992).

6. Interestingly it is Monsieur Verdier's unnamed daughter, a student, who poses the question of whether there were other feelings than courage in the Resistance. Her father replies that for him personally it was "le chagrin et la pitié."

7. Stephen Heath, "Difference," in *The Sexual Subject,* 49.

8. A useful analysis of the connections between French fascism and femininity is provided by Alice Kaplan in *Reproductions of Banality: French Fascism, Literature and French Intellectual Life* (Minneapolis: University of Minnesota Press, 1986).

9. Madame Solange, *L'Avant-Scène,* 64–65. All French quotations and page references, unless otherwise noted, are taken from the special issue of *L'Avant-Scène: Cinéma* 127/128 (July–Sept. 1972), dedicated to Ophuls's film. For the English text of *The Sorrow,* see Marcel Ophuls, *The Sorrow and the Pity: A Film,* Introduction by Stanley Hoffmann, filmscript trans. Mireille Johnston (New York: Outerbridge and Lazard, 1972).

10. Guehenno, cited by W. D. Halls, *The Youth of Vichy France* (Oxford: Clarendon Press, 1981), v.

11. See Miranda Pollard, "Women and the National Revolution," in *Vichy France and the Resistance: Culture and Ideology,* ed. Roderick Kedward and Roger Austin (Totowa, N.J.: Barnes & Noble, 1985), and "La Politique du Travail Féminin," in *Vichy et les français,* ed. Jean Pierre Azéma et François Bédaria (Paris: Fayard, 1992).

12. Anthony Eden, *The Sorrow and the Pity,* 168.

13. At the Studio Saint-Séverin, and then Paramount-Champs-Elysées.

14. At lest one archivally based history of Clermont-Ferrand contradicts the evidence offered by *The Sorrow* about resistance, collaboration, and public opinion. See John F. Sweets, *Choices in Vichy France* (New York: Oxford University Press, 1986).

15. "La Critique," *L'Avant-Scène,* 73.

16. Stanley Hoffmann.

17. Ophuls, "Regardez donc dans vos greniers," *L'Avant-Scène,* 10.

18. On the perils of an unproblematized historical "experience," see Joan W. Scott in *Feminists Theorize the Political,* ed. Judith Butler and Joan W. Scott (New York: Routledge, 1992), 22–40.
19. See Miranda Pollard, "Vichy, Femmes et Représentations," unpublished paper given at the Colloque Femmes et Fascismes, held in honor of Rita Thalmann, at University of Paris VII, 1992.
20. M. Leiris, former mayor of Cambronde, *L'Avant-Scène,* 52.
21. One of the most shocking and moving sections of the film is Claude Lévy's account of the Vélodrome d'Hiver roundup of Jewish families by the French police in July 1942 and the brutal separation of 4,051 children from their parents. It is this account of Pierre Laval's indifference to *family* that is used to indict him, especially set against his paternalistic relations with his Auvergnat neighbors, his son-in-law's persistent apologia and assertions that Laval "resisted" the Germans. *L'Avant-Scène,* 59.
22. *The Sorrow and the Pity,* 70.
23. I am especially grateful to Roderick Kedward for a paper given at Trinity College Dublin in 1981, in which he analyzed these critical issues, and for many subsequent conversations that prompted me to think further about the politics of the home-space under Vichy. For an alternative interpretation of rural women's actions and responses under the Occupation, see H. R. Kedward, *In Search of the Maquis: Rural Resistance in Southern France, 1942–1944* (Oxford: Clarendon Press, 1994). On the general problems of representing women's resistance activities, see Paula Schwartz, "Partisans and Gender Politics in Vichy France," *French Historical Studies* (spring 1989). On the experience of POW wives, see Sarah Fishman, *We Will Wait.*
24. Question to Raphael Germiniani, *L'Avant-Scène,* 39.
25. *L'Avant-Scène,* 62.
26. Ibid., 63.
27. On the Liberation, see *The Liberation of France: Image and Event,* ed. H. R. Kedward and Nancy Wood (Oxford: Berg, 1995).
28. See Robert Paxton and Michael Marrus, *Vichy France and the Jews* (New York: Basic Books, 1981).
29. Madame Solange, questioned by Ophuls, *L'Avant-Scène,* 65.
30. *The Sorrow and the Pity,* 174.

Vichy's Female Icons

1. Francis Szpiner, *Une Affaire de femmes: Paris 1943, exécution d'une avorteuse* (Paris: Balland, 1986). All translations from the French are my own.
2. Tear gas was reportedly thrown by protesters in Europe to keep the film from being shown. See Eva H. Kissen's review in *Films in Review* 41 (March 1990), 172–73.
3. Abortion was legalized in France in 1975.
4. Although the debates concerning the precise nature of fascism's relationship to Vichy are far from being settled (often because few can agree on a definition of

fascism), it is possible to locate in Pétainist ideology certain traits that are consonant with fascist propaganda. Pétain's speeches preach an explicit condemnation of
capitalism, individualism, and fruitless (immoral) pleasures. This moralizing ideology affirms "family values" (to use today's term), spiritualism over materialism, as
well as the constant sacrifice for the Fatherland. To be sure, Pétain is also fervently
anticommunist and anti-Semitic. All of these traits align Vichy's social agenda
with certain aspects of fascist propaganda. During the latter part of the war (from
1943 on), Vichy's neo-Nazi alignment becomes increasingly clear, culminating in
1944 with such figures as Joseph Darnand, head of the Milice (the French police
auxiliary of the Gestapo), and the fierce propagandist Philippe Henriot. By the time
Marie is guillotined (in 1943), France's government is turning decidedly pro-Nazi.
For discussions of Vichy and fascism, see: Zeev Sternhell, *Ni Droite ni gauche:
L'idéologie fasciste en France*, new ed. (Brussels: Editions Complexe, 1987); René
Rémond, *Les Droites en France* (Paris: Aubier Montaigne, 1982), 231–38, 461–62;
Histoire des droites en France, ed. Jean-François Sirinelli (Paris: Gallimard, 1992),
vol. 1, ch. 10, "Le Fascisme," Philippe Burrin, 603–52.

5. During the Occupation, there was much interest in recuperating Joan of Arc for
Vichy propaganda, or more generally as an artistic lightning rod for patriotic values. See, for example, the work of fascist Robert Brasillach, *Domrémy*, in his *Oeuvres complètes*, vol. 4 (Paris: Club de l'Honnête Homme, 1963). This is a play written in 1933 that he reworked in 1943, adding here and there analogies between the
occupation of France in the fifteenth century and the occupation by the Germans
after 1940. Brasillach also wrote a theatrical adaptation for the trial proceedings of
Joan of Arc (vol. 4 of the *Oeuvres complètes*), probably sometime in April of 1944.
He was executed as a German collaborator in 1945. Much more recently, Le Pen's
far Right party, Le Front National, has been attempting (along with the Pope) to recuperate the early-sixth-century King Clovis as a symbol (for contemporary consumption) of French nationalism and Christianity, while many historians are decry-
ing the attempts as another example of revisionist history.

6. I am obviously using "Left" very loosely here for the purposes of contrasting Vichy
and the Gaullists. Clearly, communists and socialists would be far to the left of de
Gaulle and his followers.

7. For an early review of the films dealing with Joan of Arc's life, see the double issue
of *Etudes cinématographiques* 18–19 (1962).

8. Marina Warner, *Joan of Arc: The Image of Female Heroism* (New York: Knopf,
1981). Subsequent references to this work will be provided in my essay with corre-
sponding page numbers. Other useful sources on the image of Joan of Arc during
the Occupation include: "The Role of Joan of Arc on the Stage of Occupied Paris,"
by Gabriel Jacobs in *Vichy France and the Resistance: Culture and Ideology*, ed.
Roderick Kedward and Roger Austin (Totowa, N.J.: Barnes and Noble, 1985),
106–22; *Histoire des droites en France*, 3 vols., ed. Jean-François Sirinelli (Paris:
Gallimard, 1992). In particular, see vol. 2, "Cultures," ch. 10, "Jeanne d'Arc dans
la mémoire des droites," by Philippe Contamine (399–435).

9. Marie's haircut also recalls the politically conservative sculpture of Joan by
Maxime Réal del Sarte, whom Warner describes as "one of the most ardent adherents to the extreme right-wing movement, the Action Française" (227).

10. Although it may not be intentional on Chabrol's part, Marie's closer physical resemblance to Vichy's Joan than to the Gaullist one makes her all the more apt to represent the ambiguities of State betrayal, since she is both its victim and its representative.

11. In his account, Francis Szpiner does not say that it was the husband who turned in the anonymous accusation against the real Marie-Louise Giraud, so one may assume that this is Chabrol's touch. I will return to this issue later.

12. It should be pointed out here that Warner's interpretation tends to make it seem as if the secrecy surrounding the accusations in Joan's case was unique to that case. Michel Foucault maintains, however, that this sort of secrecy was generalized in trial cases in France and in most European countries before the eighteenth century. According to Foucault, a presiding magistrate had every right to receive anonymous accusations, to hide from the accused the nature of the case, and at times to use insinuations against the accused. See Michel Foucault, *Discipline and Punish*, trans. Alan Sheridan (New York: Vintage Books, 1979), 35.

13. See Szpiner, 31.

14. The French word for "chief" is "chef," but it is also an old term for "head" in French (a fact that any school child learns in France). It is because Marie threatens the head (of state) that she must lose her head (at the guillotine, the symbol of the power of the head of state, as noted earlier).

15. I would like to thank my student Mary Hatch for having brought this painting to my attention.

16. When Marie stands in court to have her sentence read to her by the magistrate, the camera shot cuts off her head as we glimpse her lawyer seated in front of her. Then, as if this were not enough, the camera returns to the judge, who, at the moment he pronounces her guilty, covers his own head with his official hat. The visual decapitation, like the painting, belongs to an elaborate network of images that appear to confirm the inevitability of Marie's execution.

17. In 1988, the trial of Paul Touvier, who was the Milice chief for Lyons during the war, provided much evidence of such thievery.

18. I am not trying to make the argument that the camera lens should be equated with the little boy's vision. There are many scenes that he does not witness himself. Rather, it is a question of understanding how his viewpoint, his particular gaze, inflects what we see, making us view Marie negatively, or at least judgmentally.

19. Scullion also notes this negativity, but attributes it almost exclusively to Chabrol's own sexism (88–89). While this interpretation is possible, there is another one that stresses more the film's internal dimensions: the intervention of Pierrot at the end provides a key perspective that need not be identical to Chabrol's. As an artistic device, the voice-over at the end establishes an internal male viewpoint for the film.

20. The food in question may well be the nettle bushes themselves, given that a "nettle soup" was said to have been concocted during the Occupation when food became very hard to come by. See Célia Bertin, *Femmes sous l'Occupation* (Paris: Stock, 1993), back cover.

21. This is before the return of her husband from the prisoner-of-war camp.

22. Pierrot's curious explanation of this wish, that he could then be invisible or unrecognizable, suggests an identification (no doubt unconscious) with his mother, who

is constantly the object of his and others' dangerous gazes. In an era of proliferating denunciations and false accusations, it is not perhaps so surprising that the boy would seek refuge in an all-powerful image of anonymity.

23. The sword itself is an explicit phallic symbol for Marie and Lucien that connotes the latter's sexual prowess as well as his political power and athletic skills.

24. Female solidarity is by no means absolute in the film, but it is certainly predominant. The most notable group exceptions are of course the nuns who guard Marie in prison, and some of the inmates themselves.

25. Vichy, in the early years of the war, provided subsidies to allow mothers to stay home to care for their children. The problem was that the money was insufficient to live on, so the mothers still needed to work, particularly later on, when so many men were sent to camps, leaving families with no means of support. In the United States, the debate about a return to orphanages makes one think back to Vichy's handling of family issues and values.

26. This conjecture would confirm the pattern of vengeance against women by men who feel excluded.

27. Marie is also attracted to Rachel because of her looks.

28. See H. R. Kedward, *Vichy France: Collaboration and Resistance, 1940–1944* (New York: Blackwell, 1985), 49.

29. This individual Catholic woman does, however, plant in Marie the seed of doubt (telling her that babies in the womb have a soul) that in the end will help push Marie into accepting culpability and hence the role of Vichy's victim.

30. Szpiner, 136.

31. Naomi Greene, "'La vie en rose': Images of the Occupation in French Cinema," in *Auschwitz and After: Race, Culture, and "the Jewish Question" in France*, ed. Lawrence D. Kritzman (New York: Routledge, 1995), 283–98.

32. New Novelist Nathalie Sarraute, herself a Jew, refused to wear the yellow star during the war and had to hide her origins in order to avoid being deported. Part of her concealment involved posing as the governess of her own children. Eventually, however, she was denounced by a local merchant and had to flee her home.

33. The adjectives I have used here to describe Marie are those of a male colleague (the negative image) and a female student (the positive image).

34. At one point Marie hesitantly offers to pay her maid/assistant to sleep with her husband, Paul, a situation that has the potential to please all parties, but Paul realizes that the whole thing is Marie's idea and refuses.

35. Marcia Polly, "Women's business," *Film Comment* 25.5 (1989), 16.

36. This research was supported by a grant from the Amherst College Research Award Program.

Righting Gendered Writing

1. For example, only one out of fifteen essays of Rita Thalmann's *Femmes et fascismes* (Paris: Tierce, 1986) is devoted to the French context.

2. An exception to this was the publication (in 1996, after this essay was written) of Francine Muel-Dreyfus's *Vichy et L'éternal féminin* (Paris: Seuil, 1996).

3. Nancy R. Reagin, *A German Women's Movement: Class and Gender in Hanover*, 1880–1933 (Chapel Hill: University of North Carolina Press, 1995).

4. Dealing with gender by celebrating women's roles in resistance movements is a common approach. Recent examples include books on women and resistance in Spain (Shirley Mangini González, *Memories of Resistance*, New Haven: Yale University Press, 1995) and in Greece (Janet Hart, *New Voices in the Nation*, Ithaca: Cornell University Press, 1996).

5. Célia Bertin, *Femmes sous l'Occupation* (Paris: Stock, 1993).

6. The history of antigay prejudice may be compared to the history of anti-Semitism in Germany, and the literature by gay camp survivors offers many examples of the way the treatment of homosexuals paralleled the treatment of Jews. In *Hitler's Willing Executioners*, Daniel Goldhagen has recently argued that anti-Semitism also preexisted Hitler's rise to power. Although Goldhagen deals only with the persecution of Jews, the treatment of homosexuals bears many points of resemblance. Goldhagen argues that Germans were so saturated with anti-Semitism that they did not even view Jews as human, and willingly followed Hitler's orders, sometimes exceeding them or anticipating them. Moreover, the evidence from work camps and death marches suggests that the intent all along was to exterminate the Jews, not simply to punish or extract labor from them. These points are echoed in the testimony of gay concentration camp victims. Heinz Heger, for example, records that those with the pink triangle were "prioritized for medical experiments" (34) and were "victims of a deliberate operation of destruction by the Hitler regime" (37). Homosexuals were frequently assimilated to the Jews when it came to meting out punishments and worse treatment. Only Jews and homosexuals (not criminals or political prisoners, for example) were assigned the arduous and dangerous work of quarrying in the Flossenbürg camp (49), where the guards amused themselves by picking sadistically on inmates, forcing them onto the wire fences where they would be shot as escapees. "'Games' such as these were a favorite pastime for some of the SS guards, who had no need to fear any disciplinary measures, their victims being just the homosexuals and Jews whose extermination was planned for in any case" (51). When orders came down to treat prisoners working in factories more leniently, these were ignored by the camp commanders, who voluntarily meted out harsher punishments than they were required to do. "All these favors bestowed on the German prisoners, however, did not apply to German Jews, let alone the Jews from the occupied territories. And as far as we were concerned, the pink triangle prisoners, besides being allowed to let our hair grow we received hardly any other favors, and were still equated with the Jews in our treatment by the SS" (89–90). Despite the promises of release in return for work, the pink triangle prisoners knew that "the intention was to exterminate us, as had already been decided in 1938" (101), and gays were disproportionately represented in the lists of those slated for liquidation (103). Toward the end of the war, when the prisoners were sent on death marches as an evacuation measure, they sensed that the real purpose was to finish the work of extermination: "We couldn't help thinking that the purpose was not to transport us to Dachau, but rather to kill us off on the way, by exhaustion or by shooting us" (112). As in the case of the Jews, there was little to be gained by such cruelty, when the end of the

war was imminent, except extermination and torture for their own sake. In numerous ways, then, the treatment of homosexuals mirrored the treatment of Jews, both stemming from widespread, shared cultural assumptions about their fundamental inhumanity. But the similarites ended with the war. Whereas the Jews were recognized as victims, no such compassion was extended to the pink triangle prisoners. And where historians such as Goldhagen see the pervasiveness of anti-Semitism prior to Hitler's rise as a factor contributing to the easy implementation of Nazi exterminationist policy, the same pattern was used to disallow the claims of gay survivors, as the 1957 West German Supreme Court decision illustrates. Goldhagen's work is persuasive in showing what ordinary people are capable of when their social demons go unexamined, and his study points chillingly to the danger that unacknowledged prejudices such as homophobia continue to pose.

Bibliography

Annales: Economies, sociétés, civilisations. 48.3 (May-June 1993). "Présence du passé, lenteur de l'histoire: Vichy, l'Occupation, les juifs."

Aron, Robert. *Histoire de Vichy.* Paris: Fayard, 1954. Trans. *The Vichy Regime.* New York: Macmillan, 1958.

Aubrac, Lucie. *Ils partiront dans l'ivresse: Lyon, mai 43, Londres février 44.* Paris: Seuil, 1984. Trans. *Outwitting the Gestapo.* Lincoln: University of Nebraska Press, 1993.

Azéma, Jean-Pierre, and François Bédarida, eds. *Vichy et le Français.* Paris: Fayard, 1992.

Bard, Christine. *Les Filles de Marianne: Histoire des féminismes, 1914–1940.* Paris: Fayard, 1995.

Bertin, Célia. *Femmes sous l'Occupation.* Paris: Stock, 1993.

Bertrand, Simone. *Mille visages, un seul combat: Les femmes dans la Résistance, témoignages recueillis.* Paris: Français Réunis, 1965.

Blee, Kathleen M. *Women of the Klan: Racism and Gender in the 1920s.* Berkeley and Los Angeles: University of California Press, 1991.

Blum, Cinzia Sartini. *The Other Modernism: F. T. Marinetti's Futurist Fiction of Power.* Berkeley and Los Angeles: University of California Press, 1996.

Bock, Gisela, and Pat Thane, eds. *Maternity and Gender Policies: Women and the Rise of the European Welfare States, 1880s–1950s.* New York: Routledge, 1991.

Bridenthal, Renate, Atina Grossmann, and Marion Kaplan, eds. *When Biology Became Destiny: Women in Weimar and Nazi Germany.* New York: Monthly Review Press, 1984.

Burrin, Philippe. *La France à l'heure allemande.* Paris: Seuil, 1995.

———. "La France et le fascisme." *Le Débat* 32 (1984): 52–72.

Butler, Judith. *Gender Trouble: Feminism and the Subversion of Identity.* New York: Routledge, 1990.

Caldwell, Lesley. "*Madri d'Italia*: Film and Fascist Concern with Motherhood." *Women and Italy: Essays on Gender, Culture and History.* Ed. Zygmunt Baranski and Shirley W. Vinall. Basingstoke: Macmillan, 1991.

Cannistro, Philip V., and Brian R. Sullivan. *Il Duce's Other Woman.* New York: William Morrow, 1993.

Carpi, Daniel. *Between Mussolini and Hitler: The Jews and the Italian Authorities in France and Tunisia.* Hanover, N.H.: University Press of New England, 1995.

Carroll, David. *French Literary Fascism: Nationalism, Anti-Semitism, and the Ideology of Culture.* Princeton: Princeton University Press, 1995.

Chatel, Nicole, ed. *Des Femmes dans la Résistance.* Paris: Julliard, 1972.

Chebel d'Appollonia, Ariane. *L'Extrême Droite en France: De Maurras à Le Pen.* Brussels: Editions Complexe, 1988.

———. *Histoire politique des intellectuels en France, 1944–54.* 2 vols. Brussels: Editions Complexe, 1991.

Cheles, Luciano. "*Dolce Stil Nero*? Images of Women in the Graphic Propaganda of the Italian Neo-fascist Party." *Women and Italy: Essays on Gender, Culture and History*. Ed. Zygmunt Baranski and Shirley W. Vinall. Basingstoke: Macmillan, 1991.

———, Ronnie Ferguson, and Michalina Vaughan, eds. *The Far Right in Western and Eastern Europe*. 2nd ed. London: Longman, 1995.

Chevrillon, Claire. *Code Name Christiane Clouet: A Woman in the French Resistance*. College Station: Texas A&M University Press, 1995.

Cobb, Richard. *French and Germans, Germans and French: A Personal Interpretation of France under Two Occupations, 1914–1918/1940–1944*. Hanover, N.H.: University Press of New England, 1983.

Conan, Eric, and Henry Rousso. *Vichy, un passé qui ne passe pas*. Paris: Fayard, 1994.

Cooke, Miriam, and Angela Woolacott, eds. *Gendering War Talk*. Princeton: Princeton University Press, 1993.

Coudert, Marie-Louise. *Elles, la Résistance*. Paris: Messidor/Temps Actuels, 1983.

De Grazia, Victoria. *How Fascism Ruled Women: Italy, 1922–1945*. Berkeley and Los Angeles: University of California Press, 1992.

Eco, Umberto. "Ur-Facsism." *The New York Review of Books*. 22 June 1995. 12–15.

Esprit Créateur. 33:1 (1993) "The Occupation in French Literature and Film, 1940–1992."

Ezekiel, Raphael S. *The Racist Mind: Portraits of American Neo-Nazis and Klansmen*. New York: Viking, 1995.

Les Femmes dans la Résistance. Paris: Editions du Rocher, 1977.

Fischer, Erica. *Aimée and Jaguar: A Love Story, Berlin 1943*. New York: Harper-Collins, 1995.

Fishman, Sarah. *We Will Wait: Wives of French Prisoners of War, 1940–1945*. New Haven: Yale University Press, 1991.

Fouché, Pascal. "Les Listes Otto pendant l'Occupation allemande. Des saisies par millions." *Censures: De la Bible aux larmes d'Eros*. Paris: Centre Georges Pompidou, BPI, 1987.

Fourtouni, Eleni. *Greek Women in Resistance*. New Haven, Conn.: Thelpini Press, 1986.

Francos, Ania. *Il était des femmes dans la Résistance*. Paris: Stock, 1978.

Frevert, Ute. *Women in German History: From Bourgeois Emancipation to Sexual Liberation*. Providence, R.I.: Berg, 1989.

Friedlander, Judith. *Vilna on the Seine: Jewish Intellectuals in France since 1968*. New Haven: Yale University Press, 1990.

Gaspard, Françoise. *Une Petite ville en France*. Gallimard, 1990. Trans. *A Small City in France*. Cambridge: Harvard University Press, 1995.

Gättens, Marie-Luise. *Women Writers and Fascism: Reconstructing History*. Gainesville: University Press of Florida, 1995.

Goldhagen, Daniel Jonah. *Hitler's Willing Executioners: Ordinary Germans and the Holocaust*. New York: Knopf, 1996.

Golsan, Richard J., ed. *Fascism, Aesthetics, and Culture*. Hanover, N.H.: University Press of New England, 1992.

Grau, Günter, ed. *Hidden Holocust? Gay and Lesbian Persecution in Germany, 1933–45*. London: Cassell, 1995.

Griffin, Roger. *The Nature of Fascism*. 1991; rpt. London: Routledge, 1993.

Grossman, Atina. *Reforming Sex: The German Movement for Birth Control and Abortion Reform, 1920–1950*. New York: Oxford University Press, 1995.

Guérin, Daniel. *The Brown Plague: Travels in Late Weimar and Early Nazi Germany*. Durham, N.C.: Duke University Press, 1994.

Hart, Janet. *New Voices in the Nation: Women and the Greek Resistance, 1941–1964*. Ithaca: Cornell University Press, 1996.

Heger, Heinz. *The Men with the Pink Triangle: The True, Life-and-Death Story of Homosexuals in the Nazi Death Camps*. Boston: Alyson, 1980, rpt. 1994.

Hewitt, Andrew. *Political Inversions: Homosexuality, Fascism, and the Modernist Imaginary*. Stanford: Stanford University Press, 1996.

Hyman, Paula. *From Dreyfus to Vichy: The Remaking of French Jewry, 1906–1939*. New York: Columbia University Press, 1979.

Jeansonne, Glen. *Women of the Far Right: The Mothers' Movement and World War II*. Chicago: University of Chicago Press, 1996.

Joplin, Patricia Klindienst. "The Authority of Illusion: Feminism and Fascism in Virginia Woolf's *Between the Acts*." *South Central Review* 6.2 (1989): 88–104.

Les Juifs sous l'Occupation: Recueil des textes français et allemands, 1940–1944. Paris: Centre de Documentation Juive Contemporaine, 1945.

Kaes, Anton, Martin Jay, and Edward Dimendberg, eds. *The Weimar Republic Sourcebook*. Berkeley and Los Angeles: University of California Press, 1994.

Kahn Annette. *Le Fichier*. Paris: Laffont, 1993.

Kaplan, Alice Yaeger. *Reproductions of Banality: Fascism, Literature, and French Intellectual Life*. Minneapolis: University of Minnesota Press, 1986.

Kedward, H[arry] [Roderick]. *In Search of the Maquis: Rural Resistance in Southern France, 1942–1944*. Oxford: Clarendon Press, 1993.

———. *Resistance in Vichy France: A Study of Ideas and Motivation in the Southern Zone, 1940–1942*. Oxford: Oxford University Press, 1978.

———. *Vichy France: Collaboration and Resistance, 1940–1944*. New York: Blackwell, 1985.

———, and Roger Austin, ed. *Vichy France and the Resistance: Culture and Ideology*. Totowa, N.J.: Barnes and Noble, 1985.

———, and Nancy Wood, eds. *The Liberation of France: Image and Event*. Oxford: Berg, 1995.

Klarsfeld, Serge. *Vichy-Auschwitz: Le role de Vichy dans la solution finale de la questions juive en France*. Vol. 1: 1942. Paris: Fayard, 1983. Vol. 2: 1943–1944. Paris: Fayard, 1985.

Koonz, Claudia.: *Mothers in the Fatherland: Women, the Family, and Nazi Politics*. New York: St. Martin's Press, 1987.

Lacey, Kate. *Feminine Frequencies: Gender, German Radio, and the Public Sphere, 1923–1945*. Ann Arbor: University of Michigan Press, 1996.

Laska, Vera, ed. *Women in the Resistance and in the Holocaust: The Voices of Eyewitnesses*. Westport, Conn.: Greenwood Press, 1983.

Lebovics, Herman. *True France: The Wars over Cultural Identity: 1900–1945*. Ithaca: Cornell University Press, 1992.

Lévy, Bernard-Henry. *L'Idéologie française*. Paris: Grasset, 1981.

Macciocchi, Maria-Antonietta. "Female Sexuality in Fascist Ideology." *Feminist Review* 1 (1979): 67–82.

Mangini González, Shirley. *Memories of Resistance: Women's Voices from the Spanish Civil War*. New Haven: Yale University Press, 1995.

Marrus, Michael, and Robert Paxton. *Vichy et les juifs*. Trans. *Vichy France and the Jews*. New York: Basic Books, 1981.

Martin, Elaine, ed. *Gender, Patriarchy, and Fascism in the Third Reich: The Response of Women Writers*. Detroit: Wayne State University Press, 1993.

Mason, Tim. *Nazism, Fascism and the Working Class*. Cambridge: Cambridge University Press, 1995.

Mehlman, Jeffrey. *Legacies of Anti-Semitism in France*. Minneapolis: University of Minnesota Press, 1983.

Milza, Pierre, and Serge Berstein. *Dictionnaire historique des fascismes et du nazisme*. Brussels: Editions Complexe, 1992.

Mizejewski, Linda. *Divine Decadence: Fascism, Female Spectacle, and the Makings of Sally Bowles*. Princeton: Princeton University Press, 1992.

Modernism/Modernity 1:3 (1994). "Marinetti and the Italian Futurists."

Monestier, Marianne. *Elles étaient cent et mille: Femmes dans la Résistance*. Paris: Fayard, 1972.

Monferrand, Hélène de. *Les amies d'Héloïse*. Paris: Editions de Fallois, 1990.

———. *Journal de Suzanne*. Paris: Editions de Fallois, 1991.

Musil, Robert. "Ruminations of a Slow-Witted Mind." *Critical Inquiry* 17:1 (Autumn 1990): 46–61.

Owings, Alison. *Frauen: German Women Recall the Third Reich*. Brunswick, N.J.: Rutgers University Press, 1993.

Payne, Stanley G. *A History of Fascism, 1914–1945*. Madison: University of Wisconsin Press, 1996.

Paxton, Robert O. *Vichy France: Old Guard and New Order, 1940–1944*. 1972; rpt. New York: Columbia University Press, 1982.

Péan, Pierre. *Une Jeunesse française: François Mitterand, 1934–1947*. Paris: Fayard, 1994.

Phayer, Michael. *Protestant and Catholic Women in Nazi Germany*. Detroit: Wayne State University Press, 1990.

Pickering-Iazzi, Robin. *Mothers of Invention: Women, Italian Fascism, and Culture*. Minneapolis: University of Minnesota Press, 1995.

Pinkus, Karen. *Bodily Regimes: Italian Advertising under Fascism*. Minneapolis: University of Minnesota Press, 1995.

Plant, Robert. *The Pink Triangle: The Nazi War against Homosexuals*. New York: Henry Holt, 1986.

Poznanski, René. *Etre juif en France pendant la Seconde Guerre mondiale*. Paris: Hachette, 1994.

Raymond, Philippe Ganier. *Une certaine France*. Paris: Balland, 1975.

Reagin, Nancy R. *A German Women's Movement: Class and Gender in Hanover, 1880–1933*. Chapel Hill: University of North Carolina Press, 1995.

Rémy, Dominique, ed. *Les Lois de Vichy: Actes dits "lois" de l'autorité de fait se prétendant "gouvernement de L'Etat français."* Paris: Romillat, 1992.

Rittner, Carol, and John K. Roth, eds. *Different Voices: Women and the Holocaust.* New York: Paragon House, 1993.

Roberts, Mary Louise. *Civilization Without Sexes: Reconstructing Gender in Postwar France, 1917–1927.* Chicago: University of Chicago Press, 1994.

Rossiter, Margaret L. *Women in the Resistance.* New York: Praeger, 1986.

Rousso, Henry. *Le Syndrome de Vichy: De 1944 à nos jours.* Paris: Seuil, 1987. Trans. *The Vichy Syndrome: History and Memory in France since 1944.* Cambridge: Harvard University Press, 1991.

Ruaux, Jean-Yves. *Vichy-sur-manche: Les Iles Anglo-normandes sous l'Occupation.* Rennes: Editions Ouest-France, 1994.

Schoppmann, Claudia. *Days of Masquerade: Life Stories of Lesbians During the Third Reich.* New York: Columbia University Press, 1996.

———. *Nationalsozialistische Sexualpolitik und weibliche Homosexualität.* Pfaffenweiler: Centaurus, 1991.

Seel, Pierre. *Moi, Pierre Seel, déporté homosexuel.* Paris: Calmann-Lévy, 1994. Trans. *I, Pierre Seel, Deported Homosexual.* New York: Basic Books, 1995.

Sirinellei, Jean-François. *Histoire des droites en France.* Paris: Gallimard, 1992.

Soucy, Robert. *Fascism in France: The Case of Maurice Barrès.* Berkeley and Los Angeles: University of California Press, 1972.

———. *Fascist Intellectual: Drieu la Rochelle.* Berkeley and Los Angeles: University of California Press, 1979.

———. *French Fascism: The First Wave, 1924–1933.* New Haven: Yale University Press, 1986.

———. *French Fascism: The Second Wave, 1933–1939.* New Haven: Yale University Press, 1995.

Spackman, Barbara. *Fascist Virilities: Rhetoric, Ideology, and Social Fantasy in Italy.* Minneapolis: University of Minnesota Press, 1996.

Sternhell, Zeev. *Maurice Barrès et le nationalisme Français.* Paris: A. Colin, 1972.

———. *Ni Droite ni gauche: L'idéologie fasciste en France.* Paris: Seuil, 1983. Trans. *Neither Right nor Left: Fascist Ideology in France.* Berkeley and Los Angeles: University of California Press, 1986.

———, Mario Sznajder, and Maia Ahersi. *Naissance de l'idéologie française.* Trans. *The Birth of Fascist Ideology: From Cultural Rebellion to Political Revolution.* Princeton: Princeton University Press, 1994.

Stephenson, Jill. *The Nazi Organisation of Women.* London: Croom Helm; and Totowa, N.J.: Barnes and Noble, 1981.

———. *Women in Nazi Society.* London: Croom Helm, 1975.

Suleiman, Susan Rubin. *Authoritarian Fictions: The Ideological Novel as a Literary Genre.* 1983. Princeton: Princeton University Press, 1992.

Sweets, John. *Choices in Vichy France: The French under Nazi Occupation.* New York: Oxford University Press, 1986.

———. *The Politics of Resistance in France, 1940–1944: A History of the Mouvements Unis de la Résistance.* Dekalb: Northern Illinois University Press, 1976.

Tatar, Maria. *Lustmord: Sexual Murder in Weimar Germany.* Princeton: Princeton University Press, 1995.

Telos. "The French New Right: New Right—New Left—New Paradigm." 98–99 (Fall 1993–Winter 1994).

Thalmann, Rita, ed. *Femmes et fascismes*. Paris: Tierce, 1986.

Theweleit, Klaus. *Male Fantasies*. Vol. 1. *Women, Floods, Bodies, History*. Minneapolis: University of Minnesota Press, 1987. Vol. 2. *Male Bodies: Psychoanalyzing the White Terror*. Minneapolis: University of Minnesota Press, 1989.

Tucker, William R. *The Fascist Ego: A Political Biography of Robert Brasillach*. Berkeley and Los Angeles: University of California Press, 1975.

Usborne, Cornelie. *The Politics of the Body in Weimar Germany: Women's Reproductive Rights and Duties*. Ann Arbor, University of Michigan Press, 1992.

Utne Reader. 72 (Nov.–Dec. 1995)."The Familiar Face of Fascism."

Veillon, Dominique. *Vivre et survivre en France, 1939–1947*. Paris: Payot, 1995.

Verdès-Leroux, Jeanine. *Refus et violences*. Paris: Gallimard, 1996.

Weber, Eugen. *The Hollow Years: France in the 1930s*. New York: Norton, 1994.

Weitz, Margaret Collins. *Sisters in the Resistance: How Women Fought to Free France, 1940–1945*. New York: Wiley, 1995.

Wilhelm, Maria de Blasio. *The Other Italy: The Italian Resistance in World War II*. New York: Norton, 1988.

Willson, Perry R. *The Clockwork Factory: Women and Work in Fascist Italy*. New York: Oxford University Press, 1993.

Winock, Michel. *Histoire de l'extrême droite en France*. Paris: Seuil, 1993.

———. *Nationalisme, antisémitisme, et fascisme en France*. Paris: Seuil, 1990.

Contributors

Richard J. Golsan teaches French at Texas A&M University.

Mary Jean Green teaches French, Women's Studies, and Film Studies at Dartmouth College.

Martine Guyot-Bender teaches French at Hamilton College.

Melanie Hawthorne teaches French and Women's Studies at Texas A&M University.

Andrew Hewitt teaches comparative literature at the State University of New York—Buffalo.

Leah D. Hewitt teaches French at Amherst College.

Elizabeth A. Houlding formerly taught French at the University of Nevada, Reno, and is now an independent scholar.

Andrea Loselle teaches French at the University of California, Los Angeles.

Miranda Pollard teaches history at the University of Georgia.

Willa Z. Silverman teaches French at the Pennsylvania State University.

Index

University Press of New England publishes books under its own imprint and is the publisher for Brandeis University Press, Dartmouth College, Middlebury College Press, University of New Hampshire, Tufts University, and Wesleyan University Press.

Library of Congress Cataloging-In-Publication Data
Gender and fascism in modern France / edited by Melanie Hawthorne and Richard J. Golsan.

    p.   cm. — (Contemporary French culture and society)

    Includes bibliographical references and index.

    ISBN 0–87451–812–1 (cl : alk. paper). — ISBN 0–87451–814–8 (pa : alk. paper)

    1. French literature—20th century—History and criticism.   2. French literature—19th century—History and criticism.   3. Fascism in literature.   4. Fascism and women—France.   5. Homosexuality and literature—France.   6. Fascism and literature—France.   I. Hawthorne, Melanie.   II. Golsan, Richard Joseph, 1952– . III. Series.

PQ307.F3G46   1997

840.9'358—dc21   97-5530